IRISH BOSTON

A Lively Look at Boston's Colorful Irish Past

Second Edition

Michael Quinlin

Guilford, Connecticut

ISBN 978-0-7627-8834-7

Printed in the United States of America
10 9 8 7 6 5 4 3 2 1

A previous edition was cataloged as follows:

Library of Congress Cataloging-in-Publication Data

Quinlin, Michael
    Irish Boston / Michael Quinlin.
        p. cm.
    Includes bibliographical references and index.
    ISBN 0-7627-2901-5
1. Irish Americans—Massachusetts—Boston—History. 2. Boston (Mass.)—Ethnic
relations. 3. Boston (Mass.)—History. 4. Boston (Mass.)—Guidebooks. 5. Historic
sites—Massachusetts—Boston—Guidebooks. I. Title.
    F73.9.I6Q46 2004
    974.4'61—dc22   2004042549

For Colette Minogue Quinlin

Contents

Acknowledgments

FRIENDS, COLLEAGUES, AND STRANGERS all come to the fore when a book is getting written, and I am grateful for the assistance of many people for helping me along the way. My sister Margaret Quinlin shared her publishing expertise at every turn, and Michael Coffey has offered sound publishing advice and friendship through the years. Judith Rosen of Cambridge shaped my original proposal for the first edition, and editor Erin Turner guided me on the revised edition with patience and encouragement. Speaking of patience, thanks to Ellen Urban, book project manager, for her forbearance along the way. And to copy editor Eileen Clawson for her fine-tuning of the text.

I am grateful to my friends Seamus Connolly and Brian O'Donovan and the late Michael Cummings and David R. Burke for sharing their knowledge and perspective with me. I salute the late professor Thomas O'Connor, who read my original manuscript and whose books continue to instruct me. Thanks to Ray O'Hanlon of the *Irish Echo* and Patricia Harty of *Irish America* magazine for allowing me to publish my research on Boston Irish history over the years.

I am indebted to librarians and archivists who helped me locate obscure and relevant material for this project. At the Boston Public Library, these include Henry Scannell and staff in the Microtext Department, Aaron Schmidt in the Print Department, and Susan Glover and staff in the Rare Books Department. Beth Sweeney at the Irish Music Archives, John J. Burns Library, Boston College; Robert Johnson at the Boston Archdiocese Archives; Dr. John McColgan and Kristen Swett at City of Boston Archives; Susan Greendyke at the Massachusetts State House Art Commission; Tom McNaught and Colleen Cooney at the John F. Kennedy Library and Museum; and James Feeney at the Boston Athenaeum provided invaluable assistance.

Finally, my love and affection go to my wife, Colette, and son, Devin, for their encouragement and good humor throughout this project; to Leo McLaughlin; and always to my family—the late Johnny Quinlin and to Marie, Margaret, Sheila, Patricia, Kathleen, and Ann—for their unwavering support and devotion.

Introduction

When I wrote the first edition of *Irish Boston* a decade ago in 2003, I thought of Boston's Irish community as monolithic, especially as it pertained to politics and religion, the twin towers of Irish-American life for much of the twentieth century. Those two subject matters were already deeply investigated by other writers, and besides, I was more interested in the cultural, social, and grassroots dimensions of the Irish community, so that became the focus of this book.

That remains my perspective in this new edition: to share the story of how the Irish came to Boston, how they navigated the fears and prejudices that all immigrants face, how they relied on family, faith, and community in times of trouble, how they kept their culture alive, and how they kept a genuine belief in the promise of America, a belief that never wavered in over three hundred years.

There is an assortment of sturdy Ulster Presbyterians and desperate Famine refugees alongside optimistic sculptors, talented athletes, musicians, and dancers, and dedicated preachers, politicians, and poets to be found in this edition. The rascals and rogues are still here, too, though they interest me less than they did a decade ago. Perhaps these particular typecast Irish are beginning to fade away, except in Hollywood, of course.

When updating this edition I was struck by the patterns of immigration to Boston, typically dictated by how Ireland fared at any given time and also by American immigration laws over the decades. I noticed that Irish immigrants tended to cluster together when they came, preferring their own company and their own pubs, social events, and neighborhoods, rather than mixing right in with the American mainstream. Perhaps this is an impulse of all immigrants initially, to stay on familiar footing before moving toward a realization of this nation's motto, E Pluribus Unum—out of many, one.

Much has occurred since the new century turned, and I no longer think of the Boston Irish as monolithic, ruled by titans, chieftains, cardinals, and bosses. There is now room to look at the unsung heroes, generous organizers, and individual geniuses who stepped into the limelight to display their athletic skills, artistic talents, and musical accomplishments.

I remain guided by the perspective of historian James O'Toole, who wrote that "the purpose of history is not merely to praise great and famous men; it must also document and reveal the lives of ordinary men, women and children." I have tried to document those lives, with hopes of claiming a value for them in the grand scheme of Boston's history.

God Almighty, in his most holy and wise providence, hath so disposed of the condition of mankind, as in all times some must be rich, some poor, some high and eminent in power and dignitie; others mean and in submission.

—*John Winthrop, 1632*

So let us begin anew. . . . With a good conscience our only sure reward, with history the final judge of our deeds, let us go forth to lead the land we love.

—*John F. Kennedy, 1961*

CHAPTER ONE

Puritans, Presbyterians, and Papists (1700–1770)

I MAGINE WHAT the early Irish immigrants saw when they arrived in Boston, dreaming of the Promised Land.

They had crossed an arduous ocean to arrive at a severe frontier town, a brave speck of civilization perched on the edge of a vast wilderness stretched across a dark continent. The English Puritans who settled in Boston constantly battled extreme weather, food shortages, and outbreaks of diseases, while facing enemies on all sides. Wild Indians hid in the woods, conspiring with the French trappers encroaching from Quebec. African slaves were sullen in their chains, ready to mutiny at any moment. Pirates on the open seas were waiting to pounce on supply ships coming in and out of the harbor. Raggle-taggle drifters, vagabonds, and criminals came from other parts of the colonies, jumping off ships coming in from the West Indies or getting run out of New York and Pennsylvania.

The Puritans refused to yield to these tribulations. They were on a mission from God to purify their lives, to build a "city upon a hill, with the eyes of the world upon us," as John Winthrop preached. They believed they were the chosen people, on an errand into the wilderness, as the Reverend Samuel Danforth described it.

The Irish observed various religious groups—Quakers, Anabaptists, and Catholics—trying to get a foothold in this colony of dissenters so they could practice their own brand of faith. They learned quickly that the Puritans had no tolerance for toleration, as Roger Williams discovered when he was banished to Rhode Island for advocating liberty of conscience.

In this new land, you would imagine the Irish would be circumspect and discreet, given that they already had two strikes against them. As Irish they were considered second-class citizens by the English, who had conquered them time and again in the British Isles. The English had proscribed their Gaelic language and customs and confiscated their land; in fact, Ireland was Great Britain's first colony, even before America. But more importantly, as Catholics they were despised by the righteous Puritans. Indeed, the Puritans had left England seventy years earlier, hoping to purify their Anglican faith of the remnants of Catholicism, so being anti-Catholic was part of their raison d'être. In 1647 a statute threatened to hang priests caught in the colony. In 1688 Goody Glover, an Irish Catholic servant who had come to Boston after being enslaved in the West Indies, was hanged in Boston for allegedly practicing witchcraft. At her trial she spoke only Gaelic and was accused of speaking in the Devil's tongue. In 1700 the Massachusetts legislature voted to eject all Jesuit priests and Catholic missionaries. Cotton Mather, the Puritan preacher, warned that letting Irish Catholics into the Bay Colony was a "formidable attempt of Satan and his sons to unsettle us."

But the Irish weren't always circumspect and discreet, they were daring, desperate, and sometimes dangerous, acting as if they had nothing to lose. Their names appeared frequently in newspaper classified sections and selectmen's proceedings, typically for being on the wrong side of the law. In 1704 the *Boston News-Letter* ran this item: "Stolen out of the house of James Cooper, near Charlestown Ferry, several sorts of men's apparel, both woolen and linen, by an Irish man, speaks bad English. He is a young man about 22 years of age, low stature, dark colored hair. . . . whoever discovers said person shall have sufficient reward."

Many of the original Irish to Boston were indentured servants who gained passage to America by agreeing to work in servitude for up to seven years. But once they got here, many of them quickly absconded from their masters, as evidenced by the number of classified ads in the first half of the eighteenth century like this one: "Runaway servant girl Mary Farrel, last seen on January 29, 1725 . . ." She wore a "black griffet gown, an old grey petticoat, and a pair of ticken shoes, with red heels."

Sometimes the runaway servants were caught and punished, then returned to their master, only to escape again. Edmund Murphy absconded from Milton resident Thomas Craddock in November 1737, was captured and returned to Craddock, then ran away again in March 1738. A companion of Murphy who didn't fit the servant persona was Edmund Butler, who escaped from Craddock in May 1738. Butler was described as "a good scholar who speaks English, Latin, Greek, and French, a thin-looking fellow of middle stature."

The fact was that in the eighteenth century, Puritans needed the Irish, along with Indians and Africans, for manual labor and skilled trades as the city grew. By 1700 Boston had become Britain's major port for trade in New England, a key link to Virginia and Maryland and to the West Indies, which supplied sugar for the burgeoning rum trade. Seventy-eight wharves lined the shores around Boston and Charlestown, and the harbor was abuzz with ships coming and going from around the world.

Evan Thomas, biographer of naval hero John Paul Jones, notes that "in the 18th century, the world was sharply divided into a great chain of being in which you were born to your class." Most Irish and Scots, along with American Indians and African slaves, were decidedly at the bottom of the chain of being in Boston, designated to bend to the will of the Puritans. And that dynamic— between the rulers and the underclass, the haves and the have-nots—would become one of the recurring tensions of America as it evolved from a colony of the chosen few to a republic of the people.

This caste system led to early inklings of America's melting pot, since the underclass were often lumped together as commodities in the marketplace, to be traded, bartered, punished, or imprisoned. Boston merchant Samuel Sewall advertised a sale at his warehouse in Merchant's Row in September 1714, offering to dispose of "several Irish maid servants, most of them for five years, one Irish man servant, who is a good barber and wigmaker, and four or five likely Negro boys." In 1738 Irishmen Michael Dullowin and Patrick Shangasseys ran away from gingerbread baker Thomas Pearson, and Hugh McCan escaped from His Majesty's Prison, the Bridewell on Beacon Hill. They were joined on the run by fugitive slave George Tilley, American Indian Jo Daniels, and Scottish servant William Cobb. The following year, nine more prisoners escaped from the Bridewell. Five of them were Irish men, led by twenty-five-year-old Thomas Dwyer, and the group also included a one-armed Indian named John Baker, a twenty-year-old Negro named Jocco, a woman, and an Englishman. They each had a three-pound bounty on their heads.

This is not to suggest that slavery and indentured service were comparable. Africans were sold into bondage for life and were mistreated in the most brutal manner, often whipped, mutilated, and raped, whereas Irish—as well as English and Scottish—servants typically entered voluntarily into an indenture contract for five to seven years, as a means of getting over to America. They were often physically abused, too, but after serving their time they were able to settle as free men in America. Skilled tradesmen were generally well treated and often made a good living after their service was finished. In Virginia George Washington once hired bricklayer Michael Tracy, shoemaker Thomas Ryan, and tailor Caven Bowe, paying about twelve pounds for each Irishman in exchange for three years of service. The most notable indentured servants in New England were Irish immigrants John Sullivan and his wife Margaret Browne, who settled in Maine in 1730 and raised five sons, all of whom played prominent roles in the Revolutionary War.

Many servants from the British Isles came to America involuntarily. Researcher Frances McDonnell writes that more than sixty thousand adults and children were sent against their will to the colonies. Many were felons or vagabonds, but there were political and religious dissenters, too. In skirmishes across the British Isles, marauding soldiers often captured Irish and Scots and sent them to New England or the West Indies. This eliminated dissenters in the British Isles while also providing manpower to colonize British holdings abroad. In 1672 Irishman Robert Collins won a landmark case in Boston's Suffolk County Court after he was captured against his will and shipped to Boston. He was relieved of having to serve a Bostonian who had purchased his indenture contract. Abbot Emerson Smith, author of *Colonists in Bondage*, describes the practice as "licensed kidnapping on a large scale, with the [English] magistrates and officers of the law conniving at it under some pretense of statutory sanction."

Given the Puritan impulse to keep a tight rein on Bay Colony citizens, Boston officials kept track of all "foreigners and strangers" coming into town. Newspapers ran regular lists of "Inward Bound" and "Outward Bound" travelers who stayed more than a few days. Those staying too long were ordered to leave, as noted in the selectmen's minutes. In 1719 Mary Newell from Ireland was "warned to depart," after being in Boston for seven weeks, and so were John Walker, his wife, and three children, who "came last from Ireland and had then been in this town about one month."

The Presbyterian Strangers

Not all Irish came to Boston as indentured servants. Many small landholders and merchants in Ireland could afford the passage and the means to get started in Boston, and were attracted by the promise of opportunity. They were mostly Scots-Irish Presbyterians from Ulster, the nine northernmost counties in Ireland. As early as 1611 England's King James the First had

MAJOR GENERAL JOHN SULLIVAN,

General John Sullivan, who drove the British naval fleet out of Boston Harbor on March 17, 1776, was a son of indentured servants.

sent Scottish "planters" to Ulster to subdue the native Irish. Many of the planters' descendants retained their Scottish identity and were commonly known as Ulster Scots. But after a few generations they, too, were disillusioned with their situation in Northern Ireland, having to fend off dissident Catholics whose land they had taken, while also getting overtaxed by the Crown. So when they had the opportunity to come to the New World, many of them jumped at the chance. An article in the *New England Weekly Journal* in 1729 noted that the idea of "going to the plantations in America is spreading throughout this kingdom to an incredible degree," and that included "the common people." The British government immediately acted to put into effect a law "to restrain His Majesty's subjects from transporting themselves and their effects to places beyond sea." While the British were content to ship the poor Irish to America, they preferred to keep the merchants and farmers in place, especially those paying taxes to the Crown.

When the Ulster Presbyterians began making overtures to bring their congregations to New England, Puritan leaders such as Cotton Mather encouraged them, perceiving the newcomers as like-minded religious renegades from Anglicanism. A more practical reason was that the Bay Colony needed valiant, sturdy colonists willing to settle and protect its frontiers, beyond the Boston pale in New Hampshire and Maine, where American Indians and Frenchmen posed a threat. Ironically, the Scots-Irish, as they later came to be known, had experience in settling among indigenous populations that were hostile to them. They had already done so in Ireland.

In August 1718 five boats, containing about seven hundred Ulster Irish Presbyterians, arrived in Boston Harbor. They had been assured beforehand that they could purchase a parcel of land in the city, but when they arrived city leaders informed them they would need to join the Puritans' Congregational Church to reside in Boston. A few of them did, but the rest refused to change religion. At Governor Samuel Shute's suggestion, the Presbyterians moved to twelve square miles of land in Casco Bay, Maine, and eventually settled Worcester, Massachusetts, and Londonderry, New Hampshire.

The arrival of these new settlers caused some concern. Alluding to grain shortages in the city, Thomas Lechmere complained in 1718, "These confounded Irish will eat us all up, provisions being most extravagantly dear and scarce." The Boston Town Records in 1723 noted that "great numbers of people have lately been transported from Ireland into this Province, many of which by reason of the present Indian war and other accidents befalling them are now residents in this town. . . . If due care [is] not taken, they may become a Town Charge or be otherwise prejudicial to the well fair and prosperity of the place."

As the city neared its centenary in 1730, the strenuous tenets of Puritanism had diminished somewhat, and Irish Presbyterians got their chance to gain a foothold in Boston. In 1729 they established the Church of the Presbyterian Strangers with thirty parishioners, led by the Reverend John Moorhead, formerly of Newtownards, County Down. They built an Irish meetinghouse in a converted barn at the corner of Berry Street and Long Lane. Church historian Harriett E. Johnson wrote that the Presbyterians were "good, quiet, law-abiding citizens. . . . [W]ith their sober, steadfast, hard working, moral philosophy of life they constituted an excellent balance to the idealistic, variable [Puritan], who so often preached freedom, but practiced intolerance and bigotry."

The Irish Presbyterians appeared more tolerant than their Puritan neighbors, or perhaps they were simply proselytizing. Church records indicate a number of African-American children were baptized into the congregation. James Mayes baptized "three Negro children, Rosanna, John, and Sarah," all presumably the children of slaves. In 1742 a slave named Jeffrey baptized his son Jeffrey, while church member William Baird had a "Negro boy baptized Thomas." Also in 1742 "Cato and Flora, a Negro man and woman," were married at the church by Rev. Moorhead.

The Church of the Presbyterian Strangers prospered in its first decade, and in 1744 the modest barn was replaced by a proper church. By 1749 Rev. Moorhead had baptized more than twelve hundred children. The congregation prospered over the years, and Rev. Moorhead remained the pastor until his death in 1773.

The Charitable Irish

Even as Boston grew, the Puritan leaders remained suspicious of newcomers and immigrants. Bostonians still struggled with the same concerns of their forefathers a century earlier: economic uncertainty, food shortages, the threat of disease, and severe weather. The year 1737 was particularly difficult. Bostonians rioted in March when officials attempted to centralize food markets at Dock Square and a severely harsh winter temporarily froze the harbor. Ships carrying Irish passengers were quarantined at Spectacle Island because of measles or smallpox. Boston's poorhouse already held more than a hundred impoverished people, and about three dozen inmates were imprisoned in the Bridewell.

It was during this year that a group of Boston Irishmen banded together to help their fellow countrymen and women who were falling on hard times. On March 17, 1737, twenty-six "Irish gentlemen, merchants and others" came together to form the Irish Society in New England, later to be known simply as the Charitable Irish Society. Their mission was to help their fellow countrymen "reduced by sickness, shipwreck, old age and other infirmities and unforeseen accidents, [and] for the relief of their poor and indigent countrymen." They were mirroring a tradition that had been established eighty years before, when local Scots formed the Scottish Charitable Society to help their fellow Scotsmen, many of whom had been sent as prisoners to Boston by Oliver Cromwell.

The Irish Presbyterians formed the nucleus of the Charitable Irish Society, and initially only Protestants could become officers. Dues were ten shillings (or approximately fifty dollars) per year and an additional two shillings (ten dollars) each quarter. The original society members came from all walks of life,

Good Deeds: The Charitable Irish Society in Boston

The **Charitable Irish Society** is the oldest Irish organization in North America, created by Irish Protestants to help fellow Irish men and women in the eighteenth century. The society holds its annual dinner every March 17 and since 1997 has presented a Silver Key Award to a worthy recipient doing good deeds on behalf of Irish immigrants. The silver key is the symbol of the Charitable Irish Society, bearing the arms of Ireland on one side and those of King George II on the other. The actual key, made of coin silver and about eight inches long, is engraved with the motto With Good Will Doing Service.

Past presidents of note have included Boston mayors Hugh O'Brien and Patrick Collins, architect Charles D. Maginnis, and historian Henry Lee. Historian Catherine B. Shannon was the first woman elected president in 1990. The society's papers dating from 1737 through 1937 are stored at the Massachusetts Historical Society; more recent papers from the 1930s to the present are kept at the John J. Burns Library at Boston College. The core mission of the society remains the same, writes Shannon: "to help immigrants, to nurture unity and harmony among Irish people, and to advance their social, moral and civic interests on both sides of the Atlantic."

For more information visit charitableirishsociety.org.

and many of the early members appear to have been tradesmen. William Hall, the society's first recorded president, was a leather dresser and town constable; John Little was a groundskeeper; and George Glen was a tailor. Rev. Moorhead remained a member throughout his life. Daniel Gibbs was a sea captain, whose ship, the *Sagamore*, had brought 408 Irish to Boston Harbor in 1737, where they were quarantined at Spectacle Island for measles. Member Andrew Knox was listed as a mariner.

In its early years the society rescued dozens of people in need. In 1740 Abigail Richardson, an Irishwoman, found herself destitute and resigned to die a lonely death on the streets of Boston. Society member James Downing saw her one night lying in the cold darkness behind his house on Wing's Lane, off Hancock Street in the North End. He picked her up and carried her to his house, then petitioned the society to help provide relief. Another recipient of charity was privateer John Ryan, who had been on trial in the 1770s for piracy after sailors from the British frigate *Rose* boarded an American vessel and tried to arrest the crew. Ryan's arm was shattered by a musket in the fracas. His lawyer, future president John Adams, helped him beat the charge of piracy. The crippled Ryan received a small settlement, but he had to depend upon the society to survive.

Keeping Track of Papists

Irish Catholics, meanwhile, continued to feel unwelcome in the Bay Colony, even as restrictions against Presbyterians, Quakers, and Baptists eased. An entire literature of anti-Catholic sentiment in New England existed during this time, writes Catholic scholar Arthur J. Riley, including "sermons, catechisms, school books, diaries and almanacs." Similar to the witch scare phenomenon of the seventeenth century, much of the anti-Catholic literature bordered on the absurd, as when almanac publisher Benjamin Harris searched through astrological data "to find in the position of the planets signs of impending doom for the Church of Rome."

On theological grounds, Catholics believed that the pope in Rome was the head of an established church set up by Christ and that the pope had the authority to expound on the scriptures and interpret matters of faith, morals, and dogma. The Puritans, on the other hand, believed that Christ came down to Earth and left the scriptures for man to rely upon as a direct link to God's will. There was no intermediary needed, and anyone claiming otherwise was an imposter.

The Catholic problem in New England went beyond theological differences, important though they were; it had to do with economic and political matters. The English were battling for colonial jurisdiction in Northern New England with the Catholic French Canadians, who had formed alliances with Indian tribes and were encroaching on valued fishing and fur-trapping regions. The Ulster Presbyterians were dispatched to Maine and New Hampshire partly to help establish a "continuous frontier line" that would define British territory.

Local authorities were always on the watch for Catholic activity. In 1731 Governor Jonathan Belcher, hearing there were "papists now residing within the town of Boston," ordered his officers to "break open their dwelling places, shops and so forth and bring them to the court of justice." Rumors flew that local Catholics were planning to hold a secret Mass on Saint Patrick's Day, 1732, in the West End, near the present-day Saint Joseph's Church on Cardinal O'Connell Way. Three days later the *Weekly Rehearsal* reported, "We hear that Mass has been performed in town this winter by an Irish priest among some Catholics of his own nation, of whom it is not doubted we have a considerable number of them."

The annual Pope's Day holiday held in Boston each November 5 was a chilling warning for any Catholics wishing to profess their faith openly. Also known as Guy Fawkes Day, Pope's Day celebrated a failed Catholic plot by Fawkes to blow up the English Parliament in 1605. It was one of those bizarre and archaic pastimes that reveal a lack of progress in the human condition. To mark the occasion groups of men from Boston's South End and North End marched from their respective neighborhoods into the center of Boston, holding effigies they had studiously constructed of the pope and the Devil. Upon meeting, the two sides, by now fueled by rum and the excitement of old grudges, attempted to destroy the other team's effigies. Often fights broke out between the two groups of Protestants over who despised the pope more, and constables had to be called. It wasn't until decades later, during the Revolutionary War, that the brutish pastime died out in Boston, when more immediate enemies were at hand.

Chapter Two

Tories and Patriots, Pirates and Painters (The 1770s)

I RISH IMMIGRANT James Forrest backed the wrong side in the American Revolution. He shared the dilemma of many of his fellow Boston Irish: whether to stay loyal to the British Crown or to join the rebellious colonists intent on overthrowing British sovereignty. Since emigrating from Ireland to Boston in 1761, Forrest had become a successful merchant and a customs official with strong ties to the British establishment and to Irish circles. He joined the Charitable Irish Society in 1772 and was named the Keeper of the Silver Key, a ceremonial position he held for two years. Like many others, Forrest never dreamed that a handful of colonial gentry and a ragged army of indentured servants, felons, immigrants, and other castaways would one day defeat what was then the world's mightiest empire. So he backed the British.

Boston was fast splitting into two camps: those loyal to the Crown and those opposed to Britain's draconian tax acts. The Stamp Act, which levied a tax on newspapers and legal documents, and the Townsend Act, which taxed tea and other items, were cutting into the profits of Boston merchants, and confrontations with customs officials increased. A face-off between British officials and Boston merchants was inevitable. To quell the opposition, the Crown sent British troops to Boston to keep order in the town. On May 17, 1768, the warship HMS *Romney*, armed with fifty guns, entered Boston Harbor followed by a fleet of warships and two regiments from Halifax, Nova Scotia. The

Twenty-Ninth Regiment camped on Boston Common, while the Fourteenth Regiment took over Faneuil Hall. A few months later the Sixty-Fourth and Sixty-Fifth Regiments arrived from Ireland.

Branded a Tory by the rebellious Bostonians, Forrest became ubiquitous in local British circles, tending to socialize with like-minded Irish soldiers in the British army, such as Captain Brabazon O'Hara of the Fourteenth Regiment and Captain Jeremiah French of the Twenty-Ninth. All three men were drinking at the British Coffee House on King Street in September 1769 when patriot James Otis lost a bloody fistfight with loyalist John Robinson, an incident referred to as the Coffee House Brawl by historian Hiller B. Zobel in his masterful book, *The Boston Massacre*. Forrest was good friends with fellow Irishman Captain Thomas Preston of the Twenty-Ninth Regiment, an Irish battalion where "the average man was over thirty, medium tall, and Irish." It was his friendship with Preston that cast Forrest as a minor player in the infamous Boston Massacre.

The trouble started on Friday, March 2, 1770, when local rope maker Samuel Gray got into a fistfight with Private Matthew Kilroy of the Twenty-Ninth Regiment. Gray got the better of Kilroy, but the two vowed to finish the fight the following Monday, and their respective friends agreed. More scuffles occurred over the weekend, and by Monday the Bostonians and the soldiers were itching for a showdown. Several small confrontations broke out in early evening, and eventually a crowd of two to three hundred Boston men converged upon the Custom House, which was guarded by a lone sentry, Hugh White of the Twenty-Ninth Regiment.

Captain Preston was called in to protect White from the unruly mob, and he arrived along with Corporal William Wemms and six privates—James Hartigan, William McCauley, Matthew Kilroy, William Warren, John Carroll, and Hugh Montgomery. As Preston approached the site, Henry Knox, whose father had been one of the original members of the Irish Presbyterian Church on Long Lane, came out of his bookstore and warned Preston not to shoot into the crowd, which was throwing snowballs and ice chunks while taunting the soldiers.

Preston ordered his men to present arms to keep the crowd at bay, but the taunting continued. Crispus Attucks, described as a mulatto of African and American Indian blood, stepped out of the crowd and wrestled Montgomery's rifle away from him. In the confusion that followed, someone yelled, "Damn you, fire!" The troops fired into the crowd. Samuel Gray was the first to go down, shot in the head by a musket ball. Montgomery wrestled his gun back from Attucks and shot him in the chest. Two other Boston men quickly went down: James Caldwell was shot in the back as he turned to run, and seventeen-year-old Sam Maverick was shot on the spot.

Thirty-year-old Patrick Carr, an Irish sailor, had come out of a house on Court Street and was moving toward the ruckus with fellow sailor Charles Connor when he became the last man to be shot. The bullet tore through Carr's hip and backbone, and he suffered for nine days before dying. The soldiers escaped back to their barracks, and the crowd dispersed to a local tavern in absolute shock and anger about the turn of events. Captain Preston was arrested and jailed at three o'clock on Tuesday morning, March 6, and the eight soldiers were also rounded up.

The town was in an uproar. Distraught at the prospect of his friend Preston being convicted, Forrest rushed around Boston that Tuesday, begging lawyers to take his friend's case. No one volunteered. Finally Forrest barged into the law offices of thirty-five-year-old John Adams, the future president of the United States, who would give Forrest his nickname, the Irish Infant. Adams later recalled the encounter in his autobiography:

> The next morning, sitting in my office near the steps of the townhouse stairs, Mr. Forrest came in. . . . With tears streaming from his eyes, he said, "I am come with a very solemn message from a very unfortunate man, Captain Preston, in prison. He wishes for counsel, and can get none. I have waited on Mr. Quincy, who says he will engage, if you will give him your assistance; without it, he positively will not. Even Mr. Auchmuty declines, unless you will engage."

Adams agreed to represent the soldiers, understanding that the decision could harm his career. Even so, he recognized the importance of conveying to the world the capacity of the American colonies to hold a fair trial. He engaged attorneys Josiah Quincy and Robert Auchmuty to assist him. Their opponent in the courtroom was chief prosecutor Robert Treat Paine, who traced his ancestry back to the O'Neill clan of County Tyrone. Assisting Paine was Sam Quincy, the older brother of Josiah Quincy.

As the trial of Preston and his men loomed, an interesting Irish dimension emerged. Local newspapers such as the *Boston Gazette* suggested that many of the soldiers the British had sent to Boston were Irish Catholics, feeding into the paranoia about a papist conspiracy extant from the Puritan days. The *Providence Gazette* suggested that Pope's Day should take place on the anniversary of the Boston Massacre so as to include Preston and the others in the effigy burnings. In a cruel twist of history, beleaguered Irish Catholics, many of whom were conscripted and forced to join the British forces, were now being blamed for the riot that occurred in Boston.

Defense attorney John Adams pushed back, describing the rioters as "a motley rabble of saucy

Remembering the Massacre

The **Boston Massacre Memorial** on Boston Common, along Tremont Street near West Street, was erected in 1888 to honor the five men killed by British soldiers in 1770. The memorial's proponents were surprised to discover opposition to the plan from old-line Bostonians who considered the victims to be nothing more than rabble rousers.

The memorial proceeded despite the objections. Editor and poet John Boyle O'Reilly, Boston's best-known Irish leader in the late nineteenth century, wrote a poem called "Crispus Attucks," using the occasion to comment on the race relations between blacks and whites. His verses asked "whether we learned what Crispus Attucks knew, when right is stricken, that white and black are one, not two."

The actual site of the massacre is marked by a medallion of cobblestones next to the Old State House, at the corner of State and Washington Streets. The Boston Massacre victims are buried at the Old Granary Burying Ground on Tremont Street, where their tombstone faces the street.

boys, Negroes, mulattos, Irish teagues and outlandish jack tars . . . shouting and hazing and threatening life . . . whistling, scream[ing] and rendering an Indian yell . . . throwing every species of rubbish they could pick up in the street." The term "teague" was and is a slang and derogatory name for Irish Catholics. So the Irish were taking the blame on both sides of the melee.

In the end it was Carr's dying testimony that helped to exonerate Preston and his men. Dr. John Jeffries, who had treated Carr on his deathbed, became a star witness at the trial. He testified that Carr "was a native of Ireland, and had frequently seen mobs, and soldiers called upon to quell them. . . . He had seen soldiers often fire on the people in Ireland, but had never seen them bear half so much before they fired in his life." As a final gesture of contrition, Carr told Jeffries that "he forgave the man whoever he was that shot him, he was satisfied he had no malice, but fired to defend himself."

On December 5, 1770, nine months to the day after the Boston Massacre, only Kilroy and Montgomery were found guilty of manslaughter for the killing of Crispus Attucks; the others were exonerated. At their sentencing on December 14, both men invoked a medieval English plea for mercy called "the benefit of clergy," originally offered to clergy and later extended to felons facing a first conviction. The plea involved showing their God-fearing ways by reciting Psalm 51; both Kilroy and Montgomery did so and thus had their execution commuted. They were branded with an M for murder on their thumbs and were released back into their regiment. Years later, when Governor Hutchinson's diaries became public, it turned out that Hugh Montgomery had admitted to his lawyers that it was he who yelled out the fatal call to fire that helped start the American Revolution.

The Fighting Irish

The Irish fought on both sides in the Revolutionary War, and it was not uncommon for Irish soldiers to face each other in battle. Colonel Daniel O'Brien's Fifth Regiment of British Foot Soldiers, composed primarily of Irish soldiers, fought at the Battle of Lexington, against a colonial force that included three Burkes, five Collinses, eight Kellys, six Kennys, and eight Welshes. After Lexington a cartoon in a local newspaper depicted the retreating British troops as "Irish asses defeated by the brave American militia."

Ever mindful of maintaining the might of the empire, or the perception of it, the British dutifully planted stories in Boston papers suggesting that all of Ireland was against the American insurrection. In September 1775 *Draper's Gazette* reported, "A brigade of Irish Roman Catholics is forming in Munster and Connaught in order to be sent to Boston to act against the rebels."

What the story did not reveal is that many of the Irish soldiers were recruited by force. The British employed press gangs to scour the Irish countryside and forcibly conscript young men into military service. A letter printed in a Philadelphia paper during the war and later found by historian Michael O'Brien states, "The recruiting officers were driven out of the towns [in Cork and Kerry] by angry mobs . . . and many of the Irish soldiers in the English regiments destined for America swore they will never draw a trigger against the Americans, amongst whom they all have relations."

Once they were in America, it wasn't unusual for Irish soldiers in the British regiments to desert and join the other side, forcing the British to recruit new soldiers constantly. British adjunct general Lord Francis Rawdon, Earl of Moira, led a regiment called the Volunteers of Ireland. On Saint Patrick's Day His Lordship, hoping to stave off further deserters, treated the Irish regiment to a fancy banquet that included "beef and good liquor" in New York City.

It makes sense that disaffected Irish servants and stubborn Ulster Presbyterians would join the colonial army and navy. As much as they disliked certain aspects of New England, they recognized that Olde England, with its class system, empire building, and feudal remnants, was much worse. And while they regarded the Boston Puritans as narrow-minded and intolerant, especially in religious matters, they also admired their independence and tenacity in bucking authority, regardless of whether that authority came from Rome or London. Bostonians correctly saw parallels in the struggles of the Irish and the thirteen colonies. Benjamin Franklin, whose sister Mary had married Irishman Robert Holmes from Fermanagh, spoke of this parallel when he visited Europe to establish lasting alliances with France and Ireland during the war. In 1778 Ben Franklin wrote a letter entitled "To the Good People of Ireland":

> *The misery and distress which your ill-fated country has been*
> *so frequently exposed to, and has so often experienced, by such a*
> *combination of rapine, treachery and violence, as would have disgraced*
> *the name of government in the most arbitrary country in the world, has*
> *most sincerely affected your friends in America, and has engaged the most*
> *serious attention of Congress.*

In return for Ireland's support, Franklin promised that America would someday find the means to "establish your freedom in the fullest and amplest manner."

The marquis de Chastellux of France, who recorded his travels in America between 1780 and 1782, noted the camaraderie between Irish and Americans during this time:

> *An Irishman, the instant he sets foot on American ground, becomes, ipso*
> *facto, an American. While Englishmen and Scotsmen were regarded*
> *with jealousy and distrust, even with the best recommendation of zeal*
> *and attachment to their cause, a native of Ireland stood in need of no*

The Tracys and O'Briens: Irish Privateers

When British ships began to stop American ships along the New England coast in 1775, two Irish families in particular engaged in a daring cat-and-mouse game with the British fleet. The O'Brien brothers of Maine and the Tracy brothers of Massachusetts were considered pirates by the British, but grateful colonial leaders such as George Washington preferred the name "privateers" for the captains and sailors who joined the struggle for American liberty.

Jeremiah O'Brien and his four brothers—Gideon, William, John, and Joseph—started the first naval battle of the Revolutionary War. The sons of Cork immigrant Maurice O'Brien, they captured the British warship *Margaretta* on May 11, 1775, in the waters next to Machias, Maine. The British called it "the first act of Colonial piracy," but the Massachusetts Provincial Congress commissioned the brothers to serve as privateers. During the war they captured numerous British vessels, including the prize schooner *Hibernia.* On September 24, 1900, the United States Navy christened a torpedo boat the SS *Jeremiah O'Brien.* A plaque honoring Jeremiah O'Brien was placed at the Massachusetts State House in 1936.

Patrick Tracy of Wexford, Ireland, settled in Newburyport, Massachusetts, in the 1740s and had three sons, Nathaniel, James, and John. Together the father and sons were successful sea merchants who traveled to Europe and the West Indies. When the war began the Tracy fleet was commissioned for privateering. The Tracy brothers, along with their brothers-in-law Jonathan Jackson and Joseph Lee, refitted twenty-three of their merchant boats, including their privateer vessels *Game Cock* and *Yankee Hero,* with mounted guns. The Tracy vessels captured 120 British vessels and 2,200 prisoners of war. Patrick Tracy's home is today the Newburyport Public Library, located at 94 State Street.

other certificate than his dialect. His sincerity was never called into question; he was supposed to have a sympathy of suffering.

English officer Major Joshua Pell wrote in his diary, "The rebels consist chiefly of Irish redemptioners [servants] and convicts, the most audacious rascals existing." Some from those servant families were numbered among George Washington's most valued officers. One such was General John Sullivan of Maine. Another was Henry Knox, the leader at the Battle of Ticonderoga whose family helped form the Irish Presbyterian church in 1729. More than two hundred Irish-born soldiers fought at the Battle of Bunker Hill on June 17, 1775, alongside Americans of Ulster stock whose families had settled New Hampshire and Maine earlier in the century. Hector McNeil of Antrim, an active member of the Irish Presbyterian church, was a seasoned navy man and close friend of Scottish naval hero John Paul Jones. John Barry of Tacumshane,

County Wexford, commander of the ship *Lexington*, captured the first British ship, the *Edward*, under the American flag.

James Forrest himself remained a steadfast loyalist. In December 1775 he raised a company of ninety-five men and five lieutenants, named the Loyal Irish Volunteers, to patrol the streets of Boston with a white cockade, or insignia, on their hats. The duties of this vainglorious group lasted for only about three months, for in March 1776 the British were forced to evacuate Boston when General Sullivan, Colonel Knox, and hundreds

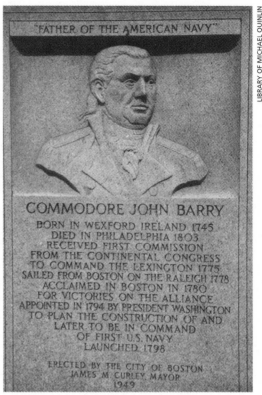

Boston Common memorial to Commodore John Barry of County Wexford, a hero in the Revolutionary War

of rebels aimed cannons at the British fleet from atop Dorchester Heights in South Boston, bringing the eight-year siege of Boston to an end.

Forrest and his fellow Tories fled to Halifax, Nova Scotia, where many of them remained in exile for the duration of the war. Charitable Irish Society loyalists were so well represented in Nova Scotia that they formed a Halifax chapter, which still flourishes today. Forrest remained active in the war and was captured by American troops while carrying supplies from the West Indies to the British army in Valley Forge. He was jailed in Philadelphia for a time. His sons Charles and James fought on the British side, with Charles losing an eye at the Battle of Germantown in 1777. That same year Forrest sunk his life savings into a cargo of tea, which was captured by the Americans on the Delaware River. He later applied for a Tory pension from the British government and was awarded recompense.

The Artists Take on the Revolution

Two of the more interesting Boston Irish personalities of the Revolutionary War period were notable portrait painter John Singleton Copley and his half brother Henry Pelham. John was born on July 3, 1738, in Boston, the only child of Mary Singleton from Quinville Abbey, County Clare, who came from a prosperous family that owned nearly two thousand acres of Irish land, and Richard Copley, "who was probably the son of Alderman Charles Copley, one of the sheriffs of Limerick," writes art historian Jules David Prown. Richard Copley became ill and died in the early 1740s, leaving his wife and son to fend for themselves in Boston. For a time Mary ran a small shop on Long Wharf, where she sold tobacco and sundries. She met Peter Pelham, a talented portrait painter from England who had ties to the Charitable Irish Society and who had done a portrait of Rev. Moorhead. After Pelham's second wife died, he and Mary married in May 1748 at Trinity Church on Summer Street and the following year had a son, Henry Pelham. Peter Pelham quickly introduced Henry and his stepson John Copley to the fine art of painting, and both boys became accomplished artists in their time.

PHOTOGRAPH © 2004 MUSEUM OF FINE ARTS, BOSTON

John Singleton Copley's first painting of his brother Henry, entitled *A Boy with a Flying Squirrel*, was completed in 1765 and established him as a significant American artist. He painted portraits of Paul Revere, Samuel Adams, George Washington, and John Hancock, who was his neighbor on Beacon Street overlooking Boston Common. But radical activists regarded Copley suspiciously, since he also painted the British elite occupying Boston,

John S. Copley's 1765 portrait of his half brother, entitled A Boy with a Flying Squirrel, *is displayed at the Museum of Fine Arts, Boston.*

including General Thomas Gage, the colonial governor of the Bay State from 1774 to 1775. Copley's reputation was further suspect when he married Susannah Clarke, the daughter of a leading Tory merchant who was the Boston agent for the East India Company. It was Mr. Clarke's shipment of tea that American colonists, disguised as Mohawk Indians, dumped in Boston Harbor on December 16, 1773, in the infamous Boston Tea Party.

Henry Pelham, a decade younger than his brother, would have a minor role to play in the Boston Massacre, gaining notoriety as the artist who captured for posterity the iconic illustration of the Boston Massacre in March 1770. The drawing has been wrongly attributed to engraver Paul Revere. Revere had taken the illustration from the twenty-one-year-old Pelham, then proceeded to engrave, print, and sell it without any credit to Pelham.

Pelham wrote Revere a furious letter on March 29, 1770:

> *When I heard that you was cutting a plate of the late Murder, I thought it was impossible, as I knew you was not capable of doing it unless you copied it from mine and as I thought I had entrusted it in the hands of a person who had more regard to the dictates of Honour and Justice than to take the undue advantage you have done of the confidence and Trust I reposed in you. But I find I was mistaken. . . . If you are insensible of the Dishonour you have brought on yourself by this Act, the World will not be so. However, I leave you to reflect upon and consider of one of the most dishonorable Actions you could well be guilty of.*

Henry Pelham was present at the Battle of Bunker Hill in June 1775. General Gage commissioned Pelham to draw a map of the battle, entitled *A Plan of Boston in New England and Its Environs*, which put him squarely on the British side of the war. He felt "a duty to his most gracious Sovereign and Veneration for the British Government," but that sentiment put Pelham in a bind once the British left Boston in 1776. He fled to Halifax and never returned. "All his books, furniture, and personal property was left behind in Boston," writes historian Alfred Jones. His beloved mother, Mary Copley, refused to leave during the exodus and remained in Boston until her death in 1789. Henry eventually settled in County Clare, where his mother had been born. He married Catherine Butler and worked as a surveyor, completing an intricate map of County Clare for the British government in 1787. He worked for a time as a land agent for the Marquis of Lansdowne, who owned considerable property in County

Kerry. In 1806 Pelham accidentally drowned in the Kenmare River when his boat overturned.

John Singleton Copley moved to London during the war and never returned to Boston. Unlike Henry, who vanished from history, Copley is still remembered fondly in Boston. Copley Square in Back Bay was named in his honor in 1883, and a plaque at 34 Beacon Street across from Boston Common marks the site of Copley's home. In 1902 the Boston School of Art was renamed the Copley Society to honor the city's most famous painter, and his portraits are cherished by the Museum of Fine Arts, the Boston Public Library, and the Massachusetts Historical Society. In 2002 the Boston Parks Department unveiled a statue of the artist at Copley Square, a testament to the artist's continuing influence on the Boston imagination.

CHAPTER THREE

Here Come the Catholics (1780–1830)

GEORGE WASHINGTON set the stage for Catholics to be accepted in Massachusetts and in America. It was Washington, after all, who had stopped the churlish celebration of Pope's Day among his troops in November 1775, at Cambridge, shortly after he arrived at camp. Knowing the colonial army's reliance on French, Irish, and German soldiers, Washington issued an order prohibiting the celebration of Pope's Day, calling the practice a "ridiculous and childish custom." Then in 1788 at Valley Forge, Pennsylvania, colonial soldiers kicking around an effigy of the pope caused "great indignation among the Irish in the camp," writes historian John Crimmins. Washington himself appeared on the scene and put an end to the pastime, saying, "I, too, am a lover of St. Patrick's Day."

After the war Washington wrote to Bishop John Carroll of Maryland, "I hope to see America as the foremost nation in examples of justice and liberality. I hope Americans will not forget the patriotic part which [Catholics] took in the accomplishment of their revolution, and the establishment of their government."

Washington also looked kindly on immigrants, especially those seeking refuge from the old-world tyrannies of Europe. In a letter to Rev. Francis Vanderkamp in 1788, Washington wrote, "I had always hoped that this land might become a safe and agreeable Asylum to the virtuous and persecuted part of mankind, to whatever nation they might belong."

Entering the nineteenth century, America reached a crossroads that it would return to time after time in its history. Would the guarantees of citizenship enshrined in the US Constitution and the Bill of Rights be available to all Americans, regardless of religion, gender, class, or national origins? Or would America remain a nation whose core character came from wealthy landowners of Anglo-Saxon Protestant ancestry?

It was in this postwar environment that Boston Catholics held their first public Mass in 1788 in downtown Boston, attended by about a hundred Catholics. An eyewitness gave this firsthand account:

> *We fitted up a dilapidated and deserted meeting house in School Street that was built in 1716 by some French Huguenots . . . and now converted by us into a popish chapel. Money was raised by subscription, a pulpit was erected, the Altar furnished, a few benches were purchased for seats and the little temple, which had served as a stable to the British in 1775, was once more consecrated to the uses of religion.*

The Mass on School Street was a defining moment in Boston's history, setting the stage for a new tolerance that followed the end of the war. A few years later Bostonians responded generously when Bishop Jean de Cheverus started a subscription drive to raise twenty thousand dollars for a Catholic church. President John Adams made a generous contribution of one hundred dollars, and Protestants donated one-fifth of the money raised. Architect James Bulfinch, who designed the Massachusetts State House and the new Irish Protestant church on Federal Street, drew up architectural plans for the church at no charge; he was later awarded a solid silver urn by the congregation. On Saint Patrick's Day, March 17, 1800, church leaders broke ground at a site on Franklin Street for the new church, and the Church of the Holy Cross was completed by 1803, serving as the centerpiece for the Catholic Church in New England. In the 1860s Holy Cross moved to its present site on Harrison Avenue in Boston's South End.

The first Irish priests serving in Boston were characterized by their commitment to the poor. In 1817 Bishop de Cheverus ordained Dennis Ryan of Kilkenny, who was posted to Newcastle, Maine, to tend to a growing congregation there, and in 1820 he ordained Patrick Byrne, also of Kilkenny, to become the bishop's assistant. Thomas Lynch of County Cavan, pastor of Saint Patrick's Church on Northampton Street in the 1830s, was "probably the best

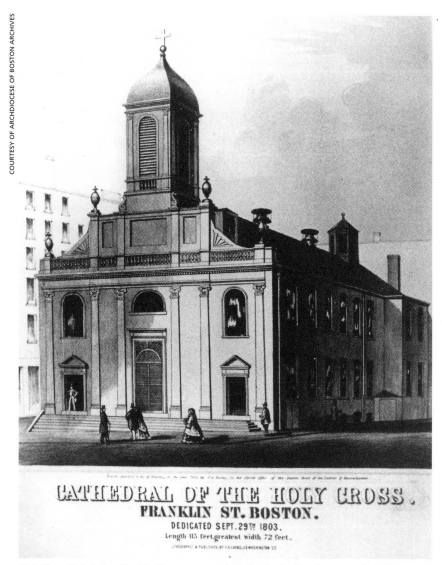

CATHEDRAL OF THE HOLY CROSS.
FRANKLIN ST. BOSTON.
DEDICATED SEPT. 29TH 1803.
Length 115 feet, greatest width 72 feet.

Holy Cross Cathedral on Franklin Street was an early anchor for the Catholic community in Boston.

classical scholar at that time in New England," according to the archdiocesan paper, the *Pilot.* "But the grand passion of his life was charity to the poor. He fed them, clothed them, and counseled them. They slept in the basement of the church till other shelter could be procured. He always had a store of boots and shoes in his house, and kept many hands busy making up clothes for the immigrant women and children. He cared little for splendid buildings."

Settling in South Boston

Just as Presbyterians flourished in Boston after establishing the Church of Irish Strangers on Long Lane more than seventy years earlier, so too did the Irish Catholic community begin to blossom with the completion of the Cathedral of the Holy Cross. In 1808 the state legislature established a new neighborhood by annexing a peninsula that was part of Dorchester and renaming it South Boston. Drawn by the cheap accommodations and the prospect of working in the shipping industry, the Irish found South Boston to be a perfect place for them. The peninsula's rugged coastline and isolated geography permitted the development of a community akin to an Irish village, and it allowed residents there to create a distinct, separate culture that would become the hallmark of South Boston for two centuries.

In 1810 Thomas Murray, a thirty-six-year-old Dubliner, set up shop in South Boston as an undertaker, and five years later Boston's Board of Health granted Catholics permission to build a cemetery in South Boston. Augustinian priest Philip Lariscy organized a fund-raising campaign and collected six hundred dollars to purchase the parcel of land at the corner of Dorchester and Sixth Streets. The cemetery and its small chapel, which opened in 1819, were named for Saint Augustine in honor of Lariscy's order. Up to this time Catholics were buried in one of the city's public cemeteries, such as the Central Burying Ground on Boston Common, or Copp's Hill Cemetery in the North End, according to Thomas H. O'Connor. This was a suitable arrangement, since only 120 Catholics were living in Boston in 1790. By 1820 that population had jumped to about two thousand.

When Saint Augustine's Cemetery opened, "over 200 parishioners of Boston's Cathedral of the Holy Cross . . . transfer[red] the bodies . . . of relatives and friends from local cemeteries to the new Catholic burial ground," writes historian O'Connor. Over time the small mortuary chapel at the cemetery was used to celebrate Mass for the growing population of Irish immigrants. Many Irish Catholics outside Boston took their loved ones from Irish settlements in Lowell and Chelmsford to be buried at Saint Augustine's, and by the end of the decade, the cemetery was filled.

A survey of the early tombstones by George F. Dwyer indicates that many of the Irish buried there were children who didn't survive past their first year on earth. This Stone Erected by Christopher Connolly in Memory of His

SON, JOHN, WHO DIED APRIL 14, 1825, AGE 16 MONTHS, reads one tombstone. A majority of Irish buried in the cemetery came from Cork, Tipperary, and Kilkenny, followed by Donegal, Longford, Waterford, and Wexford. All thirty-two counties are represented in the cemetery, underscoring the pervasiveness of Irish immigration to Boston in the nineteenth century.

Irish citizens continued moving into South Boston, but so too did numerous institutions that Boston officials didn't want downtown. These included the Massachusetts School for Idiots, the House of Industry, the Almshouse, and detention centers for adults and juveniles. Ironically, the Irish migration to South Boston increased by midcentury, when many of the impoverished immigrants fleeing the Irish Famine ended up in these institutions. In the 1840s neighborhood leaders, mostly Yankees, accused the city of turning South Boston into another Botany Bay, home of the world's most famous penal colony in Australia, and they threatened to secede from Boston. The city eventually transferred several of these facilities to Deer Island in the 1850s, and the Irish migration to South Boston continued.

Taking a Chance on Charlestown

Boston's increasing Irish population prompted Catholic leaders to seek out more cemetery space. They set their sights on Charlestown, a separate municipality that would not be incorporated into Boston until 1874. Bishop Benedict Fenwick purchased a twenty-four-acre plot of Charlestown land in 1825 for an order of Ursuline nuns who had been living on Franklin Street across from the cathedral. On this land they built a religious educational complex that included a three-story brick convent for the nuns to live in, a chapel, and a school for girls. It featured terraced gardens and greenhouses and was enclosed from public view by a wooden fence surrounding the property. The school provided a quality education and within a few years included up to sixty girls from wealthy Protestant families, along with Irish immigrant girls.

The school caused resentment in the town from working-class Yankees, especially as Fenwick continued to expand the Catholic presence in Charlestown, opening Saint Mary's Church on Richmond Street in 1829 and the following year purchasing a plot of land behind Bunker Hill for a Catholic cemetery. Fenwick got an inkling of the trouble ahead when the stable on the cemetery grounds was deliberately burned to the ground. The Charlestown residents were sending a message: they didn't want Irish Catholics buried in their town.

In addition to an anti-Catholic sentiment, Charlestown people feared that the Irish would bring religious superstitions and disease to their town. In the nineteenth century the entire world was worried about the spread of diseases, and rightly so, since they were responsible for so many deaths, especially among children. Boston had long taken pains to quarantine ailing passengers arriving by ship. Passengers were checked for measles, smallpox, and cholera, and Spectacle and Rainsford Islands had quarantine stations for ships coming in from Europe. Charlestown had its first smallpox epidemic in 1752 and was always thereafter vigilant against scourges. When faced with cholera epidemics in 1829 and again in 1832, local health officials successfully prevented the spread of the disease by literally scrubbing down streets, water pumps, and latrines.

Marie Daly of the New England Historic Genealogical Society believes that Charlestown residents feared that contact with the Irish would literally make them sick. Daly, an expert on early Catholic cemeteries, notes, "In those days, before the development of germ theory, people believed that disease was spread by people emitting fumes that passed from one person to the other. Bostonians considered the Irish to be a very dirty, immoral people who were bringing epidemics to their town. Disease was seen not as a health issue but a moral issue."

The conditions of poverty—poor sanitation, lack of clean drinking water, overcrowded living quarters, and poor nutrition—were characteristic of Irish immigrant life during this time, and the mortality rate of the Boston Irish was disproportionately high. In the 1830s the majority of Irish children died before the age of five. The infant mortality rate was bad too, with one out of every five Irish babies dying under the age of twelve months as late as 1850. A high rate of birth defects also occurred as a result of malnutrition. Those factors probably accounted for the tendency of Irish Catholic couples to have large families, Daly says. In fact, it was frequent early deaths of Irish children that created an urgent need for burial space.

In November 1831 the town selectmen in Charlestown tried to prevent Catholic burials by voting to prohibit "the dead bodies of a particular class of people, brought from the city of Boston." The decision expressed concern for the "proper regard for the future health, security and improvement of the town." Bishop Fenwick immediately contested the selectmen's ruling, appealing to the Massachusetts General Court in March 1832. His appeal stated:

> *More than 100 interments have already taken place . . . tombs have likewise been marked for the accommodation of families, which have been purchased. . . . Surely the legislature will not pass a law [to] forever . . . prevent the ashes of a husband [or] parent from mingling with those of his once beloved and cherished spouse or of his dear children.*

The state's ruling supported the right of Charlestown officials to make Bishop Fenwick seek permission in writing from the selectmen every time he wanted to bury someone at Bunker Hill Cemetery from outside of Charlestown. This was an outrageous notion, and everyone knew that it was intended to prevent burials from ever taking place.

On May 19, 1832, Fenwick attempted to comply with the ruling to bury two Boston children, three-year-old Florence Driscoll, who died from teething, and three-month-old James Kinsley, who died from infantile disease. Fenwick's request was denied the same day it was written by Selectman Nathan Austin, who stated, "The object of the town in adopting the rule was to prevent the bringing of the dead from the surrounding towns and country. . . . We feel constrained from a sense of duty to decline giving the permission you request."

Fenwick decided he would test the validity of the state ruling and went ahead and buried the children without the town's permission. The matter went to a higher court, and ultimately the church was recognized as having the right to bury its dead on its own property. But the victory did not soften the harsh mood that many folks had toward the Irish, and the disdain for Irish Catholic funerals continued for decades to come.

During the Famine years, Marie Daly notes, officials in other towns such as Roxbury and Cambridge tried to revive the Charlestown model of obstructing Catholic funerals by transferring authority to local selectmen. In 1849 Boston's Board of Health tried to shut down South Boston's Saint Augustine's Cemetery, claiming that the graves were too shallow, and the following year the city passed an ordinance to this effect. Once again the ordinance was struck down by the lower courts, and the city appealed to the state legislature to pass what became known as the Paddy Funeral Acts, ceding to town authorities the power to influence who could be buried and who could not. Bishop John

Fitzpatrick, who succeeded Bishop Fenwick in 1846, convinced the moderate members of the state legislature to let the appeal languish in committee, and burials continued. The Yankees, it seemed, were not just unhappy about the Irish living in Boston and Charlestown. They were also displeased about their dying there.

Chapter Four

Fighting Over the Irish (The 1830s)

A DINNER PARTY on Thanksgiving night, 1833, ended up as a full-blown riot the next day, when a mob of angry townsmen came to Rodger McGowan's house in Charlestown and tore it to the ground piece by piece. The several thousand nervous Irish Catholics living around Boston had to ask themselves, could it get any worse? The answer was yes, it could get a lot worse, for what took place at McGowan's was just part of an escalating chain of violent episodes directed at the Irish through much of the 1830s.

The troubles began on the evening of Thanksgiving, one of the holidays most revered by Bay State residents. Governor Joseph Dudley had proclaimed Thanksgiving a holiday in 1713, asking all Bostonians to "attend and perform the duties of the day with a religious and becoming devotion." The Puritans had banned Christmas celebrations in Boston, considering it a Catholic holiday with pagan overtones, so Thanksgiving had emerged as the city's chief winter celebration, commemorating the harvest feast shared nearly one hundred years earlier when American Indians had helped struggling Pilgrims survive a harsh winter. In later years Irish humorist Finley Peter Dunne would quip that Thanksgiving "'twas founded by the Puritans to give thanks for being preserved from the Indians, and we keep it to give thanks we are preserved from the Puritans."

On Thanksgiving night Irish immigrant Rodger McGowan and his wife were hosting an Irish party at their home, which doubled as an unlicensed speakeasy, or *shabeen* as the Irish called it, at the corner of Main and Water Streets in Charlestown. On this night they were charging one dollar per couple, offering dancing and fiddling in two rooms below and refreshments in the bar upstairs. About fifty people attended the affair, mostly immigrants who had walked over from Boston and crossed the Charles River Bridge to enjoy the Irish soiree.

Just down the road some of the local Charlestown boys went into town for a few beers in Langley's barroom after their own Thanksgiving feasts. Before too long a gang of them, including Ira Greene, Caleb Carter, William Bullard, Benjamin Daniells, and Cornelius Harding, were getting drunk. Around ten o'clock they decided to head over to the Irish party, intending to cause some mischief. They began to throw rocks, chunks of ice, and snowballs against McGowan's house. At one point in the ruckus, an Irishman reached over the fence and hit Ira Greene on the head with a stick. Then some Irish came around the fence and confronted the Charlestown men, and threats were exchanged.

Ben Daniells bent down to pick up a club and said sarcastically, "I'll have a shillelagh too." The two groups circled each other tensely. One of the Irishmen, later described in court as a tall man in a light frock coat with a cap on his head, pointed at Greene and Daniells and said, "I mark you and shall know you again." The two groups circled each other some more, then went their separate ways, with the townsmen going back to the hotel for a few more drinks and the Irish returning to McGowan's.

Around midnight a few dozen Irish men and women were heading back to Boston, with the men still roiling about the ice-throwing incident earlier that evening. Suddenly the Charlestown men appeared out of the darkness. As town watchman Cyrus Blanchard later testified, he walked with the Irish back toward the bridge "so that they should not be insulted. . . . The young men followed us down and two or three times sung out, I should think insultingly, to the party. I told the young men to go back and let the Irish people alone."

The Irish men walked the women to the bridge, then suddenly turned and chased down the Charlestown men. On the wharf next to Davidson's Granary, the two sides caught up with each other a final time. Daniells and Bullard picked up clubs from a nearby woodpile and began swinging them, witnesses recalled.

"They had clubs in their hands about four feet long and as thick round as my arm," one testified in court.

"I came from the woodpile, struck an Irishman with a club, kicked an Irishman and knocked him down," Bullard admitted.

Witness Jacob L. Kean picked up the story from that point: "Two [men] getting clubs from the wood pile . . . came round and went upon the side walk. The Irishmen attacked one of these men and knocked him down; he was dressed in a light dress coat and light pantaloons. I saw one man strike another, afterwards, a second strike him, and after he had fallen, then a third and a fourth." The brawl ended quickly, with the townsmen retreating back to the town and the Irish racing back across the bridge to Broad Street, a notorious Irish enclave in Boston where the poorest immigrants lived and where trouble was routine.

Hearing the noise, the Dailey sisters, who ran a shop right next to the bridge, looked out their window and saw a man lying in the gutter. Ellen Dailey ran over to the man, clapped her hands, and began screaming, "It's Ben Daniells," then lifted his head up to help him breathe. "I see no one coming [so] I screeched and I screeched" until others came along.

Dr. Walker, the town physician, arrived upon the scene, where he pronounced Daniells, a thirty-six-year-old married blacksmith, dead from injuries around his head. On the way back home Walker passed McGowan's and was surprised to hear Irish dancing and fiddling still going on. He stopped a watchman and asked him to stop the party, but the watchman said he was too scared to go in. Walker called the police captain, who went into the house and found about twenty-five people there. He told the Irish what had happened, and the party broke up at once.

The next day rumors of the "cold-blooded murder of an American citizen" spread through the town, and a "just indignation" took hold of the townspeople, the *Bunker Hill Aurora* weekly newspaper later reported. Daniells, people said, was an innocent passerby who met up with a group of Irish who were "undoubtedly intoxicated and armed with billets of wood." There was talk of tearing down McGowan's house, where all the trouble had started.

McGowan had heard the rumors and immediately armed himself with "muskets, powder and balls." But the town's selectmen confiscated McGowan's weapons, leaving him defenseless. At about six o'clock in the evening the townsmen began to assemble outside, whipping up the fury needed to invade the house. Armed with pickaxes, bats, guns, and fire hooks, they threw McGowan and his family out, then began to break up the furniture and dump the liquor from the bar onto the street. Several rioters grabbed the fire hook from the local hook and ladder company and pulled down a corner of the house.

Meanwhile, Judge John Soley appeared upon the scene and proceeded to read the Riot Act "amid the uproar and assaults of the rioters." This proved ineffective, so town officials called upon a local battalion of US Marines, who marched to the site and were immediately attacked by the rioters. With no direct orders to intervene, the Marines returned to their quarters.

Around eleven o'clock about thirty citizens attempted to quell the riot, coming to the scene with light infantry guns, under the command of Captain Pritchard. The mob corralled the citizens with ropes, dragging them away from the scene en masse, and they fled back to Town Hall. Now the rioters had "unlimited sway," according to the *Bunker Hill Aurora*. They found a large cable and attached it to McGowan's roof and finally managed to demolish the house.

Irish Landmarks in Charlestown

The **Bunker Hill Monument** marks the famous battle of June 17, 1775, in which one hundred Americans died. Historian Michael J. O'Brien's book, *The Irish at Bunker Hill*, identifies 176 Irish-born colonists and hundreds of Irish Americans who fought in the battle.

Winthrop Square contains the Bunker Hill Memorial Tablets, which list the names of the battle's casualties. It also is the site of the Charlestown Civil War Monument, erected in 1871 and created by Sligo-born sculptor Martin Milmore. Across the street from the square, at 34 Winthrop Street, is the former home of poet John Boyle O'Reilly, now a private residence.

The **Charlestown Historical Society** is housed with the National Park Service at 43 Monument Square.

The **USS Constitution** in the Navy Yard became famous during the War of 1812. It was commanded by Charles Stewart, the maternal grandfather of Ireland's Home Rule leader Charles Stewart Parnell and poet Fanny Parnell.

The **Bunker Hill Cemetery** is Boston's second Irish Catholic burying ground, opened in 1832. Over nine thousand people, including a large number of Irish children who died from typhus, cholera, and other diseases, are buried here. In 2009 the people of Charlestown erected a Celtic cross in remembrance of the nineteenth-century Irish.

As a final act of defiance, the rioters took two dressed hogs from the kitchen and threw them in the river.

A Decade of Rioting

The McGowan incident was part of a frenzy building up against the city's growing Irish community. The goodwill that had been established in the aftermath of the Revolutionary War was quickly fading. As Professor O'Connor writes, the "veneer of religious and ethnic tolerance was already beginning to wear thin."

And the veneer was wearing thin across the nation. Historian Tyler V. Johnson notes, "Only after 1830, as the increasing tide of Irish emigration threatened to revolutionize the previously Anglicized and inoffensively small Catholic community . . . , did the somewhat dormant anti-Catholic prejudice reawaken and begin to fuel an increasingly virulent nativist movement."

What should the Irish do? A few months after the McGowan incident, "A Naturalized Irishman" wrote a letter to the *Catholic Intelligencer* newspaper expressing astonishment at the "apathy with which Irishmen in this city bear the insults that are continually cast upon their religion and their country." Why, he asked, after fighting English tyranny all these centuries, would Irishmen cross the Atlantic and "submit to insult and mockery" in a land where they came to be free?

Why, indeed. By 1830 about 11 percent, or seven thousand of the city's sixty-one thousand residents, were Catholics, of mostly German, French, and Irish descent, and Boston itself was growing dramatically. The city's second mayor, Josiah Quincy, who served between 1823 and 1828, made great strides in modernizing the city and expanding its infrastructure as the population increased. It wasn't only Irish and German immigrants who pushed the city to its limits; rural workers from New England and the Maritimes were also pouring into Boston looking for work.

Quincy, who had been a close friend of Bishop de Cheverus, seemed sympathetic to the immigrant plight, and he made considerable improvements to sanitary conditions in the city by putting restrictions on livestock, collecting garbage regularly, and cleaning the streets. But the rapid expansion of the city brought attendant urban ills. Crime was on the rise, and so were public drunkenness, arson, prostitution, and vagrancy. Rioting seemed to come into fashion as rival volunteer fire companies, neighborhood gangs, and other public audiences engaged in fights as if they were sporting events. Much of the rioting was directed against the newcomers. Professor Jack Tager writes in his book *Boston Riots* that "hatred against Catholicism by Yankee plebeians was an intrinsic part of their heritage."

The Boston Irish seemed timid, trying not to draw attention to themselves. Perhaps they were falsely optimistic that the situation might improve if they kept their heads down. As the goodwill established in previous decades continued to deteriorate, Irish Catholics had become the whipping boys for the city's collective fears, anxieties, and resentments.

Conservative Protestant preachers kept the emotional flames high. Tager points out that in the 1830s a "nationwide evangelical movement" targeted Catholicism and liberal Protestantism as "a danger to American democracy." The movement, called the Second Awakening, was a sequel to the Reverend Jonathan Edwards's Great Awakening of the 1740s, which sought to restore a pure Puritanism in New England. The stern, rigorous outlook some Bostonians yearned for seemed to personify the quip that journalist H. L. Mencken made about Puritanism: the haunting fear that someone, somewhere, may be happy.

The Jesuits Keep Watch

Boston's Catholic community received a shot of self-esteem in 1829 when Bishop Fenwick established the first Catholic newspaper in Massachusetts, initially called the *Jesuit* or *Catholic Sentinel.* The editor was the Reverend Doctor Thomas J. O'Flaherty, a scholar and physician from County Kerry who had studied theology and medicine in Dublin and Rome. He had translated a tome on the Spanish Inquisition and was said to be the intellectual equal of any preacher in town. In 1830, when the Reverend Lyman Beecher began a series of anti-Catholic sermons, O'Flaherty rose to the occasion and challenged every one of the sermons, pointing out the theological flaws and the non-Christian attitude toward Catholics.

O'Flaherty would soon be supported in the fray by Patrick Donahoe, who had arrived in Boston from Munnery, County Cavan, in 1825 at the age of fourteen. Patrick was a Catholic novelty at the predominantly Protestant Adams School in Boston, and the older boys liked to chalk a cross on his back, wrote historian Francis R. Walsh. Donahoe took a job as a typesetter with the local paper, the *Columbian Sentinel,* and by the time he was twenty-four had established the first boat-ticketing service between Ireland and America. In 1834 he took over the *Jesuit* newspaper, which had undergone several name changes since 1829, then in 1836 rechristened it the *Pilot,* a paper dedicated to the region's Catholic community with an emphasis on the Irish. The *Pilot* became a nationally renowned weekly newspaper that influenced many of the conversations Americans were having about the future of their country as it pertained to religion, immigrants, and ethnic communities.

In the 1830s Irish activities in Boston continued to increase. A literary group named the Hibernian Lyceum held weekly meetings at Columbian Hall behind the courthouse. The Boston Roman Catholic Mutual Society brought Irish businessmen together. Thomas Mooney's bookstore, at the corner of Federal and Franklin Streets, opened a singing school for young Catholics, using the new *Catholic Music Book* that Bishop Fenwick had paid to publish.

The Charitable Irish Society was approaching its centennial and had been energized by James Boyd, an Ulster Irish Presbyterian who patented the first fire hose in America. President of the society from 1836 to 1837, Boyd delivered a rousing oration on the Irish at the centennial dinner. The society, which had started as a Protestant group, began selecting Irish Catholics as its presidents. Among these were businessman Thomas Murphy, Bernard Fitzpatrick (the future bishop of Boston), and Rev. O'Flaherty.

The increasingly visible Catholic activities gave confidence and cohesion to the Irish community under siege. On Saint Patrick's Day, 1833, for example, the Cathedral of the Holy Cross overflowed with parishioners, and hundreds more waited outside hoping to get in. Reporting on the occasion, the *Jesuit* noted that the scene "afforded great edification to the good citizens of Boston, who beheld them, as they passed, at prayer, and all of them kneeling reverently with their faces turned toward the altar, on the hard pavement, and in the open street, in front of their church."

In November 1833, just a few days before the Thanksgiving incident at McGowan's, the first Catholic concert was held at the Masonic Temple. "Never was the Masonic Temple more densely crowded; and great were the numbers who could not gain admittance," the *Jesuit* reported. Organizers vowed to hold another concert on the Sunday before Christmas.

Support for the Irish

While many plebeians and preachers appeared intolerant, the Irish had gar-
nered sympathy from other parts of Boston. Writer Francis J. Grund, who
published a two-volume book in 1837 called *The Americans in Their Moral, Social,
and Political Relations*, complimented the Boston Irish as "a remarkably orderly
people . . . not usually given to intemperance but on the contrary willing to aid
in its suppression." Grund sympathized with their impoverished plight, but he
thought they had made a "noble beginning in Boston." If he had one piece of
advice, it was this: "Let the Irish, on their arrival in the United States, be, above
all things, careful not to disturb the peace of the citizens by revels of any kind."

But very often it was not the Irish who disturbed the peace. In Charlestown the townsmen grew increasing resentful as the Catholic presence
increased in the town. Bishop Fenwick had built Saint Mary's Catholic church,
opened a Catholic cemetery, and developed the twenty-four-acre Ursuline
Convent, all within the space of a decade. The convent, a boarding school for
girls, especially rankled the laboring class, since the young women came mainly
from wealthy Catholic and Protestant families in Boston. Historian Nancy
Lusignan Schultz writes that "these families paid a yearly tuition to the nuns
equivalent to a bricklayer's wages for six months' labor."

COURTESY OF ARCHDIOCESE OF BOSTON ARCHIVES

The Ursuline Convent in Charlestown was burned to the ground in 1834.

The workmen, frustrated by economic woes and the growing competition from immigrants for jobs, took on a nativist mentality that put the rights of Americans above the rights of immigrants. It didn't help that Rev. Beecher and others were preaching about a Catholic conspiracy, rekindling seventeenth-century Puritan fears of popery and Jesuit priests that had sparked anti-Catholic hysteria more than a century earlier.

All these factors came to bear in August 1834, when the Ursuline Convent was set afire by angry workmen led by John Buzzell, a New Hampshire transplant who worked as a bricklayer. The frightened nuns and their young female boarding students rushed from the school as the building went up in flames, with the bloodthirsty mob intent on burning it to the ground. A newspaper later reported that the "pianos and harps, thrown from the windows when the Convent was set on fire, were subsequently burnt, and nothing but an old chair and one or two worthless articles were saved from destruction."

Many public leaders condemned the mob of Yankee workmen who had burned the school. Lynde Walter, editor of the *Boston Evening Transcript*, wrote an editorial denouncing the episode:

> *We passed the ruins of the Ursuline Convent this morning. [It] was indeed a melancholy and mortifying sight. We hung our heads in shame whilst our spirit was indignant. We felt a great sense of degradation whilst we could have leapt into burning flames to seize upon the atrocious villains who had brought this disgrace.*

The ringleaders were arrested and went to trial, but they were not convicted, with the exception of one boy, who was later pardoned by the governor.

Assaults against the Irish continued through the decade. In June 1837 a brawl ensued in downtown Boston when an Irish funeral procession and a volunteer fire brigade returning to the station reached an intersection at the same time. In what became known as the Broad Street Riot, the volunteer firemen and their supporters chased the Irish along Purchase and Broad Streets into their houses, which were then attacked by the enraged mob. "The air was full of flying feathers and straw from the beds which had been ripped up and emptied into the streets," according to historian J. B. Cullen. Mayor Samuel A. Eliot ordered eight hundred National Lancers, a military group, to quell the riot and maintain peace.

Later that year an Irish voluntary militia group was attacked by other brigades during the annual brigade mustering on Boston Common. The Irish group called themselves the Montgomery Guards after Irish-born Revolutionary War hero General Richard Montgomery. When the Irish regiment arrived on the Common, the other groups walked off the parade ground in protest, then marched through the streets of Boston playing "Yankee Doodle" on their fifes and drums. As the Montgomery Guards returned to their barracks near Faneuil Hall, a mob attacked them, pelting them "with stones, coal, and sticks of wood all along their line of march." The Irish held formation and marched quickly to their armory, which was surrounded briefly by several thousand Bostonians. Mayor Eliot again intervened.

By the end of the decade, many Bostonians wondered whether their City on a Hill would now be destroyed by reckless, desperate Irish Catholics. Could the problem get any worse? The answer was yes, it was about to get a lot worse. In 1840 the Cunard Line ship company, subsidized by the British government, built a pier in East Boston and began direct routes from Britain to Boston, using the port as the best way to distribute mail throughout North America. As historian Oscar Handlin writes, "The line itself did not engage in the immigrant trade until 1863; but by engrossing other passenger business almost at once, it forced the established packet lines to devote themselves to the least desirable customers."

That would be the Irish, who increasing fled their homeland as Ireland continued to fare poorly under British rule. In 1836 a British report by George Nicholls suggested that emigration was a possible remedy for Irish destitution; the Irish should be encouraged to emigrate. In the 1840s Ireland's political unrest and economic instability caused by inept British policies and by a series of potato crop failures reached new heights. Between 1845 and 1849 all of those conditions forced the Irish to board rickety ships in hopes of avoiding disease and death. Unfortunately they couldn't escape either. Instead, they brought both with them.

Chapter Five

Invasion of the Fruitful Barbarians (The 1840s)

Two immigrants, each named Patrick Sullivan, left their homes in Ireland in 1847 and took passage to Boston. One of them flourished here; the other perished.

The Sullivan who survived had boarded the good ship *Unicorn* in London on July 22, 1847, and sailed into Boston that August. His only skill was dancing, so he set up a dance academy and taught boys and girls the "fine art of symmetry, of grace, of rhythm," as it was later described. He married Swiss immigrant Adrienne List, a classically trained pianist, and they settled at 22 Bennett Street in the South End, where in September 1856 they had their first and only son, whom they named Louis.

The other Patrick Sullivan spent his final days on this earth quarantined at Deer Island in Boston Harbor. He died on November 11, 1847, of diabetes at age thirty-three. He was the 260th Irish immigrant to die at the quarantine hospital since its opening on May 29 of that year. He was one of nine Sullivans who died on the island between June and December 1847.

Sullivan the dancer and his wife the pianist, along with their son Louis, lived for several more years in the South End and later moved to South Reading, enraptured first by the rhythm of city life, then by the stupendous beauty of nature. Louis would become the nation's foremost architect and generally regarded as the Father of American Architecture.

In his 1924 book *The Autobiography of an Idea,* Louis Sullivan described his father's remarkable odyssey through life. When Patrick was twelve he became separated from his father at an Irish county fair and never saw him again. "Thus . . . he was thrown upon the world to make his way," wrote Louis. "With a curious little fiddle, he wandered barefoot about the countryside, to fiddle here and there for those who wished to dance. . . . [eventually] his attention . . . focused on dancing as an art." He moved to London, where he taught dancing as "a social art of grace, of deportment, and of personal carriage. . . . [H]e was [considered] no gentleman as that technical term went, but essentially a lackey, a flunkey or social parasite.

"It is probable that, about this time," Louis continued, "the lure of America, goal of the adventurous spirit, the great hospitable, open-armed land of equality and opportunity, had been acting on his imagination." The rest, as they say, is history.

But the Patrick Sullivan who languished on Deer Island is also part of Boston's history. He was one of several hundred men, women, and children who suffered a sad, painful, lonely death at a quarantine station in a harbor far away from home. Fate has always had a hand in Irish history, and it's worth pondering what this Patrick Sullivan and the other Sullivans might have become had they actually made it to the Promised Land, which shimmered just five miles in the distance on the shores of America.

It is impossible to downplay the utter tragedy of the Irish Famine, known as the Great Hunger, which occurred in Ireland between 1845 and 1849. Out of Ireland's population of eight million, nearly one million people died, and another two million fled the island, many of them in abject poverty, selling the clothes on their backs to get ship passage and often arriving at their destination—Quebec, Boston, New York—distraught, diseased, and, in many cases, dying or dead.

Bostonians were entirely unprepared for what happened in 1847, known in Irish history as Black '47. How could they be otherwise? On New Year's Day, when the *Boston Daily Bee* cheerfully wished readers "health and prosperity . . . that they may increase and multiply," who could have imagined that the fallout from an impending calamity three thousand miles away—of such scale that it could only be described in the most extreme terms—was about to descend on Boston?

Details of the dying taking place in Ireland were described in language that strikes modern readers as apocalyptic. "Children have been found lying dead on their mother's breasts which they had gnawed in twain to procure the nourishment that was not there; and men and women devour the mantling filth of the gutters to alleviate the pangs of the awful hunger which oppresses the whole people," wrote the *Boston Bee* in February 1847. The magnitude of the despair and desperation cannot be overstated.

Over a period of twelve months, more than thirty-seven thousand Irish refugees fleeing from famine landed in Boston in the most pitiful condition imaginable. Irish paupers lay on the streets, their tongues swollen from ship fever, signaling for help with their eyes. Irish vagrants broke into people's homes and stole from shops. Irish children whose parents had died en route to Boston were put in orphanages. Fifty refugees camped out on Boston Common, with nowhere else to go. A family of seven who landed in Quebec walked the four hundred miles to Boston and, exhausted, ended up at the quarantine station. Some Irish, distraught by the carnage they had witnessed, committed suicide by jumping out of windows or by slitting their throats with a razor. Others, simply unable to cope, broke down and were placed in the lunatic asylum in South Boston.

Celtic cross at the Bunker Hill Cemetery in Charlestown, where Irish famine victims were buried

It was a year of ironies and mysteries of the human condition that neither the poet, the pundit, nor the preacher could fully comprehend, much less articulate. The swollen tongues and shrunken stomachs caused by ship fever rendered the Irish speechless and unable to eat when they arrived. Freedom of speech in the land of plenty was lost on these Irish. In Boston, Protestant ministers such as Rev. Kirk charged the English government and the Catholic

Church with doing to the Irish what Americans were accused of doing to the slaves.

And yet, in the midst of utter depravity and human suffering, there were wondrous triumphs of humanity. Even as narrow-minded Bostonians added insults to the injuries of the Irish, big-hearted Bostonians proved to be among the most generous and compassionate citizens in the entire nation. As nativists threatened to burn down the quarantine station where hundreds of immigrants battled death, the city's finest Yankee physicians were working at the hospital, tending to their patients, at personal risk to their lives.

The USS *Jamestown* Sails to the Rescue

When the full extent of the crisis became known in Boston, both the Irish and the Yankee communities sprang into action. On February 7, 1847, Bishop John Fitzpatrick gave an emotionally

Famine Memorials around Boston

Various Irish Famine memorials have been built in the Boston area to commemorate the Great Hunger that devastated Ireland from 1845 to 1849.

Cohasset Celtic Cross, unveiled in 1914 in Central Cemetery, commemorates the Galway passengers aboard the Famine ship *St. John*, which perished during a storm in 1849.

Cambridge Irish Famine Memorial, unveiled in 1997, is on Cambridge Common near Harvard Square.

Boston Irish Famine Memorial, unveiled in 1998, is at the corner of School and Washington Streets.

Lawrence Irish Famine Memorial at Saint Mary's Cemetery in Lawrence, Massachusetts, was dedicated in 2006 to honor the Irish Famine refugees who settled in the Merrimack Valley.

Providence Irish Famine Memorial, dedicated in 2007, honors the Irish Famine refugees who settled in Rhode Island.

For more information visit the website irishheritagetrail.com.

charged sermon from the pulpit of the Cathedral of the Holy Cross, and parish priests followed suit. By the end of the month, the Boston Archdiocese had raised twenty thousand dollars for Ireland. Workmen were sending in five-dollar bills, and schoolchildren were giving over their paltry savings for this urgent, desperate cause.

The city's Yankee leaders, meanwhile, called a meeting at Faneuil Hall on February 17; four thousand people attended. Harvard president Edward

Everett and Boston mayor Josiah Quincy Jr., along with the city's leading merchants, made a passionate appeal to aid the starving people of Ireland. They formed the New England Relief Committee, which raised more than $150,000 in three weeks to purchase supplies.

Four days later Robert Bennet Forbes, a wealthy China-trade merchant from Milton, petitioned Congress for the loan of a naval ship to bring supplies to the people of Ireland. Permission was granted, and the USS *Jamestown*, then anchored at the Charlestown Navy Yard, was designated to Boston, while the USS *Macedonian* was given over to Captain George DeKay for a similar enterprise in New York.

The notion of sending a ship filled with food and provisions to Ireland at once captured the imagination of the entire state, and donations came pouring in. People recalled that in 1676 the Irish ship *Katherine* brought relief supplies to Plymouth, when the colonists were fighting the Indians during King Philip's War. According to Forbes's memoir, this recollection was brought to his attention by the Reverend R. C. Waterston, who wrote in a letter, "It is an interesting fact that the people of Ireland, nearly 200 years ago, thus sent relief to our Pilgrim fathers in their time of need, and what we have been doing for that famishing country is but a return for what their fathers did for our fathers."

Rev. Waterston went on to write, "I consider the mission of the *Jamestown* as one of the grandest events in the history of our country. A ship-of-war changed into an angel of mercy, departing on no errand of death, but with the bread of life to an unfortunate and perishing people."

The Catholics were equally impressed with the *Jamestown* mission. On April 4 the *Pilot* wrote, "Captain Forbes is one of our most eminent merchants and retired sea captains. He has done himself infinite credit by his untiring exertions throughout, and his name will long be remembered by every friend of Ireland."

The 1967 book *Massachusetts Help to Ireland during the Great Famine* gives a masterful account of this episode in Boston's history:

> *Contributions of food continued to arrive from all over New England. So great was the feeling of those with relatives in Ireland, that numbers came carrying sacks of flour or potatoes entreating the crew to let them be put on board . . . [T]he cargo consisted largely of Indian corn and bread but included also hams, pork, oatmeal, potatoes, flour, rye, beans, rice, fish and sixteen barrels of clothing.*

Irish longshoremen helped load the vessel on March 17, and on the morning of March 28, the USS *Jamestown* set sail for Cork carrying eight hundred tons of supplies, with Captain Forbes at the helm and thirty-eight men who signed on as the crew. Crowds lining the wharf and the shores cheered as the ship headed

ARTIST EDWARD WALKER

The USS Jamestown *leaving Boston Harbor on its mission of mercy on March 28, 1847*

out to the open seas. The fifteen-day voyage faced foul weather and a blend of rain, sleet, wind, and fog requisite for that time of year, but finally, Forbes later wrote, "we cast anchor in the outer harbor of what had been known as Queenstown."

Back in Boston, the papers enthusiastically reported on the trip, failing to note the cruel irony that became apparent when the provincial rulers greeted the crew with an invitation to a sumptuous arrival dinner. For, as always in Ireland, a certain elite were untouched by the tragedy taking place around them. "A deputation of the gentry of Cork visited the ship. After some conversation the deputation withdrew, having previously invited Captain Forbes and officers to a public dinner, which the gallant gentleman kindly accepted. The dinner was a very special affair, and attended by the most influential classes in and around Cove," the papers reported. Forbes and his crew found this banquet most embarrassing, however, as Irish citizens lay dying in the streets nearby.

According to Lee, "Forbes strongly urged that all public demonstrations be dispensed with on account of the prevailing distress, [but] his hosts were not to be denied the satisfaction of showing their gratitude to New England and America. . . . It should be remembered that one of the terrible anomalies of the Famine years—and one which greatly surprised the Americans—was the availability of food to those who could afford to buy it."

The *Boston Daily Bee* reported, "The tables were sumptuously spread, the company most honorable, and the sentiments drank were of a high order." But Forbes was more interested in seeing firsthand the suffering everyone had heard so much about. He was escorted around Cork by Father Theobald Mathew, the famous temperance priest. Forbes later wrote,

> *I went with Father Mathew only a few steps out of the principal streets
> . . . into a lane. . . . [I]t was the valley of death and pestilence itself.
> I would gladly forget, if I could, the scenes I witnessed . . . [of] more
> actual distress and apparent poverty than I ever saw in my whole life
> . . . yet I am told that I saw nothing compared to the in-door suffering
> and the suffering in the country.*

Forbes was touched by the gratitude he received from the people of Cork but more affected by the plight of the dying, and when he returned home, arriving at the Navy Yard on May 16, he immediately set his sights on the USS *Macedonian*, which sat in New York Harbor only partially filled with supplies. Captain Forbes and the Boston Committee took over the task of funding and organizing the ship, which sailed for Cork on June 19, arriving there on July 16, 1847.

More humanitarian aid was sent to Ireland over the next three years, including a donation of $710 by the Choctaw Indians, according to a *Connecticut Courant* article published in 1847. The *Pilot* reported that the Shakers of New Lebanon contributed $700 worth of clothing, while the *Merrimack Courier* noted that the mill workers of Lawrence, mostly Irish immigrants, gave $2,000 for famine relief.

But the two famine relief ships organized by Forbes and others remained in the collective memory of Bostonians for years to come and became part of Irish lore. Samuel Lover, one of Ireland's leading poets and songwriters, penned a song in 1847 called "War Ship of Peace." It captured the spirit of Irish gratitude toward the United States.

The Poorhouse of the World

During the forty-nine days when Forbes was away, Boston's public opinion of the Irish Famine had undergone a dramatic shift. Historian Cecil Woodham-Smith comments on this changing dynamic in her classic book *The Great Hunger*:

> *By a curious piece of reasoning, the Irish starving in Ireland were
> regarded as unfortunate victims, to be generously helped, while the same
> Irish, having crossed the Atlantic to starve in Boston, were described*

The Forbes House

Robert Bennet Forbes (1804–1889) was a China-trade merchant described as having "the most original brain and attractive personality of any merchant of his day." In 1833 he built a Greek Revival mansion in the town of Milton, Massachusetts; it had a full view of Boston Harbor and the cargo ships coming in from the Far East. In 1967 the Captain Robert Bennet Forbes House at 215 Adams Street was designated a National Historic Landmark and made into a museum that focuses "on social, cultural and historical context of the 19th century." The museum contains many artifacts associated with the voyage of the USS *Jamestown* and with the Forbes family's friendship with the Irish through the end of the century. For more information call (617) 696-1815 or visit the website: ForbesHouseMuseum.org.

> *as the scourings of Europe and resented as an intolerable burden to the*
> *taxpayer.*

Even as the *Jamestown* unloaded its provisions, the dying Irish whom Forbes had seen in the back lanes of Cork were now turning up at Boston Harbor. Many of them had sold everything they had to get a one-way ticket, which cost twelve dollars. Others had been rounded up by their landlords and sent overseas to become someone else's problem.

The debate went up a notch when a new paper published by the Reverend Charles W. Dennison and named the *American Signal* hit the newsstands on May 20, 1847, keeping up a relentless attack on the immigrants:

> *Is this Boston? Or is it Dublin? Did our Pilgrim Fathers land on*
> *Plymouth Rock or was it in the Cove of Cork? Have we a right to the*
> *streets of the city where we were born or do they belong to his holiness,*
> *the Pope? Must we submit to be overrun by the paupers of English*
> *government? Shall our beloved country be forced by despots to become the*
> *POOR HOUSE OF THE WORLD?*

It seemed the indelible fears that Bostonians carried with them since the Puritan days—of economic uncertainty, religious instability, and the spread of disease—had exploded to the surface in a raucous debate that threatened to undermine civility and authority. The spread of disease was the most potent fear because it combined both medical ignorance and religious superstition, as a report of the Boston Society for the Prevention of Pauperism later acknowledged in 1865:

> *Good health and clean living were synonymous in the mid-19th*
> *century. . . . [I]t was still acceptable in certain quarters to characterize*
> *contagious diseases as God's form of moral cleansing, and there were*
> *many instances where the lack of moral character of the Irish was*
> *blamed for their medical woes.*

Fortunately for the Irish, a group of Yankee doctors stepped forward to help the dying refugees in the face of a growing nativist revolt. The names of Dr. Albert G. Upham, Dr. Joseph Moriarty and his brother Dr. John Moriarty, Dr. Thomas Welsh, Dr. C. A. Walker, Dr. Henry Grafton Clark, and Dr. Jabez Baxter Upham may have been forgotten in Boston through the passage of time. But they, along with their dedicated nursing staff, most of whom were Irish immigrants, saved thousands of Irish lives, provided physical comfort and solace to the dying, and advanced the medical knowledge of ship fever to benefit future generations. They became the unsung heroes of the Boston Irish. Several of the doctors, including Clark and Upham, kept careful notes and later published their findings in such medical journals as the *Boston Medical and Surgical Journal*, the forerunner to the *New England Journal of Medicine*.

The setting for their brave and risky work was Deer Island, a two-hundred-acre island about five miles from downtown Boston. The island had been so named by seventeenth-century colonists because of "the deare which often swimme thither from Maine, when they are chased by the wolves." In 1717, when the first wave of Ulster Irish began arriving in the harbor, the town selectmen had voted to build a hospital on the island to contain the spread of diseases such as measles and smallpox. The crisis passed, however, and the hospital wasn't built.

More than a century later, in May 1847, city officials designated Deer Island as the site of the city's quarantine hospital, as the threat of a typhus fever epidemic loomed. The almshouse in South Boston had already filled to capacity, and an average of five patients, mostly females, were dying each day. Irish people were literally huddled on the streets of Boston, waiting to die. On May 27 the first Famine ship, the *John Clifford*, was sent to quarantine, and by the end of the week more than one hundred patients were in the Deer Island Hospital. The first patient to die at the hospital was six-year-old Mary Nelson, who succumbed to typhus fever on June 1, followed on June 3 by one-year-old Mary Connolly. The city created a cemetery on the island and named it Rest Haven. It would eventually hold several hundred Irish Famine fatalities.

The Deer Island Hospital was directed by Dr. Joseph Moriarty, who came from a merchant family in Salem and had married the niece of John Hancock. Moriarty was assisted by Dr. Thomas Welsh, according to Dr. John McColgan of the City of Boston Archives, along with a "support staff about fifty strong [which] consisted of eighteen nurses, a store keeper, a boatman, a farmer, teamsters, laborers, cooks, kitchen boys, chamber girls, a table girl, ten washerwomen, a baker, a seamstress and a teacher." Quoting from city records, McColgan notes that the hospital was run with compassion:

> *Health aides . . . were to receive patients when brought to the island, and*
> *see that they are properly prepared. . . . [T]hat they are kindly treated,*
> *and their food is properly served and distributed, that their apartments*
> *are kept clean and in good order and properly warmed and ventilated.*

The disease most fatal to the Irish was typhus fever, also known as ship fever. Typhus, from the Greek word *typhos*, "mist," was a term coined in the eighteenth century to describe the clouded mental state of the patient. In the first six months at the Deer Island hospital, it killed 188 people. Another 70 died of complications related to the disease: dropsy, diarrhea, and dysentery.

The fever, Dr. Clark reported, attacked its victims suddenly, causing chills followed by "morbid heat of the skin, in many cases very intense and pungent." It caused pains in the head, back, and limbs, dizziness, and deafness or ringing in the ears and put victims in a stupor. It was, Clark explained, "a disease of debility . . . one characteristic is the great indifference the patient manifests."

In his medical notes Dr. J. B. Upham reports treating a patient named John Salter, age forty-five, on the day after Christmas in 1847: "a strong muscular man, in an advanced stage of the fever with symptoms like low muttering delirium, inability to speak, teeth loaded with black sores, skin covered with spots, flying blisters. He died the following morning."

In all, 247 Irish patients died and were buried on Deer Island between June and December 1847. Several physicians and at least one public official also died in that six-month period. Daniel Chandler, superintendent of alien passengers, died in mid-June, followed by Dr. Albert Upham, who was noted as "a young man of much promise." Two physicians in Rhode Island—Dr. Alfred Knight in Cumberland and a Dr. Fletcher in Providence—died treating ship fever victims. In December Dr. Moriarty himself died of typhus, leaving behind a wife and three children.

Moriarty was replaced by his own brother, John, who continued the extraordinary work of saving immigrants. By December 1848 panic about an epidemic had abated, and the quarantine station was closed down. The city transferred to Deer Island inmates from the House of Industry, formerly called the Bridewell, where able-bodied paupers and petty criminals were put to work while incarcerated. Dr. John Moriarty continued to treat patients at the hospital into the 1850s. The other physicians had distinguished careers in Boston, particularly Dr. Clark, who became a surgeon at Massachusetts General Hospital. Over the next quarter century, he weighed in on every public health issue in the city.

The Deer Island hospital continued to treat Irish who were being shipped back to the island, where the unsanitary conditions of Boston's ghetto life afflicted the vulnerable just as the coffin ships had. One hundred and fifty-nine men, women, and children died and were buried on the island in 1850 alone. The youngest to die that year was Mary Aldrich, fifteen days old; the oldest was James Hurley, aged sixty-three. Donahues, Finns, Cronins, Harrigans, Kelleys, Gallaghers, Donovans, Shanahans, and McCanns were among those who died on Deer Island in 1850, a microcosm of the Irish Diaspora.

Although the threat of disease subsided, Bostonians became afflicted over the next few decades with another virulent epidemic, one that even the most dedicated of doctors were at a loss to cure. It was called Know-Nothingism, and it spread through the Yankee working-class neighborhoods throughout the city. Its symptoms were hatred, intolerance, and brutality, and it evoked a mob mentality characterized by racist threats, bodily harm, and the destruction of property. It would become the typhus fever of the 1850s.

Chapter Six

The Have-Nothings Meet the Know-Nothings (The 1850s)

O N THE VERY FIRST DAY of her job as a live-in maid, Catherine Murphy stole an expensive silk dress from her employer's wardrobe and disappeared into the night. It was May 1853, and Murphy had been hired to clean house in the Fort Hill neighborhood, where sea captains and merchants had their stately homes. After she finished dusting the furniture and putting away clothes, she retired to her room. At some point in the night she crept into the dressing room of the lady of the house and ran off with a brand-new silk dress.

The theft was discovered, and the aggrieved lady and her husband raced down the narrow streets of Boston, scouring the Irish neighborhoods along the waterfront. They passed Irish paupers begging on the streets or coming home from work muddy and tired from digging trenches for the new water lines. They saw children running around barefoot and a bagpiper playing on a street corner for spare change. Eventually they reached the notorious dance cellars in the North End. There was Catherine Murphy, wrote the *Boston Herald*, "with the striped silk on her back, dancing merrily with the boys . . . in a dark place, in which about one hundred boys and girls were dancing to the music of a single fiddle." She was arrested.

In ordinary times Murphy's infraction would have been viewed as a petty crime. But the 1850s in Boston were not normal times. The teenager's action appeared to verify what many Bostonians believed: The Irish could not be trusted. They didn't belong in this country. They shouldn't be taking jobs away from "real" Americans. They should go back to Ireland.

The suspicious, unforgiving nature of Bostonians was not new; it stretched back to the Puritan days when newcomers were called strangers, and everyone was viewed suspiciously. But it reached an ugly nadir in the 1850s, as hundreds of thousands of immigrants streamed into the city. Discrimination and disdain, political opposition and mob violence rained upon the Irish. Having just barely survived the 1840s, one of the most dismal decades in Ireland's history, the Irish coming into Boston were about to be confronted by a new brand of discrimination three thousand miles away from their tiny villages and farmlands.

In some instances certain Irish deserved the negative way in which they were depicted. They came from a suppressed peasant culture defined by religious superstition and rejection of civil authority. Many were uneducated and ignorant, prone to alcoholism and violence, and susceptible to temporal vices as an outlet to their strict Catholicism. When they arrived from their rural villages or Dublin ghettoes to big cities, whether it be London, New York, or Boston, a portion of them always fell victim to their own weaknesses, and this failure, especially as it played out in public settings, became the caricature of the race as a whole.

And in the wake of the Famine, the Irish Catholics arriving in Boston had two more disadvantages: they were dirt poor and often physically ill. It was not uncommon to see articles in local papers like the *Boston Herald* with such headlines as "More Foreign Paupers," which ran in April 1851:

> *One hundred and sixty-two foreign paupers arrived in Boston yesterday on the Worcester, Fall River and Boston and Maine Railroads. Of this number 71 were entirely destitute and 18 children from one poor house in Ireland were barefooted. A more miserable looking gang of human beings never were seen. They should be sent back at once to those who so unmercifully cast them away. In addition about 300 Irish immigrants arrived in vessels at Quarantine Wednesday.*

Edward Everett Hale, one of Boston's leading citizens, described the Irish as "a horde of disappointed, starved, beaten men and women." They had become a burden to the taxpayers and a threat to Boston's health and welfare, not to mention its quality of life. "The healthy social and moral character we once enjoyed is liable to be lost forever," complained one public official. "Pau-perism, crime, disease and death stare us in the face."

In spite of the reception they got, the Irish continued to head to Boston. By 1850 the 46,000 Irish living in Boston comprised a third of the total popu-lation of 138,000. In fact, immigrants were becoming indispensable to the city's expansion and industrialization during this time. Irish men were needed to work on backbreaking and dangerous public works projects, such as dig-ging trenches for water pipes from Lake Cochituate to Boston Common, and railroad lines from Boston to the Great Lakes. The women were hired as mill workers, domestic servants, and nannies.

The ubiquity of these immigrants in everyday life created an identity crisis for those Americans of English stock, who felt their lineage being diluted by "the fruitful invasion of barbarians," as well-known Bostonian Charles Eliot Norton later put it. Even the *New York Times* weighed in with a sarcastic review of the Fourth of July celebrations on Boston Common in 1853:

> *The whole costermongery was so preponderantly Hibernian, that, if the Pilgrim Fathers could have come out of their graves, the surprise of it would have sent them back again, shaking their heads, and telling every ghost they met that the chronic Irish rebellion had at last succeeded, and that the strongest holds of Anglo-Saxondom were overrun by the Celts— they had Boston Common in their hands!*

William E. Robinson complained in a speech in New York that "an uneducated and degraded class of foreigners has succeeded in driving away the native population, and is fast acquiring the control of this hitherto glorious city."

Meanwhile, Irish immigrants in Boston were searching desperately to find families, friends, and neighbors from whom they were separated during the Great Exodus from Ireland. The *Pilot* had been running a weekly Missing Friends column since the 1830s, in which Irish immigrants tried to reconnect with those they had been separated from by placing advertisements.

In addition, Irish leaders were trying to create safe environments for the Irish refugees coming to America in droves. The *Pilot*'s publisher, Patrick Dona-hoe, was an early advocate of the Irish Emigrant Society, whose goal was to take the newly arrived Irish and send them right out to "the fertile Western States, where the resources of a country are ready for the hands that shall cultivate them." Many other nationalities, such as the Germans, Swedes, and other northern European groups, went west and settled in the Great Lakes region, but the Irish opted to stay in the eastern cities, and by 1856 the Irish Emigrant Society had closed its doors. The Irish were in Boston to stay.

Old-line Bostonians formed numerous relief agencies to help the Irish. The Boston Society for the Prevention of Pauperism, headed by Moses Grant, sought to find work for immigrants as housekeepers, servants, farmers, laboring men, coachmen, waiters, clerks, and mechanics. The society was sincere in wanting to help, but its righteous pontifications against drinking and its interest in converting boys and girls to Protestantism turned many immigrants away from its services. One of its accomplishments was to rail against the practice of lumping together "under one roof the aged, the infirm, the sick and the virtuous poor" with "common street walkers, drunkards and vagabonds" at the facilities on Deer Island.

Dancing in the Dark

Boston prided itself on being a well-governed, clean, and morally upright city, and the hordes of Irish refugees disrupted that order. The Boston police reported that nearly three-fourths of arrests made, and of cases before the municipal and police courts, were those of foreigners. Part of the reason was that the police began raiding the places where immigrants, sailors, and transients congregated, particularly in the North End. In the mid-nineteenth century, the waterfront neighborhood where Paul Revere once lived was a bustling bowery of cheap saloons, flophouses, gambling dens, and dance halls. Jewish peddlers set up a cornucopia of imported goods and fresh fruit and vegetables that they hawked in open market stalls. Sailors came off their ships to let off steam, and travelers were constantly arriving on boat routes from New York or Nova Scotia. When the Irish began coming during the Famine years, landlords converted dozens of North End warehouse buildings into hundreds of tiny apartments where dozens of people shared tiny rooms with no running water or sanitary facilities. In 1849 an Asiatic cholera outbreak killed more than five thousand people, many of them Irish immigrants. The city's health inspector, Lemuel Shattuck, reckoned the life expectancy of Irish in Boston to be just fourteen years.

The most notorious section of the North End was along Ann Street (today it is called North Street), a boulevard packed with seventy-nine dancing cellars and numerous brothels, liquor stores, gambling dens, and flophouses. Ann Street had long had its troubles: In September 1843 four "colored seamen" were attacked by white sailors, and a group of Irish boardinghouse keepers and grog shop owners jumped into the fray, with people seriously injured on both sides. In 1850 a sensational report in the *Newburyport Herald* chronicled the dance cellars and groggeries of the North End, where "the very atmosphere was redolent with drunkenness and debauchery." The correspondent visited the Negro section of the North End, known as the Black Sea, "that foul lazar-house of corrupted and festering humanity. . . . Those who danced were negroes, mulattoes and whites, in about equal proportion. The most perfect equality prevailed, for vice and crime are great levelers."

In 1851 the Boston police sent undercover agents to Ann Street for several weeks, where they made notes and identified the ringleaders. Then in April the police made their move, rounding up vagabonds, gamblers, prostitutes, and musicians who had created a Mardi Gras atmosphere in one of America's most conservative cities. One evening the police raided the gambling dens, rounding up eighty-six people and parading them before the press. Another night the police raided the dance cellars, arresting more than two hundred people, including "40 males and the rest females of the lowest class found in the city," reported the *Boston Herald*.

"There were persons taken of all ages and of every color known to the human race—varying in hue from the purest white to the most shiny black," noted the *Herald*. Musicians and pipers were arrested and charged with disturbing the peace. One judge took pity on Michael McLaughlin, charged with being a common fiddler. The court ruled that McLaughlin "could not see what company he kept" and was set free. Another musician's wife tried to "soften the heart of the judge by stating that she had seven children, mostly of a tender age." The judge wasn't softened, and the husband went to jail.

Many of the women arrested were prostitutes, and several were brothel madams, charged with keeping houses of ill repute. In a gesture that can only be described as extraordinary for the time, the court arranged for many of these women to have their sentences suspended and instead put them to work as domestic servants to local families.

Rural Irish peasants suddenly cast into a thriving urban center like Boston were often overwhelmed by their new surroundings, but the majority of them didn't succumb to vice. Most Irish who had survived the arduous journey across the ocean were determined to make the best of their new home. They had already begun putting down roots, creating a stable family environment for their progeny. In a pattern that stretched over several generations, the Irish saved money and sent it back to Ireland so their families could eventually follow them to Boston.

For many the timeless traditions of storytelling, poetry, song, and dance helped sustain them, and many organizations formed around shared cultural values. Most Irish were encouraged to play an instrument, dance, tell a story, or sing, and they carried those skills with them to Boston. Dance masters such as Patrick Sullivan and M. H. Keenan began teaching youngsters the jigs and reels of Ireland, as well as the quadrilles and waltzes favored in New England. M. J. Mooney gave lessons on the organ and pianoforte to immigrant children and formed a Juvenile Drum Corps that played at Irish occasions. Jeremiah Cohan, father of George M. Cohan, the toast of Broadway in the 1920s and '30s, learned Irish step dancing and later transferred those skills to the minstrel and vaudeville stages. Irish dance steps had already been influential in creating a hybrid American dance known as tap dancing. Immigrant musicians such as Edward Ryan and Patrick Gilmore transferred their notable skills into classical and popular music and made their mark there. Many musicians joined temperance society and military bands.

In 1853 the Boston Irish formed the Thomas Moore Club, dedicated to the music of Ireland's famous bard. The group met monthly and convened a dinner each May that drew more than two hundred people, including poet Washington Irving and Bishop John Hughes from New York City. On Ruggles Street in Roxbury, Edward White from Galway opened a music shop in 1854 where he repaired Irish and Scottish bagpipes, gave lessons to children, and offered to play at functions around the city. Known as the Dandy Piper because he wore a tall black stovepipe hat when he went out, White opened a successful dance hall in Roxbury in the years leading up to the Civil War and helped the complex art of uilleann piping take root in Boston.

In 1850 just two musical concerts were held in celebration of Saint Patrick's Day. By the end of the decade, more than a dozen such events were offered. Mooney's choir of Irish orphans of Boston performed at Tremont Temple. The Irish Temperance Societies held a concert in Cambridge. The Charitable Irish Society held its soiree at the famous Parker House, using the Shaw and Weitz Quadrille Band, and Patrick Gilmore headed up the

prestigious Boston Brass Band. Even
the Irish Protestant Mutual Relief
Society offered its version of Irish
music. At its annual dinner in April
1853, its musical list included "God
Save the Queen," "Croppies Lie
Down," and "The Protestant Boys."

Throughout the 1850s traveling
minstrel and burlesque shows came
through Boston regularly, offering
a raw, sarcastic depiction of Irish,
blacks, Germans, Chinese, and others. Several of the most popular per-
formers of the day were themselves
Irish actors, such as John Broughton
and Barney Williams. In an effort to
give the public what it wanted, these
actors depicted the Irish as the white
equivalent of Black Sambo, another
caricature popular in the days lead-

Irish playwright Dion Boucicault explored Irish
nationalist themes in his work.

ing up to the Civil War. Indeed, the mirroring of Paddy and Sambo in the
work of cartoonists like Thomas Nast later in the century found its inspiration
in these shows. Irish comedian John Collins came through Boston frequently,
performing at the Boston Museum Theatre and other large venues. Collins
was known as the "delineator of the sashing, rollicking, thoughtless Irishman,"
and his topical comedy sketches, The Irish Ambassador, The Wrong Passenger, and Paying the Rent, were popular among Irish and non-Irish audiences
alike.

Other Irish immigrants such as Dion Boucicault from Dublin portrayed
the Irish as heroic figures. Boucicault's play *Andy Blake: Or, the Irish Diamond*
made its American debut at the Boston Theater in November 1854. Boucicault
understood the importance of defining the Irish persona in a positive way, and
he helped to keep alive nationalist sentiments of the Irish living in America,
which would prove a powerful political force in the future. In 1865 he wrote
the lyrics to the Irish anthem "Wearin' o' the Green" for his play *Arrah na Pogue*,
reminding the Boston Irish just how bad things had been in Ireland:

O Paddy dear and did you hear the news that's going round,
The Shamrock is forbid by law to grow on Irish ground . . .
She's the most distressful country that ever you have seen,
They're hanging men and women there for wearin' of the green.

The Rise and Fall of the Know-Nothings

As long as the police arrested the troublemakers and the Irish stayed to themselves, nativist Bostonians were appeased. But when the Irish started to demand
a voice in political affairs and a vote in local elections, the nativists' antagonism
toward the immigrants grew. Fearing that the emerging Irish Catholic political
bloc would "vote down intelligent, honest native citizens" and take over local
politics, nativists began organizing a political opposition. In 1854 they established an anti-Irish, anti-Catholic group known as the American Party, which
preferred to be clandestine when promoting its mission. Party members were
called the Know-Nothings, because they feigned ignorance of the party's activities when questioned by outsiders. The party adopted its constitution on June
17, 1854—the anniversary of the Battle of Bunker Hill. Ironically, hundreds of
Irish soldiers had died in that battle, fighting valiantly alongside the grandfa-
thers of the nativists who now opposed the Irish.

The Know-Nothing movement represented yet another crossroad in
American history. Would the Anglo-Saxon Protestant ethos of Puritan times
prevail, anchored in a righteous religious conviction that mistrusted strangers
and excluded people of different backgrounds and beliefs? Or would America
evolve as a nation that welcomed newcomers to share in the opportunities that
had beckoned the early colonists to the New World, anchored in constitutional
principles of equality and individual rights?

The Know-Nothing movement, which lasted about six years, was reminis-
cent of what historian Jackson Lears called an "apocalyptic fervor" that was
often at the center of national debates, whereby "defenders of the status quo
sought to restrain the release of moral energy and redirect it toward the main-
tenance of existing institutions."

The American Party was all about protecting the status quo, and its
sixteen-point platform was a sloppy, poorly written, redundant screed against
immigrants and Catholics as a direct threat to their own sense of Americanism. It wanted new immigrants to wait twenty-one years before voting, and to

exclude foreigners from forming military companies or running for office. It called for a "war to the hilt on Romanism," followed by "Hostility to all Papal influences."

Nativists started a campaign to "Americanize America" by harassing Irish immigrants at every opportunity. Storekeepers were urged not to sell them goods. City officials tried to shut down the Catholic cemetery in South Boston. State legislators tried to lengthen the waiting time for immigrants to become naturalized citizens. And police cracked down on the Irish ghettoes in a manner that was harsh and unyielding. In one year fourteen thousand of the seventeen thousand people arrested in Boston were Irish, charged mostly with petty crimes, public disturbances, and vagrancy.

The notorious "No Irish need apply" phrase began to work its way into the job marketplace, appearing in advertisements such as this one from the August 19, 1853, edition of the *Daily Evening Traveller:*

> *Wanted—an experienced COOK, who is a good Washer and Ironer.*
> *Also, a Chambermaid who is a good seamstress and fond of children.*
> *Apply at 117 Harrison Avenue, between the hours of 11 A.M. and 1*
> *P.M. Protestants preferred, and no Irish person need apply.*

That same month, a man named Ira Martin at the livery stable on Cambridge Street ran a "No Irish need apply" (NINA) ad in the *Boston Evening Transcript* twenty-one days in a row! These ads were still turning up two decades later.

In the mid-1850s the Know-Nothing mobs wreaked havoc on Irish neighborhoods in Boston and in surrounding towns. Irish immigrant Patrick Collins recalled a childhood incident involving this mob that seared his memory forever. It was 1854; ten-year-old Collins had come to Boston six years earlier with his widowed mother from County Cork. They were living in an Irish neighborhood in Chelsea on the outskirts of Boston. The *Boston Globe* picks up the story from here:

> *One afternoon after Sunday school some of the teachers and nearly all*
> *the children, went up on a high hill . . . just to see the country and bask*
> *in the sun. They saw toward East Boston a long winding serpent of*
> *people coming. It was the "Angel Gabriel" [a sectarian fanatic whose*
> *real name was Orr] and some two thousand in his train. . . . The crowd*

*marched to the Catholic Church and a number of them mounted the
roof and tore the cross off the apex and threw it into the crowd. [They]
marched through the Catholic section of town and smashed with stones
the windows and doors of all the houses in which Catholics lived. The
fury lasted for weeks. Every Irish house was a fortification. Trunks and
furniture barred every front window; some one was on guard every night
in every dwelling.*

Despite a broken forearm and a few bruises, young Collins survived the
attack. He would eventually graduate from Harvard Law School, be elected
a US congressman, and be appointed US ambassador to England. He would
also serve two terms as mayor of Boston from 1902 to 1905, only the second
Irishman to hold the post up to that time.

In later life Collins articulated the way that his generation felt about being
Irish in America:

*Those of us who were born in Ireland or who spring from the Irish race
are here to stay. [But] in American politics, we are Americans, pure and
simple. We ask nothing on account of our race or creed, and we submit
to no slight or injury on account of either. All we ask is equality for us
and ours.*

LIBRARY OF MICHAEL QUINLIN

Patrick Collins was Boston's second Irish-born mayor.

The "apocalyptic fervor"
of the movement caused many
Bostonians and New Englanders
to also reject the American Party
and its platform. When Henry
Gardner was elected governor
of Massachusetts as a Know-
Nothing candidate in 1855, the
region's press objected to the
direction the Commonwealth
was taking. "The extraordinary
bitterness . . . toward that portion of our population who are
of foreign birth is unbecoming
the Chief Magistrate of the

Commonwealth," wrote the *Pittsfield Sun*, "within whose limits is Plymouth Rock, upon which the Pilgrim Fathers, who fled from the oppressions of the Old World, and who hoped that this land would forever remain an asylum for the oppressed."

"Our system is based on individual freedom, and it aims to elevate all who live under it—to Americanism [*sic*] them," wrote the *Boston Post*, reminding Know-Nothings that "adopted citizens did not hesitate" to volunteer for both the War of 1812 and the Mexican War and were "among the first to volunteer and among the last to yield" in battle.

Before he was elected president, Abraham Lincoln weighed in on the Know-Nothing movement, equating it with the expansion of slavery efforts he was battling in the years leading up to the Civil War. In a letter to Joshua F. Speed in 1855, Lincoln wrote:

> *I am not a Know-Nothing . . . how could I be? How can any one who abhors the oppression of Negroes be in favor of degrading any classes of white people? Our progress in degeneracy appears to me to be pretty rapid. As a nation, we began by declaring that "all men are created equal." We now practically read it all men are created equal, except Negroes and foreigners—and Catholics.*

By the end of the 1850s, the Irish were not just asking for equality, they were fighting for it. When the state legislature tried to extend the waiting time for immigrants seeking to become citizens, the Irish teamed up with German immigrants to fight the proposal. On March 14, 1859, eleven-year-old Thomas Whall, a Catholic student at the Eliot school, refused to pray from the Protestant Bible, and he was severely punished. The entire Irish community rallied behind him and sparked a nationwide protest against the local school officials, who relented.

The Boston Catholic newspaper the *Pilot*, which led the fight against the Know-Nothing movement, was flexing its editorial muscles. In 1859 it noted the eighty-third anniversary of the British leaving Boston on March 17, 1776, and posed the rhetorical question, why hadn't proper Bostonians yet celebrated Evacuation Day? Everyone knew the reason: Evacuation Day happened to fall on Saint Patrick's Day. The Yankees didn't want to give the Irish an opportunity to blend American patriotism with Irish pride. As if to underscore its point, the *Pilot* wrote:

The Pride of the Famine Generation

An extraordinary generation of Irish immigrants emerged in Boston after the 1840s. Liberated from the poverty, unrest, and social restraints in Ireland, they discovered their own talents and opportunties in America.

Thomas Ryan of Cork, a clarinetist, arrived in 1845, formed the Mendelssohn Quintette, and was a founding member of the Boston Symphony Orchestra.

Jeremiah Cohan, born in 1847 to Irish parents on Blackstone Street, was a leading vaudeville performer and the father of the great song-and-dance man George M. Cohan.

Augustus Saint-Gaudens arrived from Dublin in 1848, became the leading sculptor of his generation, and was the creator of the Shaw memorial in Boston.

Patrick Collins arrived from Cork in 1848 and became the city's second Irish-born mayor, elected in 1902.

Bridget Murphy and **Patrick Kennedy** both arrived around 1848, married in Boston in 1856, and begat the nation's first family of politics.

Patrick Gilmore arrived from Galway in 1849 and became one of America's favorite bandleaders. He wrote the Civil War anthem "When Johnny Comes Marching Home."

Martin Milmore arrived from County Sligo in 1851 and along with his brothers Joseph and James created dozens of Civil War memorials throughout New England, including the Soldiers and Sailors Memorial on Boston Common.

Louis Sullivan was born in Boston's South End in 1856 to an Irish father and a Swiss mother and was recognized as the Father of Modern Architecture and mentor to Frank Lloyd Wright.

John L. Sullivan was born in 1858 to Irish immigrant parents and became the world's first heavyweight boxing champion.

The expulsion of the battalion of England from Boston was not a Know Nothing achievement; nor would the sentiments of those who accomplished it harmonize with the sentiments of that party.

By 1861 the Irish would find another way to display their patriotism as the American Civil War loomed. The Irish community was split about the pending war and the issue of slavery. Daniel O'Connell, known as the Great Liberator in Ireland, supported an antislavery petition back in 1840 and befriended the black leader Frederick Douglass. But during the 1850s many Irish didn't take warmly to the abolitionists, who proclaimed the rights of African Americans in the South while doing little for the struggling Irish who were under siege by the Know-Nothings.

Even non-Irish leaders tackled Boston's hypocrisy head-on. Among these leaders was Edward Everett Hale, author of an 1852 pamphlet entitled *Letters on Irish Emigration.*

"Here in Massachusetts we writhe and struggle, really with one heart, lest we return one fugitive who can possibly be saved to Southern slavery," Hale wrote. When it comes to the Irish, Hale continued, "we tax them first and neglect them afterwards, and provide by statute, and take care, in fact, to send them back to Ireland at the public expense, poor creatures who are as entirely fugitives from a grinding slavery as if their flight had been north instead of west."

The *Pilot*, which faltered on the issue of abolishing slavery, ended its opposition in April 1861 when Fort Sumter in South Carolina was attacked by Confederate forces and it became clear that the Civil War would very well divide the country. The *Pilot*, which "honored Southerners for their chivalry but condemned them for their cause," backed the Union's side of the war effort enthusiastically, for this war offered the Irish the ultimate chance to demonstrate their courage, valor, and patriotism for the world to see.

CHAPTER SEVEN

The Irish Come Marching Home Again (The 1860s)

T HEY CAME TO SEE the soldiers marching off to war. That splendid summer day, Tuesday, June 25, 1861, crowds of Bostonians gathered as the Irish Ninth Regiment of Massachusetts Volunteers paraded from Long Wharf to Boston Common for a final muster before heading off to fight in the Civil War. That morning they had taken a boat over from Boston Harbor's Long Island to Long Wharf and were greeted by a crowd of eight hundred men and women, who followed them up to Boston Common. Leading the procession from the wharf up State Street was Galway's own Patrick S. Gilmore, bandmaster of the city's most famous military band. The Juvenile Drum Corps of music teacher M. J. Mooney also marched in step, creating a heartbeat of excitement on their bass and snare drums. Gilmore's Band had played "Hail Columbia" and "St. Patrick's Day," the unofficial twin anthems of the American Irish.

The Ninth had formed in May 1861, heeding the call of President Abraham Lincoln for seventy-five thousand troops from across the nation to fight on behalf of the Union, assuming that the conflict would last about three months and be over by the end of summer. More than a thousand Irish quickly signed up for three years of service. They came from Boston and the nearby towns of Salem, Milford, Marlboro, and Stoughton. Initially stationed in barracks near Faneuil Hall, they spent their final weeks on Long Island in Boston Harbor, which had been converted to a training center for many of the state's fighting battalions.

The Ninth Regiment was commanded by forty-year-old Colonel Thomas Cass, a native of Queen's County (now County Laois) and a Bostonian since 1829. Cass led the 1,023 Irish soldiers through the streets of Boston, marching in strict formation, proud and determined, ready to defend the unity of a country some had been living in only for a few months. At the Massachusetts State House, the regiment met Governor John A. Andrew, who offered a heartfelt thanks to Cass and his soldiers as thousands of state and city officials and well-wishers looked on:

> *"I understand, sir, that like yourself, a majority . . . of your command, derive their origin, either by birth or directly by descent, from another country than this," the governor said, handing Cass the Massachusetts and American flags. "When you look on the Stars and Stripes you can remember that you are American citizens; when you look on this venerable ensign, you can remember your wives and families in Massachusetts."*

After Colonel Cass accepted the flags from Governor Andrew, the Ninth Regiment proudly unfurled its own regimental flag, made of green silk and inscribed on the front with gold scroll: "Thy sons by adoption; thy firm supporters and defenders from duty, affection and choice." The center of the flag showed an American coat of arms with an eagle and shield. The reverse side contained the Irish harp, with the motto "The Union must and shall be preserved."

The following day, the Irish Ninth sailed from Boston on three steamers, the *Pembrook*, the *Cambridge*, and the *Ben Du Ford*, bound for Fortress Monroe in Virginia. They took with them seventy horses, twenty-one baggage wagons, and twenty thousand rounds of ball cartridges. A correspondent for the *Pilot* described the departure in detail: "As we left the island, the tears of weeping maidens and widowed mothers . . . and the cheers of stalwart men, spoke unmistakably of the feelings of grief and joy with which our departure was regarded. . . . we were bound on a sacred mission, ready to sacrifice our lives on the altar of our country in defence of our rights, in the preservation of our liberties."

When it came to pass that the war would last longer than three months, a second group of Irish and Irish Americans began forming in October 1861,

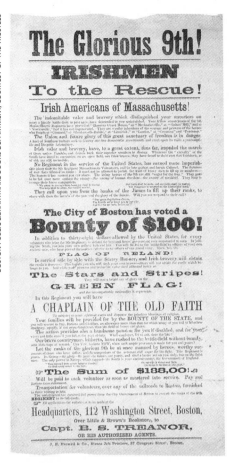

This Civil War recruitment poster called men to the Irish Ninth Regiment.

known as the Twenty-Eighth Massachusetts Volunteer Infantry. The Twenty-Eighth officially mustered into service on December 13, 1861, at Camp Cameron in Cambridge, with almost a thousand men. Governor John A. Andrew appointed Colonel William Monteith leader of the regiment. They distinguished themselves in battle throughout the course of the Civil War, fighting at Second Bull Run, Gettysburg, Fredericksburg, and Antietam. One of the main supporters and fund-raisers behind the formation of the Twenty-Eighth Regiment was the *Pilot*'s publisher Patrick Donahoe. In his book *Civil War Boston*, Professor Thomas O'Connor writes that the soldiers voted to informally call themselves the Donahoe Guard in honor of their benefactor, who also raised money to purchase the uniforms for the Ninth Regiment.

Marching bands, waving flags, cheering crowds, spotless uniforms: such was the memory of going off to war, a far cry from the muddy trenches and battlefields of broken limbs and broken hearts the soldiers encountered. Just over a year after leaving Boston Harbor to great fanfare, on July 1, 1862, the Ninth Regiment was fighting for its life at the Battle of Malvern Hill in Virginia, an epic seven-day battle pitting Union general George McClellan against Confederate general Robert E. Lee. The bloody battle was later described as murder, not war.

In July the local newspapers reported the grim news that "Colonel Cass of the 9th Mass Regiment has returned to Boston via New York and Fall River,

Flag of the 28th Irish Regiment

accompanied by his wife and little son, who met him at New York. He was most shockingly wounded in the head while rallying another regiment next to his own. The bullet entered over his ear, traversing obliquely downward taking out six teeth in its passage, and coming out under the opposite jaw. He is also wounded in the leg. He has to be moved on a stretcher." Cass died from his wounds on July 12 and was buried with honors at Mount Auburn Cemetery in Cambridge. Cass's successor, Patrick Guiney from Tipperary, had his eye blown away at the Battle of the Wilderness in 1864.

As the war lagged on, the Irish in Boston, along with many Americans North and South, grew weary of the conflict and lost enthusiasm for the fight. In March 1863 President Lincoln and the US Congress passed a Conscription Act calling for three hundred thousand more troops to fight the war on the Union side. The law was immediately controversial, especially the clause that allowed a man to opt out of his military duty by paying three hundred dollars or finding another person willing to take his place. Donahoe, who had been instrumental in forming the Ninth and Twenty-Eighth Irish companies, objected when Lincoln's Emancipation Proclamation put the war emphasis on freeing the slaves, as opposed to saving the Union. Writing in the *Pilot* in May

1863, he told his readers that Lincoln had changed, "and so have we. It is now every man's duty to disagree with him."

That disagreement took a violent turn on July 14, 1863, when army marshals went to Prince Street in Boston's North End and tried to enforce the conscription draft. The marshals were set upon by an angry mob of Irish, and one of the marshals was beaten. The police and a company of soldiers from Fort Independence were called in to quell the fighting. When the mob attacked a nearby armory filled with ammunition, the soldiers fired into the crowd, killing men, women, and children, mostly Irish.

After the war, the *Pilot* continued to extol the gallantry and courage of the Irish who fought in the Civil War. In 1873 the *Pilot* ran a series called "Irish Valor: The Irish American Regiments in the Late Civil War," which included testimony of commanders, eyewitnesses, and journalists, plus profiles of leaders of the Ninth and Twenty-Eight Massachusetts, as well as New York's famous Irish brigade. "The Irish-American people were almost unanimous for the Union," wrote the *Pilot*. "They had no local or sectional prejudices at stake in the conflict; and when the climax came, they took up arms against disunion— to prevent the dissolution and dismemberment of a great nation."

The Art of War

When the Civil War ended, families whose fathers and sons went to the battlefront, and hundreds of towns and villages across the nation, sought a permanent, tangible expression of their gratitude, grief, and pride. Public memorials became those expressions, while serving as symbols for the nation to decipher and reflect upon the democratic ideals for which men fought and died. One of the most stirring public memorials in this era was the Soldiers and Sailors Memorial on Boston Common, the city's tribute to the soldiers who fought to preserve the Union. It was unveiled on September 17, 1877, some sixteen years and three months after the Irish Ninth mustered on that very ground. A crowd of twenty-six thousand people gathered on Frog Pond Hill, now renamed Flagstaff Hill, to attend the dedication. The memorial, six years in the making, featured various allegorical figures representing History, Peace, and the Genius of America. Instead of praising generals and admirals, the memorial paid tribute to the foot soldier and the sailor, ushering in a new era of art that was more democratic in its sensibility about war.

The memorial was created by Irish immigrants Martin and Joseph Milmore, two brothers from Killmorgan, County Sligo. Martin Milmore was awarded the commission on December 30, 1870, winning over fifteen other proposals. City officials laid the cornerstone of the memorial in September 1871, and in 1872 Milmore moved to Rome, Italy, and spent the next five years modeling his designs. The shaft of the monument was made of white Maine granite, with pedestals at each of the four corners, upon which stood four bronze figures, representing Peace, History, the Army, and the Navy. At the apex of the monument stood the statue representing America, a woman "majestically proportioned, clad in a flowing robe, with a crown of thirteen stars upon her head."

"There is nothing of haughtiness nor defiance in attitude or expression," read the notes published at the monument's unveiling. "The figure does not symbolize America the conqueror, proud in her strength and defiant of her foes; but rather America the mourner, paying proud tribute to her loyal dead, whose bones lie upon every battle field of the great South, toward which her face is turned."

The Milmore brothers were an incredible American success story. They had emigrated to Boston in 1851 with their widowed mother, Sara (née Hart), and three other brothers, Patrick, Charles, and James. Patrick had died shortly after arriving, and the other boys enrolled in Boston's public schools. They changed their family name from Milmoe to Milmore, at the suggestion of a schoolteacher who thought it would be advantageous for the young brothers to have a name similar to Patrick S. Gilmore, the city's popular bandleader and an Irish immigrant himself.

All of the boys showed an inclination for art, and after school they began apprenticeships in local studios. Joseph began carving marble for sculptor John Foote and was already considered one of the best craftsmen in Boston. Martin, who graduated from the Boston Latin School and at first wanted to be a cornetist like Gilmore, took some art classes at the Lowell Institute. Then he began sweeping the studio floors of Thomas Ball, one of Boston's leading artists, who was then working on the equestrian statue of George Washington for the Public Garden.

The Irish had few opportunities in the mid-nineteenth century to prove they were on par with native Bostonians. Being a soldier was the most expedient path, which many Irish chose when the Civil War began. Being an artist was a less likely path, since it required a period of study and apprenticeship that most Irish could not afford or would not be invited to join. But America gave the Irish a freedom of expression that Ireland hadn't offered, especially to those of modest background and education. Art historian and sculptor Lorado Taft noted in his 1903 masterwork *The History of American Sculpture,* "The versatile Irish have found in America a favorable field for artistic development; transplanted into this spacious land, not a few of the race have revealed an unusual gift for sculptural expression."

Of all the Milmore brothers, Martin had the most promising career. He surprised the art world in 1864 by winning an important commission to do three Roman goddesses, Ceres, Flora, and Pomona, for the prestigious Horticulture Hall. His first war statue was the Roxbury Civil War soldier at Forest Hills Cemetery in Jamaica Plain, completed in 1868, followed by the Charlestown soldier in 1871. Editor John Boyle O'Reilly understood the significance of that occasion when he wrote in the *Pilot,* "In the list of those whose death the statue commemorates, will be found a full representation of Celtic names. This pillar will be the common tombstone of Irish and American, telling us, by their union in death, to walk in union while living. And it is even more than this to us, for the artist who designed the splendid column, Martin Milmore, is one of our race and creed."

The Milmore brothers opened a studio on Harrison Avenue in the South End and produced dozens of Civil War statues that stand on town commons across New England. Martin Milmore died suddenly at age thirty-nine from liver complications; in his will he instructed sculptor Daniel Chester French to create a fitting memorial for him and his brothers at Forest Hills Cemetery. French's masterpiece, entitled *Death and the Sculptor,* is considered one of the finest public sculptures in all of Boston.

Another Irish-born sculptor of note, now considered one of America's greatest nineteenth-century artists, was Augustus Saint-Gaudens, son of a French father and an Irish mother, Mary McGuiness. Born in Dublin on March 1, 1848, he "was not destined to remain long in Ireland," according to his son Homer Saint-Gaudens. For when he was but six months old, "red headed, whopper-jawed, and hopeful," as he often explained, "the famine in Ireland compelled his parents to emigrate with him to America, setting out from Liverpool, in the sailing ship *Desdemona.*"

The family landed in Boston in September 1848, but finding no suitable situation, the father went down to New York City, found a job and an apartment, and sent for mother and child. Augustus's brother, Louis, was born there in 1854. Augustus apprenticed in New York as a cameo cutter and as a teenager moved to Rome and Paris to study classical sculpture. In Rome Augustus met Augusta Homer of Roxbury and married her in 1877. His first commission, of Civil War admiral David Farragut, was unveiled at Madison Square Garden in 1881, and from that point on Saint-Gaudens remained busy as an artist until his death in 1907.

His most notable sculptures—of Abraham Lincoln and General William Sherman—satisfied the American public's yearning for larger-than-life heroes in the late

Irish-born sculptor Augustus Saint-Gaudens was one of America's foremost artists in the nineteenth century.

nineteenth century. Saint-Gaudens himself was larger than life in many ways, with an "unfailing sense of humor and dislike of morbid introspection." He later moved to Cornish, New Hampshire, and set up a vibrant artists' colony there.

Saint-Gaudens's most famous work of art is the Colonel Robert Gould Shaw Memorial, which depicts the Fifty-Fourth Massachusetts Volunteer Infantry. He spent fourteen years creating the memorial, and he took great care to carve individual features for the sixteen black soldiers in the piece. The 1897 unveiling was attended by such luminaries as Booker T. Washington and philosopher William James.

Augustus's son Homer provided an interesting insight into his father's view of Boston during the time. He noted, "His anxiety was increased by the fact that they were to go to Boston, a city which he regarded with ingrown hyper-criticism." This may account for the fourteen years he took to complete the Shaw memorial and why he never completed the exterior sculptures at the Boston Public Library, which had been commissioned from him and his brother Louis. Louis created the majestic twin marble lions that flank the grand stairway in the McKim Building of the Boston Public Library, a memorial that is dedicated to the Second and Twentieth Regiments.

Other Irish-American sculptors contributed to the development of American sculpture through both war memorials and classical figures. Launt Thompson, who moved from County Laois to Albany with his widowed mother in 1847, created the Civil War Monument in Pittsfield. Thomas Crawford, born of Irish parents in New York City, built the Soldiers and Sailors Memorial in Peabody, Massachusetts, as well as the Armed Freedom statue sitting atop the United States Capitol Building in Washington, DC. Stephen O'Kelley of Dublin, who lived in Boston for many years, built memorials to the New York and Pennsylvania infantry regiments, though he is best known locally for his statue of Miles Standish, which stands in Duxbury, Massachusetts.

Why did this group of Irish and Irish-American sculptors excel at war memorials? Most likely they were inclined to demonstrate their patriotism to their new country, a litmus test of loyalty that all immigrants faced. Their sensibilities may have been shaped by their own culture of war, steeped as they were in a centuries-long conflict with England. The Irish were particularly sensitive to the notions of valor, honor, horror, pain, and loss associated with war. While their work captured the power and glory inherent in battle, it also revealed the humanity of those who did the actual fighting and an attention to detail that is the foundation of great art. To produce the carefully etched portraits of the infantrymen in the Shaw memorial, Saint-Gaudens enlisted forty black men to model so he could carve out individual features for the sixteen foot soldiers represented on the monument. In his work Martin Milmore carved young, introspective soldiers and sailors to portray the common-man aspirations of American democracy.

That generation of Irish was also shaped by the Famine, which was indelible in the minds of everyone affected by the catastrophe. The trauma of boarding a boat to flee one's country, leaving behind death, suffering, and anguish, rippled through the survivors and helped to shape a particular Irish-American ethos for decades afterward. The Famine experience, or the memory of it, unleashed a remarkable period of energy and ambition in the Boston Irish, of which artistic expression and political organizing were its creative and practical outcomes.

Civil War Monuments in Massachusetts

Statues and memorial tablets and monuments created by Boston sculptors dot the landscapes of towns and cities throughout the nation. A great number of these honored the fallen soldiers as well as the political and military heroes of the Civil War period. Among them are these notable public monuments in Massachusetts:

Soldiers and Sailors Memorial on Flagstaff Hill in Boston Common, the **Roxbury Civil War Soldier,** and the **Charlestown Civil War Soldier** were created by the Milmore Brothers.

The **Robert Gould Shaw Memorial** on Beacon Hill facing the State House and the Civil War Soldier on Cambridge Common were created by Dublin-born sculptor Augustus Saint-Gaudens.

Twin marble lions in the Boston Public Library McKim Building to commemorate the Twentieth and Second Regiments were created by Louis Saint-Gaudens.

The **Thomas Cass Memorial** in Boston's Public Garden on Boylston Street commemorates the fallen leader of the Irish Ninth Regiment.

Soldiers and Sailors Memorial in Peabody was created by Irish American Thomas Crawford.

The **Civil War Monument** in Pittsfield was created by Irish-born sculptor Launt Thompson.

The **Boston Public Library** has rare photographs by Civil War photographer Mathew Brady, who studied briefly in Boston, and his assistants, Timothy O'Sullivan and Scottish-born Alexander Gardner.

The **Irish flags display** at the State House on Beacon Hill shows dozens of different flags and banners that were carried into battle by the Ninth and Twenty-Eighth Regiments.

When Johnny Comes Marching Home

One of the enduring songs from the nineteenth century is "When Johnny Comes Marching Home," published in September 1863 by musician Patrick Sarsfield Gilmore, an Irish immigrant from Ballygar, County Galway, who moved to Boston in 1849, when he was twenty. The song was part of the musical literature of the Civil War, and subsequent wars for that matter, since it captures the sentiments of families waiting anxiously for their loved ones to return home safely from battle. The melody and lyrics were clearly influenced

by an old Irish ballad called "Johnny I Hardly Knew Ye," said to be popular
with Irish soldiers fighting for the British Empire in Ceylon in the early 1800s.
The Boston Public Library's Rare Books Department has a copy of the original lyrics, which are dark and foreboding:

> *Where are the legs with which you run,*
> *When you went to carry a gun?*
> *Indeed, your dancing days are done,*
> *Oh, Johnny I hardly knew ye.*

Gilmore's lyrics were decidedly more upbeat:

> *When Johnny comes marching home again*
> *Hurrah! Hurrah!*
> *We'll give him a hearty welcome then*
> *Hurrah! Hurrah!*
> *The men will cheer and the boys will shout*
> *The ladies they will all turn out*
> *And we'll all feel gay*
> *When Johnny comes marching home.*

These lyrics captured the universal fears and hopes of a deeply divided
nation touched by the sad knowledge that their loved ones may not have
arrived home, but they're expected any day. There is no reference to victory or
defeat, or to North or South. Written in 6/8 time, the song is played as an up-
tempo march, evoking the crisp motion of soldiers mustering on Boston Common or marching in a Fourth of July parade. It is a song about optimism in the
face of pessimism, of love in the face of hatred, and reconciliation in the face
of division.

Gilmore knew about the war firsthand. A popular bandmaster in the
1850s, he was ubiquitous, organizing Boston's first Fourth of July concert on
Boston Common and playing at high-profile events, such as President Buchan-
an's inauguration in 1857 and in 1860 at both national conventions—the
Democratic in Charleston and the Republican in Chicago—the year Abraham
Lincoln won the Republican nomination and the election.

When war broke out in 1861, Gilmore and his band enlisted in the
Twenty-Fourth Regiment, Massachusetts Volunteers, that September and
spent several years playing music around the country, for soldiers on the front

and for their families back home. They also served as stretcher bearers at battles in Gettysburg, Richmond, and Antietam. Gilmore became the bandmaster of the Union Army and spent a few years in New Orleans.

Gilmore historian Michael Cummings, founder of the Patrick S. Gilmore Society, noted that Gilmore penned a number of other wartime anthems popular with both

LIBRARY OF MICHAEL QUINLIN

Patrick S. Gilmore was a Galway native and music impresario.

the troops and the public, including "God Save the Union," "Coming Home to Abraham," and "Good News from Home." His tune "John Brown's Body," written for the slain civil rights leader of the 1860s, became the most famous marching song of the Civil War. But nothing came close to the popularity of "When Johnny Comes Marching Home," which debuted at Tremont Temple on September 26, 1863, in a concert conducted by Gilmore himself. The song became wildly popular during the 1898 Spanish-American War and has since entered the pantheon of American patriotic songs. It was reportedly the favorite song of President John F. Kennedy.

Gilmore made another significant contribution to the memory of the Civil War by staging a gigantic National Peace Jubilee in Boston in June 1869, to "commemorate the restoration of peace throughout the land." Gilmore had a keen instinct for recognizing public longings and understood that Americans needed a singular event that would take the country out of its postwar doldrums. He vowed to create the largest musical concert in the history of the world. Against all odds, he raised the capital to build a temporary coliseum in Back Bay, just west of where Copley Square and the Fairmont Copley Plaza sit today. He invited musicians from across the country, and when the coliseum doors opened on June 15, 1869, for the start of the five-day concert, Gilmore had amassed a thousand musicians and ten thousand singers to perform. A highlight of the jubilee was on the second day, when President Ulysses S. Grant arrived in Boston to attend the concert, along with his war cabinet. It was a rare opportunity "to forge national memory" and to jump-start the "era of great harmony" to which Grant had aspired.

Even as the Civil War and its aftermath consumed much of its energy and resources, Boston's Irish community continued to make strides on a local level. On March 17, 1862, Irish Bostonians established the city's first Saint Patrick's Day parade. It began on Boston Common at 8:00 a.m., proceeded through the North End, over to Charlestown, then to East Cambridge, then back to Boston and over to South Boston and the South End, and finally ended back at the Common. Not a single neighborhood was missed as the marchers raised the spirits of all of Irish Boston.

The Irish Reconstruction

Despite death and injury to the soldiers of the Irish regiments, and the gradual disillusionment with the war, the Boston Irish were buoyed by their pervasive demonstration of patriotic valor. The veterans of the Irish regiments returned back into civilian life, considered heroes by their communities. Families were reunited, wounds were healed, monuments were built, songs were written, and the returning soldiers tried to resume normal lives.

One group of Irish soldiers, belonging to the Irish Republican Brotherhood (IRB), was not finished fighting. The secret society of Irish expatriates, which had formed in 1858 in New York City, was on a mission to win Ireland back from England through violent methods. Thousands of IRB members, known as Fenians, had enlisted in America's Civil War, hoping to gain an alliance with the United States against Britain, as well as firsthand experience in military fighting that could one day be directed against Britain.

One of the leading Fenians was Timothy Deasy of Lawrence, Massachusetts, whose family emigrated from Clontakilty, Cork, in 1847. Deasy and his brother Cornelius were among the first to enlist in the Fighting Ninth on June 11, 1861, and both were wounded in May 1864 at the Battle of the Wilderness and a month later mustered out of the Union Army. Shortly afterward Timothy took a military oath to the Fenian movement:

*I, Timothy Deasy, do solemnly swear that I will bear true allegiance
to the cause of Ireland, and that I will serve it honestly and faithfully
against all enemies and that I will obey all orders of the President,
Secretary of War, or officers appointed over me according to the rules and
regulations established for the government of her armies for the liberation
of Ireland so help me God.*

Deasy's oath of allegiance was soon put to the test when he became part
of the IRB's audacious, reckless scheme to invade Canada, a part of the British
Commonwealth. The mission was to create "a provisional Irish government
and a base from which they could liberate Ireland," wrote Robert J. Bateman,
Deasy's great-grandnephew, and also to "engineer a border incident that would
entangle British forces in a war with the United States," according to historian
Ian Kenneally.

Canadian authorities got wind of the attack and dispatched armed troops
along the border while US gunboats patrolled the Saint Lawrence River and
Lake Erie. On the night of May 31, 1866, General John O'Neill and his band
of more than a thousand Fenians crossed over to Fort Erie, took down the British flag, and hoisted the Irish flag. They won a small scrimmage near the village
of Ridgeway and seemed poised to continue. But ultimately O'Neill was forced
to surrender when the United States Army cut off his supplies and reinforce-
ments and Canada sent more troops to subdue the rebels, some of whose leaders were temporarily arrested, then released.

Four years later the Fenians regrouped and attempted another invasion of
Canada, with General O'Neill in command again. In late May 1870 O'Neill
and his fellow officers began moving Irish troops up to Saint Albans, Vermont,
and Malone, New York, the staging areas for the invasion across the Canadian
border. The *Pilot* newspaper sent a rookie reporter named John Boyle O'Reilly
to cover the war effort. O'Reilly's dispatch from the front captured the short-
lived attack as well as the ludicrous notion of the enterprise itself:

*At six o'clock on the morning of May 25 I arrived in St. Albans.
There were about 60 Fenians on the train—forty from Boston under
the command of Major Hugh McGuinness, and about 20 who were
taken in at various stations. . . . We proceeded to the front . . . and at
about 10 o'clock we arrived in Franklin [near the Vermont/Canadian
border]. For the first time, we saw the uniformed Fenians here in very*

considerable numbers. The uniform was a capital one for service and most attractive—a green cavalry jacket, faced with yellow, army blue pantaloons, and a blue cap with green band.

At eleven o'clock General George P. Foster, United States Marshall for Vermont, arrived at the encampment. He formally ordered O'Neill to desist from his "unlawful proceeding." The order was coolly received by General O'Neill, [who] ordered the men to fall in. . . . As soon as the column had reached the border, and before the company could deploy, the Canadians opened a heavy fire upon them. Almost at the first discharge, Private John Rowe of Burlington was shot through the head, and fell dead in the center of the road.

After a few hours of fighting, the Fenians fell back, and O'Neill was arrested by the US marshal. As he was being led away, O'Neill turned the command over to O'Reilly, who was then arrested and detained overnight. The Fenians fought for a few more days but "were utterly demoralized and disheartened" against overwhelming forces. The men disbanded and drifted back to their old lives. Some continued the struggle in Ireland. O'Reilly returned to Boston, intent on starting a new phase of his adventurous life.

Chapter Eight

Poets, Patriots, and Publishers of the Gilded Age (1870–1900)

John Boyle O'Reilly may have been a rookie journalist covering the failed Fenian invasion of Canada, but he was a veteran when it came to armed insurrection and battling the British Empire.

Born in Drogheda, County Meath, in 1844, O'Reilly and his family survived the Irish Famine decade of the 1840s. As a teenager O'Reilly became an Irish rebel, devoted to driving the British out of Ireland. He joined the British army—the sole job option for so many Irish—planning not to defend the empire but rather to undermine it by learning military skills. When the British discovered his sedition, they tried him for treason and sentenced him to twenty-two years of hard labor. After two years in an English jail, he was shackled with sixty other political prisoners on a prison ship that took him to remote Western Australia, where he toiled in the boiling sun for the empire.

Within months O'Reilly hatched a daring, dangerous plan to escape, running at night through the jungle, dodging guards and their hunting dogs, until he reached the ocean, where he rowed a small boat out to sea and was picked up by an American whaling ship out of New Bedford named the *Gazelle*. He boarded the ship, then transferred to another whaler, dodging British naval ships and avoiding capture until he made his escape complete.

He arrived in Boston in 1870 at twenty-six, penniless but impassioned by the potential of American democracy and ready to change the world. And

LIBRARY OF MICHAEL QUINLIN

John Boyle O'Reilly was a poet and a patriot.

that's what he sought to do over the final twenty years of his life. O'Reilly's stint covering the Fenian invasion opened up a new career to him as a writer, and he expressed his ideals at a prolific pace through poetry, fiction, lectures, and essays in the *Pilot,* where he served as editor and later as publisher. He became a great orator, reciting his poems at large public gatherings or debating others on civil rights, human rights, and civil liberties at Faneuil Hall and other public venues. His ideals transcended race, religion, and nationality, and he spoke out forcefully and consistently on the plight of blacks in postwar America, on immigrants, on American Indians, and on other downtrodden people seeking a foothold in American life.

He wrote a poem praising Boston Massacre victim Crispus Attucks, the nation's first black martyr, and befriended black leader Frederick Douglass, inviting him to write columns in the *Pilot* and to march in Boston's Saint Patrick's Day parade. He defended Chinese immigrants and Jewish immigrants and objected to the way Native American Indians were treated in America's westward expansion.

As the state's poet laureate, he celebrated in his verses some of New England's most cherished moments in history: the *Mayflower's* landing at Plymouth Rock, the Pilgrim Fathers, and the Boston Massacre.

O'Reilly lived in Boston for just twenty years, but during that time he became Boston's leading reconciler, ushering in a new era of acceptance for the city's Irish. He admonished the Boston Brahmin political establishment while also gaining their respect for his sincerity and his intellectual gifts. His poem on the death of his friend Wendell Phillips, the abolitionist, sums up his philosophy:

There are no classes or races,
But one human brotherhood.
There are no creeds to outlaw,
No colors of skin debarred.
Mankind is one in its rights and wrongs.
One right, one hope, one guard.
The right to be free, the hope to be just,
and the guard against selfish greed.

One of the first controversies he tackled at the *Pilot* was the "stage Irish-man," taking aim at a group called the Hibernian Minstrels, who were portraying the Irish as comic buffoons. O'Reilly wrote:

> *The stage Irishmen [invented by the English] seems to be accepted by*
> *the Irish people, who not only laugh at and applaud his vagaries, but*
> *even become more English than the English themselves in performing*
> *them. . . . This exaggeration by our own people is unworthy. No wonder*
> *people who do not know us should judge us harshly and wrongly.*

It was O'Reilly who first brought national and international notoriety to Boston as a distinctly Irish city, and he helped to spawn an Irish cultural renaissance in the city that lasted about three decades. He welcomed dozens of Irish visitors, from writer Oscar Wilde to rebel John Devoy, and helped organize fund-raising rallies for Ireland's home rule leader Charles Stewart Parnell and Michael Davitt, founder of Ireland's Land League movement. He served as a mentor to the young Chicago sculptor John Donoghue, who created the masterpiece *Young Sophocles,* now at the Isabella Stewart Gardner Museum in Boston. He supported the young poet Fanny Parnell, who headed up the Ladies' Land League, and other women poets seeking to be published.

In addition to his activism and commitment to the public good, O'Reilly was a happy family man. He married Mary Murphy of Charlestown, and they settled in the neighborhood at 34 Winthrop Street near Saint Mary's Church, where the couple raised their four daughters. They had a summer home in Hull, which later became the town's public library.

While in Boston, O'Reilly became an avid sportsman and outdoorsman, cherishing the joy of paddling down a river by himself, or attending giant Irish picnics with races and games. He was athletic and active, and that's why it was

John Boyle O'Reilly Memorial

John Boyle O'Reilly's sudden death on August 10, 1890, shocked and saddened his family, friends, and many admirers throughout the world. His supporters quickly raised twenty-two thousand dollars to build a fitting memorial, selecting Daniel Chester French as the artist. The **John Boyle O'Reilly Memorial** at Boylston and Fenway Streets in the Fens was officially unveiled on June 20, 1896. The memorial features a bust of O'Reilly encircled by a Celtic design. On the reverse side are three bronze figures representing Ireland (the female figure) and Poetry (the male figures).

O'Reilly's summer home is today the Hull Public Library, located at Main and Spring Streets. O'Reilly's residence at 34 Winthrop Street in Charlestown is a private home. In 1988 Charlestown unveiled an O'Reilly plaque at Thompson Square, near the corner of Main and Austin Streets. Sculptor John Donoghue's bust of O'Reilly is in the Fine Arts reading room of the Boston Public Library, with a facsimile at the John J. Burns Library at Boston College. O'Reilly is buried at Holyhood Cemetery in Brookline. Each June the Ancient Order of Hibernians holds a special ceremony at his gravesite. For more information visit the website irishheritagetrail.com.

a shock when he died suddenly from an accidental overdose of medication at age forty-six on August 10, 1890. O'Reilly was mourned by thousands who attended his funeral mass at Saint Mary's, and his death was covered by newspapers around the world.

People from every walk of life sent tributes to O'Reilly, including Edwin Walker, a leader in Boston's African-American community, who said at the funeral, "As long as Mr. O'Reilly lived and spoke, we felt that we had at least, outside of our own people, one true, vigilant, brave and self-sacrificing friend who . . . claimed for us just what he claimed for himself."

Reading for the Irish

As the Irish community grew between 1830 and 1880, nativist Bostonians continued to snipe at the Irish, especially in the newspapers. "No Irish need apply" ads were regular fare in some publications, along with a steady stream of racist jokes known as Irish Bulls. These latter insults portrayed Paddy as unintelligent, belligerent, cunning, or immoral, depending on the punch line. A more odious stream of criticism arose when legitimate issues (such as the matter of parochial school versus public school education or the process of becoming a voting citizen) became points of contention between the Irish and the Know-Nothings, and opponents resorted to caricature to make their points.

German-born cartoonist Thomas Nast created a stir with a series of anti-Irish, anti-Catholic drawings that ran in *Harper's Magazine* and *Puck* magazine from the 1860s through the 1880s, portraying the Irish as simian primates replete with base emotions, characteristics, and impulses.

In Boston perhaps the most vile and racist tract on the subject appeared on July 25, 1868, in *Every Saturday,* a weekly magazine distributed by Ticknor and Fields publishers. The twelve-hundred-word article by F. P. Cobbe, entitled "No Irish Need Apply," was filled with a hatred and malice that shocked decent people and made the NINA classified ads seem paltry by comparison. The *Irish-American Weekly* responded, "the article puts into condensed form, double distilled and concentrated, the venomous essence of that bigotry which exists in certain quarters among us, to a much greater extent than we are sometimes apt to imagine."

But the NINA ads, and the general stereotyping of the Irish, was gradually eclipsed during the Gilded Age by the emergence of an Irish-American publishing and writing scene that gave voice to the positive aspects of Boston's Irish community. Technological advances in the printing process and the growing popularity of sheet music and inexpensive books allowed the Irish to create their own literature rather than allow their detractors to tell the story.

The public defender of the Boston Irish had long been the *Pilot* newspaper, the official standard-bearer of Irish and Catholic causes. Other sympathetic papers such as the *Boston Vindicator* and the *Irish Illustrator* had appeared briefly on the scene, but it was the *Pilot* that had lifted up the Irish-American persona while also challenging the remnants of the parochial Puritan mind-set reluctant to accept a world outside itself.

Since launching the *Pilot* in 1835, Patrick Donahoe had become the most influential Irishman in Boston in the nineteen century, and in many ways the premier Irish-American publisher in the nation. The weekly *Pilot* had subscribers across the country, and around 1850 Donahoe started a book publishing business as well, issuing dozens of books on Irish and Catholic subjects. For several decades he ran a bookstore as part of his publishing enterprise on Franklin Street. After a series of fires and business setbacks forced him to sell the *Pilot* to John Boyle O'Reilly and the Archdiocese of Boston in 1876, he returned in 1878 to launch *Donahoe's Magazine*, a monthly journal containing "tales, drama, biography, episodes in Irish and American history, poetry, music and miscel-lany." The *Pilot*, under O'Reilly and then Kathleen Conway, continued to serve as the voice of the Irish and Catholic communities in Boston, eventually evolv-ing into largely a Catholic publication.

Other Irish newspapers were starting up around this time. Patrick Ford, whose family had moved to Boston from Galway in 1845 when he was eight, was already a veteran newspaperman by the time he was thirty, having worked for William Lloyd Garrison's abolitionist paper, the *Liberator*, as a teenager, then becoming editor and publisher of the *Boston Tribune* in his twenties. In 1870 Ford launched the *Irish World* newspaper, which was immediately praised for its "brave, fearless, honest, effective work" on behalf of Ireland. Based in New York, the *Irish World* had a strong following in Boston and covered many of the local political races and Irish activities in New England.

The Irish community found a solid ally in a start-up mainstream newspa-per, the *Boston Globe*, which formed in 1872. "A new Boston newspaper seeking a new readership would find a natural clientele in the new Irish, and in sup-porting the causes of labor and the underdog element it would naturally form associations with Democratic politicians, who were chiefly Irish," wrote Louis M. Lyons. The *Globe* hired many Irish-American writers, including Michael Curran in 1873, who was promoted to night editor in 1875 and Sunday *Globe* editor in 1877. Described as "an active Land Leaguer," Curran gave extensive coverage to visits by Charles Stewart Parnell, Michael Davitt, and other Irish leaders coming to Boston in the 1870s and 1880s.

In 1882 Patrick J. Maguire, a native of County Monahan, launched the *Republic*, a feisty weekly newspaper whose mission was to "intelligently give shape to the desires and aspirations" of the Boston Irish while disproving James Russell Lowell's view that "it is impossible for a man to be an Irishman and an American at the same time." The paper, whose circulation quickly jumped to thirty-five thousand copies and surpassed one hundred thousand in its first year, became a forceful platform for the Democratic Party, since Maguire was, as historian John T. Galvin noted, an influential "back-room operator" and possibly "the only city-wide boss Boston ever had." It was Maguire who coor-dinated Irish and Yankee leaders to nominate the city's first Irish-born mayor, Hugh O'Brien, who served from 1885 to 1889. Maguire also helped launch the political career of Patrick A. Collins, who became the city's second Irish-born mayor from 1902 to 1905.

The issue of whether an immigrant could be a good American while remaining a true Irishman was at the very heart of the Irish struggle to gain acceptance in nineteenth-century Boston. O'Reilly, Maguire, and others knew that it was possible to balance love of one's native land with loyalty to one's adopted country, but the difficult task was to present such largesse to the skeptics of Boston. This Irish generation sought to blend the two urges together by creating a singular Boston Irish persona.

When the Irish of the 1830s realized they could openly practice their Catholic faith in Boston, despite the often brutal objections of the nativists, that breakthrough served as an epiphany for the entire community. A similar epiphany occurred in the 1880s when the Irish realized they could be, in the best sense of the words, Irish Americans. They could enter the world of local politics as Americans, working themselves up the political ladder on the Boston Common Council and School Committee. They could retain their Irish roots by supporting Ireland's continued struggle for independence. And they could create their own cultural revival right in Boston, passing on to the younger generation the language, music, dance, literature, and sports of ancient Ireland.

Focusing on the cultural life of the Boston Irish was the newspaper the *Irish Echo*, launched in 1886. The *Echo* (no relation to the New York paper started in 1928) was a bilingual newspaper in Irish and English issued by members of the Philo-Celtic Society, a group formed in 1874 to promote the Irish language and Gaelic culture in Boston. Its leader was P. J. Daly, a committed Irish speaker who helped create dozens of Irish language schools in Greater Boston that lasted well into the twentieth century. The society displayed a middle-class gentility to which many Boston Irish aspired. Beneath the veneer, however, was a forceful and earnest mission, as described in the first issue of the *Echo:* "to aid and assist in the vindication of the character of the Irish race from the foul slanders of centuries by English writers."

The foremost mission of Boston Irish newspapers in the nineteenth century was to speak on behalf of the Irish community, not simply about it. The strong editorial stance of the *Pilot*, the *Republic*, the *World*, and the *Echo* prevented the Irish community from becoming languid and disinterested, as it would later in the twentieth century. The constant flow of opinion, news, and activities made sure the Irish community took a stance in its own affairs.

Irish writers became active participants in an era of increased publishing growth in the United States. John Boyle O'Reilly himself was widely published during his twenty years in Boston. He published four volumes of poetry and two prose collections. Upon his death his friend and protégé James Jeffrey Roche wrote O'Reilly's biography, entitled *Life of John Boyle O'Reilly, Together with His Complete Poems and Speeches*, published in 1891.

Other Irish-American journalists emerged during this period, including Timothy Murnane, Michael Curran, Arthur Forrester, William Kenney, Thomas Maguire, and Helen O'Neill.

Publishing the Irish

Boston was a favorable setting for many immigrants who want to get involved in book publishing. One of the early works was *A History of Ireland*, written and self-published in Boston in 1845 by Thomas Mooney, originally from Dublin. Mooney writes in the introduction: "It speaks truth of the living and the dead—is published in the land of freedom and speaks in a freeman's tone." The 1,650-page book contained an eclectic assortment of essays about oghams (secret writing), how the Irish invented poetry, and how Gothic architecture is actually Irish architecture, along with profiles of famous men. One of the valuable portions of the book was the music section, which introduced American readers to the works of Irish harpist Turlough Carolan and other composers not yet known in the United States.

Patrick Donahoe became the premier book publisher of Catholic and Irish works in the nineteenth century. Among the outstanding Irish titles,

Celtic Studies at Harvard

Fred Norris Robinson, a Chaucer scholar, taught the first Gaelic course at Harvard University in 1896. The **Celtic Languages and Literatures Department** was later established in 1940 by Henry Lee Shattuck, a descendant of famous privateer Patrick Tracy. He contributed $51,000 to launch the program. Charles Dunn headed the department from 1962 to 1984, and John V. Kelleher held the first Chair of Irish Studies. Patrick Ford headed the department from 1991 to 2005. Catherine McKenna is head of the department today. The department awards advanced degrees in Celtic studies and offers introductory courses to the public through the University Extension program. The Friends of Harvard Celtic Studies group, headed by Phil Haughey, raises funds so graduate students can conduct research in the Celtic countries. For more information, call (617) 495-1206 or visit their website fhcs.fas.harvard.edu/.

Irish Women Writers

In the late nineteenth century, Boston Irish women emerged as poets, journalists, novelists, and authors of nonfiction and children's literature. These women published frequently in the *Pilot, Donahue's Magazine,* and the *Republic,* as well as the *Atlantic Monthly,* and the daily Boston papers.

Annie Sullivan (1866–1936), who taught Helen Keller, was a lucid writer as well as a brilliant teacher. Her reports to the Perkins School for the Blind are included in Keller's best-selling autobiography, *The Story of My Life.* They reveal Sullivan's sure grasp of language, style, and structure.

Sarah Orne Jewett (1849–1909) was born in Maine, and after a visit to Ireland in 1882, she wrote numerous short stories about Irish immigrants for *Scribner's, McClure's,* and other leading magazines.

Louise Imogen Guiney (1861–1920) first published her poems under the initials P.O.L., and everyone assumed she was "a bright Harvard boy."

Mary McGrath Blake (1840–1907), born in Dungarvin, County Waterford, was the mother of eleven children and published several poetry and travel books.

Katherine E. Conway (1853–1927) served as the only woman editor of the Boston *Pilot,* between 1905 and 1908. A published poet, Conway organized the O'Reilly Reading Circle for young women, in memory of her mentor, John Boyle O'Reilly.

Fanny Parnell (1848–1882) was frequently published in the *Pilot,* which compiled her poems into a booklet when she died.

Katharine M. O'Keeffe O'Mahoney (1852–1918) immigrated with her family from Kilkenney to Lawrence when she was ten months old. She taught poetry to Robert Frost at Lawrence High School and wrote *Sketch of Catholicity in Lawrence and Vicinity, Famous Irishwomen, An Evening with Longfellow,* and *Moore's Birthday: A Musical Allegory.*

some copublished with companies in London or Dublin, were *Moore's Melodies* by Thomas Moore, *History of the Irish Insurrection of 1798* by Edward Hay, and *A History of the Irish Settlers in North America* by Thomas D'Arcy McGee. His Catholic titles included *Discourses Addressed to Mixed Congregations* by John Henry Newman, *History of the Christian Church, from its First Establishment to the Present Century* by Rev. Joseph Reeve, and *The Monks of the West: From St. Benedict to St. Bernard* by Count de Montalembert.

In 1889 James Bernard Cullen wrote and self-published one of the significant Irish volumes of the era, entitled *The Boston Irish: Together with Biographical Sketches of Representative Men and Noted Women.* The 444-page book took the reader on a fascinating journey that started in the 1620s and wound its way through the tumultuous odyssey of the Irish throughout Boston history. A historical narrative, which takes up a third of the book, was written by William Taylor Jr., while Cullen himself wrote nearly four hundred profiles of individuals, including 47 distinguished men of history. He wrote thumbnail sketches of 59 lawyers, 24 doctors, 63 journalists, and 189 politicians. It demonstrated the road to respectability the Irish had taken in the latter half of the nineteenth century.

Becoming Irish Yankees

As the Irish moved into the ranks of respectability, they often tried to duplicate the trappings of comfort and influence enjoyed by the Yankees, coveting and then re-creating the old Brahmin institutions to which they had long been denied access. In April 1882 the *Republic* announced the need for an Irish-American men's club, "such as the Union and St. Botolph clubs . . . which shall be first class in every respect and a credit to the race in the city." The following year Thomas Riley established the Clover Club of Boston, a men's association whose "object shall be the social enjoyment of its members." Most of the members were Irish natives or Irish Americans, and they seemed to relish the opportunity to be frivolous in a bourgeois sort of way. Still, it was a good-natured gathering where wit was the supreme arbitrator. John Boyle O'Reilly himself was a member, even though he had been invited into some of Boston's old-line gentleman's clubs. In 1900 the Clover Club was making a grand occasion out of the fact they had a Ladies Night each year where the wives and girlfriends were invited to join the merrymaking in the strictly male club.

The Irish were keen to be part of the city's civil and cultural life. When Irish playwright Oscar Wilde visited Boston in 1882, O'Reilly took him to meet Henry Wadsworth Longfellow, Wendell Phillips, Oliver Wendell Holmes, and Julia Ward Howe. When Hugh O'Brien was mayor in 1888, he laid the cornerstone for the new Boston Public Library, which had been created in 1848 to educate the immigrants. The Irish were proud when Henry Doogue, an Irish immigrant, became the city's chief horticulturalist and turned the Public Garden into a nationally acclaimed botanical garden. When sculptor John Donoghue from Chicago had an exhibit at Horticultural Hall, O'Reilly praised his work and suggested that Donoghue be considered an American master. The Irish were always delighted when a Yankee acknowledged their positive

characteristics, as in 1896, when Mayor Josiah Quincy told a Charitable Irish
Society gathering, "I feel that the members of your race . . . set an example
which the members of other nationalities upon this continent may emulate. No
one can look around Boston today and [not] note the progress which the Irish
race has made in Boston."

The Boston Irish gained national attention during this era. In 1893 several notable Bostonians participated in the Columbian Exposition in Chicago,
celebrating Christopher Columbus's visit to America in 1492. More than 25
million visitors attended this world's fair, and every nation had its own pavilion. Augustus Saint-Gaudens, along with Daniel Chester French, was brought
in early to help promote the expo and to help design the American pavilions.
Saint-Gaudens recommended that one of his students, Frederick MacMonnies,
whose parents were Scottish, be brought in to design the Columbian Fountain,
one of the centerpieces of the show. Louis Sullivan, by now an established
architect in Chicago, designed the massive Transportation Building in the
American exhibit. And Patsy Touhey, the uilleann piper from South Boston,
played his exciting style of music at the Irish pavilion.

With a firm footing in the city's political, business, and social circles, Irish-
American leaders turned their attention to history. Irish leaders were long
offended at the way Anglo-American historians had minimized the Irish contribution in America. Even the Irish who had come from Ulster in the eighteenth
century and made such a contribution to this country were now being called
Scots-Irish to distinguish them from the hordes of Irish Catholics who had
arrived since the 1840s. On January 20, 1897, a group of forty distinguished
Boston Irish convened a meeting at the Revere House to form the American-
Irish Historical Society, which set out "to correct the erroneous, distorted and
false views of history in relation to the Irish race in America; to encourage and
assist in the formation of local societies; and to promote and foster an honorable national spirit of patriotism." It was to be influenced "by no religious
or political divisions, for with us the race stands first, its qualifying incidents
afterwards."

The society swiftly became a national organization, with hundreds of
members subscribing from more than a dozen states. The early roster of members included writer Thomas J. Gargan; James J. Roche, editor of the *Pilot;*
Thomas Hamilton Murray, editor of the *Lowell Sun;* Thomas Lawler of the
publishing house Ginn and Company; and Augustus Saint-Gaudens. Its most

distinguished member, though, was Theodore Roosevelt, who claimed Irish roots on his mother's side of the family.

The society held numerous meetings and published a journal that uncovered some fascinating genealogical and historical material on the American Irish in the seventeenth and eighteenth centuries. Michael J. O'Brien from Fermoy, County Cork, emerged as the society's leading Irish-American historian. For more than sixty years, O'Brien patiently waded through libraries, archives, court records, genealogy papers, and military records to track down early Irish settlers in North America dating back to the seventeenth century. His book *A Hidden Phase of American History: Ireland's Part in America's Struggle for Liberty* traced the migration of thousands of Irish from all parts of Ireland, north and south, to the American colonies, since the very beginning of European travel to North America. O'Brien's sequel, *The Irish at Bunker Hill*, published after his death in 1960, determined that hundreds of Irish and Scots-Irish were involved in that famous fight, a sharp retort to historians who insisted it was an Anglo-American occasion. O'Brien was certainly intense about his work, and he openly quarreled with those who put forth the Scots-Irish as a way of minimizing the role of the Irish in America. Having proved conclusively that the Irish were involved in many significant episodes throughout American history, the society tried to avoid being vainglorious and self-laudatory. The evidence spoke for itself.

CHAPTER NINE

The Irish Take the Field (1890–1920)

JAMES BRENDAN CONNOLLY of South Boston decided he would be an Olympian. When he learned that French nobleman Pierre de Coubertin was planning to revive the Olympic Games in April 1896, after they had been dormant for almost fifteen hundred years, the pride of South Boston knew that he must find a way to make the journey to Athens, Greece. "I thought of the land of Homer . . . and made up my mind that I would make that trip," Connolly told the *Boston Sunday Post*.

Thirty-year-old Connolly was already leading an adventurous life when he was bitten by the Olympic bug. He had left school in the fifth grade to help support his family and as a teenager had begun working with his uncle, Jim O'Donnell, on the fishing boats out of Gloucester and Boston. He spent a few years down in Savannah, working alongside his brother Michael with the Army Corps of Engineers, where he became a surveyor. He returned to Boston in 1895 to attend Harvard University and was awarded an engineering scholarship given to children of immigrants. He was studying the classics as a freshman when he heard about the Olympic Games.

Connolly was one of twelve children (including eight boys in a row), the son of immigrant parents John and Ann (O'Donnell) from Inis Mór, Aran Islands, off the coast of Galway. Like many young men and women growing

COURTESY OF COLBY COLLEGE

South Boston native James B. Connolly, first winner of the Modern Olympic Games

up in Boston in the late nineteenth century, Connolly was steeped in a sports culture that placed a high premium on athletic skills and competition. Groups such as the Irish Athletic Club, the Irish American Club of South Boston, and the Columbian Rowing Association flourished with the full support of political, church, and community leaders. South Boston was a sportsman's haven, with miles of coastline and acres of parks and playing fields for children.

As the national champion in the hop, skip, and jump, as the triple jump was then known, Connolly was eligible to compete in the Olympics. The American team was made up almost entirely of athletes from Harvard, Princeton, and the Boston Athletic Club. Harvard would not allow Connolly a leave of absence, so he quit the school. With his life savings of seven hundred dollars, plus funds the parishioners raised for him at Saint Augustine's, Connolly made his way down to Hoboken, New Jersey, where he boarded a freighter, the SS *Fulda*, and headed for Greece.

Connolly's athletic career blossomed just as individual athleticism and team sports were becoming popular American pastimes. The swift growth of cities throughout America in the late nineteenth century spawned a remarkable parks and playgrounds movement that had Boston roots. Frederick Law Olmsted designed the city's Emerald Necklace, a string of parks that included 527-acre Franklin Park, with playing fields, running paths, and tennis courts widely enjoyed by the Irish community. Joseph Lee, known as the Father of the American Playground, theorized that children in tenement housing needed playgrounds to grow, and sports became a legitimate outlet for poor children.

In later years Connolly looked back with pride on how his hometown of South Boston shaped his later career as a writer and public figure. "I would rather be born in South Boston than any other place I know," he wrote, citing the "mental, physical and spiritual" benefits of the neighborhood.

Years of practice and preparation served Connolly well in Athens in 1896, where an international cast, mainly of European athletes, had gathered to compete. The field was relatively small, with 285 men competing in forty-two events.

On the day the athletes arrived at the stadium, expecting to warm up and get acclimated for several days, they were informed that the events were about to begin the following day. It turned out the Greeks used the Hellenic calendar, which was twelve days ahead of the Gregorian calendar. After a few preliminary heats in the running events, and in front of 140,000 spectators, Connolly stepped up to compete in the hop, skip, and jump. Beverly Cronin of the *Boston Herald* reported the scene: "[Connolly] walked up to the line, and with Prince George of England and Prince George of Greece as judges, yelled in a burst of emotion, 'Here's one for the honor of County Galway.'" Connolly then jumped 44 feet 11¾ inches and won the first medal of the Modern Olympic Games.

According to Ellery H. Clark, his teammate from Harvard, Connolly had beaten the nearest competitor by almost six feet, causing the crowd to chant his name and yell, "Nike! Nike!"—the Greek word for victory. To further cement his status as a world-class athlete, Connolly placed second in the high jump, clearing 5 feet 5 inches, and third place in the long jump, leaping 20 feet ½ inch. (Clark won first place in both of those jumps.)

The six-man team from Boston included two other Irish Americans, Thomas E. Burke, who took first place in the 100-meter and 400-meter runs, and Arthur Blake, who took second in the 1,500 meters. Blake's mother was Mary McGrath, the noted poet and author of children's books.

Upon returning to Boston the Olympians were feted at an elaborate ceremony at Faneuil Hall, attended by Governor Roger Walcott, Mayor Josiah Quincy, the Greek Consul General, and other dignitaries, followed by an elaborate dinner at the Hotel Vendome. Then a few weeks later, on May 29, the people of South Boston threw a banquet for the Olympians, including a parade, fireworks, and marching bands. Connolly remained a popular figure in Boston throughout his life. He continued to train and returned to the next Olympics, held in Paris in 1900, taking second place in the triple jump. The *Herald*'s Cronin reported, "In typical Connolly fashion, he walked the seven miles to Paris Stadium before that competition because he couldn't afford the taxi fare."

Connolly stayed active in athletics long after his career ended, emerging as a critic of the commercialization of amateur sports. He wrote a scathing article about the 1908 Olympic Games in London, titled "The English as Poor Losers," where he accused the organizers of cheating during the competitions. He turned his hand to writing and had a successful career, writing twenty-five books and dozens of short stories about the sea. In 1898 he covered the

Spanish-American War, enlisting in the Fighting Ninth Irish Regiment, commanded by South Boston's Lawrence J. Logan, an immigrant from Ballygar, Galway. The Ninth saw action in Santiago, and Connolly sent back dispatches to the *Boston Globe* under the heading "Letters from the Front in Cuba." During World War I he traveled with the US Navy and wrote articles on the war effort. In 1921 he covered the Black and Tan war in Ireland and wrote a series of articles titled "Tortured Ireland: The Black and Tan Warfare in Ireland," published in the *Boston American.*

Connolly also took a run at politics in 1914, vying for congressman from South Boston on the Progressive Party ticket. Though he lost his only political campaign, he was praised for his positions on "social welfare, a National child labor law, a living wage law and old age pension law."

Perhaps his greatest compliment came from President Theodore Roosevelt, who told interviewer Frank Sheridan, "My ideal of an all around man is James Connolly of Boston. . . . Connolly is what I think a man should be. If my boy Theodore turns out to be as good a man I will be satisfied. Connolly has strength, agility, and perseverance. He loves outdoor, healthful life, and he is clean through and through. I want my boy to be as good a man as Connolly."

At Play in the Old Country

Growing up to be like Jim Connolly was a common notion in sports-crazed South Boston, where love of athletic competition was part of a culture that immigrants brought from Ireland. Most nineteenth-century Irish immigrants came from rural backgrounds, where people married late in life because of the shortage of land and economic prospects. A widely accepted bachelor subculture emerged in Ireland, according to sports historian Steven A. Reiss, with groups of single men often whiling away their free time engaged in sports, betting, and drinking. That subculture was transferred to Boston, where numerous sports clubs flourished in Irish neighborhoods.

Irish groups such as the Ancient Order of Hibernians, along with trade unions and church groups, frequently held outdoor picnics and field days where sports competitions were common, along with music and dancing, oratory contests, and other pleasantries, historian Dennis Ryan noted in his book *Beyond the Ballot Box.*

"Most of the older people were of high blood still keen for the field sports of the old country," Connolly once wrote. "You could find old men unable to read or write [who] could argue keenly, intelligently on any outdoor sport whatsoever. . . . Many had been themselves athletes of fame: hurlers, bowlers, wrestlers. . . . Children growing up healthy, rugged just naturally had a taste for athletics."

The Irish had a particular passion for hurling, which had taken root in America. The *Republic* newspaper published regular notices about hurling matches in the Boston area, and matches between the South Boston Athletic Club and the Worcester Hurling Club were held as early as 1882.

The City of Boston Archives has records of hurling matches on Boston Common every Fourth of July, starting in 1884 and continuing through the 1890s. Teams included the Shamrock Hurling Club, the William O'Brien Hurling Club, and the Boston Hurling Club, who played for a prize of one hundred dollars. In July 1893 team captain John W. Flynn wrote a letter to parks official Hillard Smith, complaining that the Shamrocks had been given the prize money even though they "walked off the field before the match was decided."

Hurling, along with football and camogie, was an ancient Irish sport promoted by the Gaelic Athletic Association (GAA), a sports group that formed in Ireland in 1884 and quickly spread to the United States. As part of a burgeoning nationalistic fervor in Ireland, sports became a way for the Irish to connect with their ancient traditions. This movement went hand in hand with a broader cultural renaissance taking place in both Ireland and the United States.

The Boston Irish also excelled in competitive rowing during this time. Local Irish clubs such as the Columbian Rowing Association, Shawmut Rowing Club, and West End Boat Club competed along the Charles River and in Boston Harbor. The most famous rower in the Irish community was Bill Caffrey, champion oarsman from Lawrence. Competing for the Lawrence Canoe Club and the Columbian Boat Club in Boston, the five-foot-eight-inch, 145-pound sculler worked his way up the local ranks, winning the New England single-scull championship in 1890 at age twenty-three. Later that year he stunned a field of prominent champions across the United States and Canada by winning the national rowing championships, a feat he repeated in 1891. Caffrey later became a policeman and a pillar of the Lawrence community.

Distance walking and running were also popular pastimes for the Boston Irish. Michael J. McEttrick of Roxbury entered long-distance competitions of one hundred miles, winning the American Championship crown in 1868,

Boston Irish Athletes Honored

Four public installations pay special homage to Irish track and field legends. In 1987 Boston honored Olympic champion **James Brendan Connolly** by erecting a statue at Joe Moakley Park in South Boston that depicts his winning Olympic jump in 1896. Connolly's extensive papers are kept at Colby College in Maine and at the John J. Burns Library at Boston College. In 1996 the Boston Athletic Association placed a bronze medallion at Copley Square Park to celebrate the centenary of the Boston Marathon; Irishman **John J. McDermott** won that first race. The medallion was created by Robert Shure, sculptor of the Boston Irish Famine Memorial. In 1997 the Boston Athletic Association honored marathon runner and two-time winner **Johnny Kelley** with a statue on Commonwealth Avenue, along the marathon course. In 2005 State Representative Kevin Honan and others unveiled a statue to Olympian **Harold Connolly,** who won a gold medal in the 1956 Melbourne Olympics in the hammer throw.

which he held for a number of years. In 1882 John Meagher of Lawrence and D. A. Driscoll of Lynn competed against each other in the hundred-mile heel-and-toe walk, which ended at mile 51 when Driscoll admitted defeat, noting graciously that Meagher was "the best 100 mile walker in the country."

In the 1890s the Irish began to dominate running. Thomas E. Burke of the West End, whose father was an undertaker at Saint Joseph's Church, was a track star at English High School and later Boston University. In 1896 he was on the Olympic team that went to Athens, where he won two first-place medals, in the 100 meters and the 400 meters. Burke later went to Harvard Law School, worked as a sports reporter for a time, and became the oldest pilot to serve in World War I.

Burke served as the official race starter at the first Boston Marathon, staged by the Boston Athletic Association in April 1897. It was won by John J. McDermott, an Irish-born lithographer from New York, in two hours, fifty-five minutes, ten seconds. McDermott beat a field of fifteen runners, which included a Maguire, two Sullivans, and a Harrigan. John Caffrey, son of Irish immigrants from Ontario, won in 1900 and 1901, wearing the St. Patrick's Athletic Association shirt with a shamrock emblazed on the front.

The most famous Irish-American athlete ever to participate in the Boston Marathon was, of course, Johnny Kelley, later called "Johnny the Elder" when another runner by the same name started competing in the world's best-known marathon race. Kelley did not finish his first two marathons, in 1928 and 1932, but then finished every Boston Marathon from 1933 to 1992! He finished in the top ten eighteen times, taking first place in 1935 and 1945. His best time was two hours and thirty minutes, posted in 1943. When asked by the *Boston Globe* about his Irish connections, he replied, "My people left Wexford to go to Australia. The boat stopped in Boston, and they never left."

The Perfect Pugilist of Modern Times

None of the athletes, not even James Connolly, could compete in stature and notoriety with the most famous Irish-American athlete ever to come out of Boston, John L. Sullivan. The son of Irish immigrants, he was born in 1858 on East Concord Street, growing up just a few miles from Connolly over the Broadway Bridge in the South End. John's father Mike came from Kerry and his mother, Catherine Kelly, from Galway. He quickly became known as the Boston Strong Boy because of his powerful knockout punch and his endurance in fighting dozens of rounds. He had his first boxing success in 1878 at the Dudley Opera House in Roxbury, where journeyman boxer Jack Scannell was challenging all the local boys to take a round in the ring. Sullivan's punch knocked Scannell out of the ring, and his career was under way.

He went on the national circuit, punching it out in sports arenas or in open fields surrounded by hundreds of spectators, and worked his way up the boxing chain. Four years later, Sullivan startled the sports world by knocking out Paddy Ryan, then beat a series of world champions over the next decade, including Charley Mitchell and Jake Kilrain. His brash confidence and often outrageous displays of drinking, gambling, and womanizing, combined with his sense of humor and charm, endeared him to the Boston Irish.

A number of Irish Americans opposed the art of pugilism, including Patrick Donahoe, who refused to cover the sport in *Donahoe's Magazine*. John Boyle O'Reilly, on the other hand, was an enthusiastic sportsman who had written a book called *Ethics of Boxing and Manly Sport* and had sung the praises of a sculpture of Sullivan created by John Donoghue and exhibited at Horticultural Hall in 1888. He wrote:

> It is . . . a personification of the power, will, grace, beauty, brutality,
> and majesty of the perfect pugilist of modern times. . . . This statue
> stands for nineteenth century boxing for all time. . . . It is the statue of a

magnificent athlete, worthy of ancient Athens, and distinctly and proudly
true of modern Boston.

In 1887 Sullivan took a trip to Ireland, which was widely reported in the
press and followed eagerly by Boston's Irish community. Feted and praised
every step of the way by huge crowds, the larger-than-life champion defeated
every fighter who dared to step into the ring. University of Limerick lecturer
Jack Anderson wrote that Sullivan was greeted in Dublin to the musical strains
of Handel's "Hail the Conquering Hero," followed by "Yankee Doodle." He
gave several boxing exhibitions while in Ireland and even weighed in on the
topic of Home Rule for Ireland, which he of course endorsed.

The biggest journalism scoop of the day was when Sullivan returned from
Ireland. John S. Taylor, sporting editor of the *Boston Globe*, waited in a tugboat
near the Boston lighthouse for two days for Sullivan's ship to come in and
snagged an exclusive interview with the celebrity pugilist. He had already filed
the story while the other reporters waited at Commercial Wharf to meet the
boxer, according to James B. Cullen in his book *The Story of the Irish in Boston*.

Upon his return to Boston, Sullivan was awarded a championship belt
studded with diamonds and other stones. The belt was inscribed "Presented to
the Champion of Champions, John L. Sullivan, by the Citizens of the United
States." The belt included the flags of the United States, Ireland, and the United
Kingdom. (The *British American Citizen*'s snide headline read, "Diamond Belt to
Rum-Selling Pugilist.") Sullivan continued to amass victories, defending his title
against worthy opponents or offering fifty dollars or more to anyone who could
stay with him in the ring for three rounds. In September 1892 the sporting world
was shocked, and the Boston Irish were in mourning, when their Strong Boy was
defeated by a more nimble Jim Corbett in a famous match in New Orleans. Sullivan continued to fight until 1905, when he hung up the gloves forever and, a
few months later, quit the booze. He spent years on the temperance circuit, warning anyone who would listen about the evils of whiskey. He once told reporter
Jerome W. Power, "Whiskey is the only fighter who ever licked John L. Sullivan."

Sullivan remained a popular figure, first on the temperance circuit and
finally as a vaudeville performer. Everywhere he went, until his death in 1918,
he attracted crowds of admirers. Political powerhouse James M. Curley enlisted
him on the campaign trail, and the Boston Red Sox used to invite him into the
dugout during ball games.

He became an enduring legend in Boston long after his death. "What other man," wrote James Brendan Connolly about Sullivan, "being waked out of his sleep and finding two burglars in his room—what other man in the world would lock the door, give the two burglars a beating, and then order them up a good breakfast, and turn them loose with a sermon on the error of their ways?"

The Irish Pilgrims Play the Olde Ball Game

Early efforts to name baseball teams in Boston were not so successful. In 1901 the team was nicknamed the Boston Somersets, after team owner Charles Somers. But that name conjured up unfortunate reminders of the city's exclusive gentleman's club, called the Somerset, which had been formed in 1851 as a way for the old Brahmins to escape the Irish masses in comfort and privacy with a stiff brandy and a Cuban cigar. A full century later John F. Kennedy complained to a friend, "Do you know it's impossible for an Irish Catholic to get into the Somerset Club? If I moved back to Boston even after being president, it would make no difference."

Some fans started calling the team the Pilgrims, then the Puritans. Not too many Pilgrims or Puritans, however, were apparent on a team that sported a roster with Jimmie Collins, Bill Dineen, Patsy Dougherty, Duke Farrell, Tommy Hughes, and Jackie O'Brien, with German-American Cy Young thrown in for good measure. Finally the Taylor family, which owned the team, renamed it the Boston Red Sox after the 1907 season, and the rest is history.

The first baseball teams in America formed in the 1850s as a pastime for middle-class young men, but immigrants and blue-collar athletes soon took over, forming leagues united by their trade, neighborhood, or religious affiliations. Baseball easily supplanted cricket, which had made some headway in America but was essentially viewed as an elitist sport. Baseball seemed to embody something so democratic that it ultimately became the national pastime, and the Irish, enthusiastic about anything that was both patriotic and enjoyable, quickly filled the ranks. By the 1880s Irish players dominated the game of baseball, accounting for more than one-third of the league.

The ballplayers were matched in the local sports pages by a crop of Irish-American reporters. Timothy Hayes Murnane started the respected sports paper the *Boston Referee* in 1886 and later covered sports for the *Boston Globe* and

Michael "King" Kelly, the first superstar in baseball

the *Sporting News*. Eugene Buckley published the *Baseball Record*, and Peter Kelly, a journalist from South Boston, was chosen as secretary of the Boston National Baseball League in 1910.

Journalist Ron Kaplan, writing in *Irish America* magazine, claims that the first superstar of baseball was first-generation Irish American Mike "King" Kelly, who was sold by Chicago to the Boston Braves in 1887 for ten thousand dollars and in 1890 became the team's player/manager. Kelly was an extroverted showman and "the greatest drawing card the game has ever produced," wrote T. H. Murnane in the *Boston Globe*. "Kelly could sing a song, dance a jig, throw a somerset and crack a bottle of champagne all in the hour." Kelly once stole six bases in a single game, a feat memorialized in a popular song called "Slide, Kelly, Slide."

The most famous baseball coach to come out of Massachusetts was Connie Mack, born Cornelius McGillicuddy in East Brookfield. In 1914 Mack's team, the Philadelphia Athletics, lost four straight games to the Boston Braves in the World Series Championship. Jimmie Collins, regarded as the greatest third baseman ever to play, coached Boston to the World Series title in 1903 against the Pittsburgh Pirates. Joe Cronin, who played his last ten years with the Red Sox, had a .301 batting average, including 1,424 runs batted in. William "Rough" Carrigan, from Lewiston, Maine, led the Sox to two consecutive World Series in 1915 and 1916. He was "the greatest manager I ever played for," said Babe Ruth. "He taught me how to be a big league pitcher."

Speaking of Ruth, the player who brought him to Boston was none other than Patsy Donovan, who was born in Cork but at age three emigrated to Lawrence, a mill city of Irish immigrants north of Boston. Donovan broke into professional baseball in 1886 when he was twenty-one, playing in the New England League. He spent seventeen years as a player and manager, coaching the Boston Red Sox in 1910 and 1911. He had 2,263 hits as a player and a lifetime batting average of .313.

According to his son Charles M. Donovan, Patsy was in Baltimore scouting some players when he ran into a priest he knew who was working at St. Mary's Industrial School in Baltimore. The priest suggested that Patsy take a

Irish Events at Fenway Park

Irish Hurling and Football

September 4, 1916—The Galway Men's Association enjoyed a day of hurling matches and track and field events.

May 30, 1927—The Kerry Gaelic Football played a Boston team at Fenway.

June 6, 1937—County Mayo's [Ireland] All-Ireland Football Champions beat a Massachusetts team 17 to 8. Lt. Governor John Kelly threw in the ball to start the game.

November 7, 1954 —Cork's All-Ireland Hurling Team beat a Boston team 37 to 28; then a week later a County Mayo team beat a local team 13 to 6.

Boxing and Wrestling

June 26, 1928—Irish Billy Murphy lost a close match against Portuguese champion Al Mello before twelve thousand boxing fans.

June 12, 1932—Eddie "Kid" Sullivan, "the perpetual motion machine from Walpole," fought Tony Acquaro of Lynn.

June 27, 1935—Danno O'Mahoney from Cork wrestled Jimmy "the Greek" Londos into submission before thirty thousand people.

July 20, 1937—O'Mahoney lost a tough wrestling match to fellow Irishman Steve Casey.

July 29, 1937—Two heavyweights, Al McCoy and Jack McCarthy, battled before ten thousand people.

More Irish Occasions

June 23, 1958—Television personality Ed Sullivan was master of ceremonies at Mayor John Hynes's Charity Field Day.

April 17, 1964—Robert Kennedy and the Kennedy clan attended a Memorial Game at Fenway in honor of his brother, President John F. Kennedy.

look at George Herman Ruth, then playing for the Baltimore Orioles. As journalist Arthur Daley recounted in the *New York Times*, "The instant he saw him work he fell in love with a huge southpaw pitcher of obvious skills, Babe Ruth. He . . . rushed helter-skelter back to Owner [Joe] Lannin with the demand that the Red Sox buy Ruth from the Orioles regardless of the price. Ten minutes later Lannin had closed the deal over the phone." Daley called it "the greatest bargain buy in baseball history."

The Greening of Fenway Park

At times opening day at Fenway Park, April 20, 1912, had the appearance of an old-fashioned Irish Field Day. Buck O'Brien was on the pitcher's mound. Umpire Tommy Connolly was behind home plate, and ace sports reporter Timothy Murnane was scribbling for the *Boston Globe*.

Mayor John "Honey Fitz" Fitzgerald, the grandfather of President John F. Kennedy, threw out the first pitch, officially kicking off the first major league game to take place at Fenway Park. It was the Boston Red Sox versus the New York Highlanders, later renamed the Yankees. In the stands the fanatical Royal Rooters, an Irish-American fan club led by pub owner Michael "Nuf Ced" McGreevey, cheered for the hometown team and mightily jeered the New York nine. Some things never change.

There is more than a tinge of Irish at Fenway Park, especially in the early years of the park's hundred-year history. Irish-American ballplayers and coaches dominated the rosters in the first half century, and many of the groundskeepers, ticket takers, hot dog vendors, and souvenir hawkers came from the city's sprawling Irish community.

Fenway itself was built by Charles E. Logue, an immigrant from Derry, who broke ground in September 1911 and had it finished nine months later.

COURTESY OF THE LOGUE FAMILY

Derry immigrant Charles E. Logue built Fenway Park, one of America's most cherished ballparks.

James E. McLaughlin was the park architect; he was born in Halifax, Nova Scotia, to Irish immigrant parents. Both men had successful careers in their fields, working on many fine churches, schools, and college buildings, but Fenway would become their legacy. The groundskeeper in 1912 was Jerome Kelley, who took the infield sod from the old Huntington Avenue ballpark at the end of the 1911 season and planted it in Fenway so it would be ready on opening day.

Like many ballparks in America, Fenway Park was used for more than just baseball, and in Boston that included Irish hurling and football matches, featuring All-Ireland champions against American All-Star squads. *Globe* reporter John Ahearn once described hurling as a "combination of field hockey, lacrosse and mayhem." Also popular at Fenway were numerous boxing and wrestling matches, with boxers named Billy Murphy and Eddie "Kid" Sullivan, and wrestlers like Danno O'Mahoney and Steve Casey.

Fenway was a perfect setting for monster political rallies. Éamon de Valera spoke there on June 29, 1919, before sixty thousand people. Constance Markievicz and Kathleen Barry held a rally before six thousand followers on May 28, 1922, to report on the civil war raging in Ireland that year. "The Republic still lives," Markievicz told the cheering crowd, "and we are not going to let it be swept or signed away."

In 1934 William Cardinal O'Connell held his Golden Jubilee open-air Mass at Fenway, and forty thousand faithful turned out, including the Cavan All-Stars Football Team, which happened to be in Boston at the time. There were numerous small occasions, as in September 1931 when Mayor James Michael Curley took Irish rebel Dan Breen to a game between the Red Sox and the Braves. And in April 1946 twenty-eight-year-old John F. Kennedy posed for a photo with Red Sox legend Ted Williams and others, just days before Kennedy announced his plans to run for the US Congress.

When JFK became president, he was invited to throw the first pitch at Fenway Park to open the 1962 season, but he was in Palm Beach at a family reunion and could not. In 1964, President Kennedy was instead memorialized on opening day; his siblings Bobby, Jean, Patricia, and Ted attended, and the Yawkey family donated all of the ticket sales, totaling $50,000, to the JFK Library being planned.

Irish-American Red Sox Managers

Jimmie Collins, 1901–6
Deacon McGuire, 1907–8
Patsy Donovan, 1910–11
Bill "Rough" Carrigan, 1913–16
Jack Barry, 1917
Hugh Duffy, 1921–22
Bill Carrigan, 1927–29
Shano Collins, 1932–32
Marty McManus, 1932–33
Joe Cronin, 1935–47
Joe McCarthy, 1948–50
Steve O'Neill, 1950–51
Pinky Higgins, 1955–59, 1960–62
John McNamara, 1985–88
Joe Morgan, 1988–91
Kevin Kennedy, 1995–96
Jimy Williams, 1997–2001
Joe Kerrigan, 2001
Grady Little, 2002–3
John Farrell, 2013–

CHAPTER TEN

The World's Greatest Irish City (1900–1930)

MAUD GONNE, Ireland's Joan of Arc, helped to usher in the Boston Irish Century in style. The raven-haired beauty came to the city on Sunday afternoon, February 17, 1900, as part of a national tour to tell Americans about British atrocities in the Boer War. She was greeted at South Station by a delegation of fifty men and women from the local Irish societies, who then escorted her to the Vendome on Commonwealth Avenue, the city's fanciest hotel. Dr. P. J. Timmons spoke for the entire delegation when he praised her "noble efforts" to rail against British imperialism in South Africa and in Ireland, "our suffering motherland."

The tall, slender Englishwoman-turned-Irish rebel had captured the world's imagination. She was the muse of poet William Butler Yeats, and local Boston writers seemed smitten with her, too. *Republic* newspaper editor Patrick Maguire remembered her "wealth of wavy hair and eyes that flash at will when she becomes animated in discussing the cause of Ireland." The *Boston Globe* wrote that she looked "picturesque in a black velvet gown with a silver girdle at the waist . . . her splendid voice extremely musical."

When she arrived at Tremont Temple on Monday to speak before two thousand cheering supporters, the stage was ablaze with colorful bunting and the flags of the United States, Ireland, and the Boer Transvaal. Gonne wasted no time blasting the British for "the greatest crimes in the world" and invoking a time-honored belief among many Irish nationalists. "From an Irish point of view, it matters not whether it be right or wrong, the nation that is the enemy of England is a friend and ally of Ireland." Many Bostonians, mindful of Britain's opposing role in the Revolutionary War, in the War of 1812, and siding with the Confederacy during the Civil War, agreed with that assessment.

Gonne's visit was just the kickoff to a flurry of Irish activities taking place in Boston in the first year of the new century. Composer and singer Chauncey Olcott brought his new play *A Romance of Athlone* to the Boston Theatre, featuring the hit song "My Wild Irish Rose." The Gaelic League of America held its national convention here, and so did the Ancient Order of Hibernians, the country's largest Irish-American group. South Boston's star athlete James Connolly went to the Olympic Games in Paris and came in second in the triple jump. And James Michael Curley launched a half-century political career as an elected official on the seventy-five-member Boston Common Council.

By 1900 an air of cockiness infused the spirit of the Boston Irish. Ascending in all directions, the Irish were ready to put their distinctive stamp on a city that had initially banned them from even entering the town. True, some nasty attempts were made by the American Protective Association and nativists such as Henry Cabot Lodge to slow them down, but the Irish were having none of it. Trying unsuccessfully not to gloat, John "Honey Fitz" Fitzgerald, grandfather of a future president, would announce, "The Celt has replaced the Puritan" in dear old Boston. In 1906, the year that Fitzgerald became the city's third Irish mayor, journalist Herb Classon would take that sentiment one step further, declaring in *Munsey's Magazine,* "Boston, not Dublin or Belfast, is now the greatest Irish city in the world."

Many old-line Bostonians weren't happy about that, but what could they do? By 1900 16 percent of Boston residents had been born in Ireland, and another 25 percent of the residents claimed some sort of Irish connection. They had grown in confidence and stature under the political leadership of O'Reilly, Collins, and O'Brien. Gilmore and Cohan had become household names in the entertainment world. Sullivan and Connolly were spreading fame around the world as sports stars. Labor leaders such as Mary Kenny O'Sullivan and Margaret Lilian Foley had emerged as organizers for women working in factories. The Catholic Church, which had only one church and two priests in 1800, had 260 churches and 635 priests in 1900, according to a Boston almanac entitled *Our Church, Her Children and Institutions.* The Irish had taken over

John F. Fitzgerald, mayor of Boston and grandfather to President John F. Kennedy, promenades through the streets of Boston.

South Boston, Charlestown, South End, and Roxbury, towns that had once rejected them, and were quickly moving into Dorchester, Brighton, and West Roxbury.

But the opening decade of the twentieth century also marked a changing of the guard for the Boston Irish. The incredible generation of leaders who helped beleaguered Irish immigrants weather their considerable tribulations in the nineteenth century was passing. Newspaper publisher and poet John Boyle O'Reilly had died young in 1890 at age forty-six. Hugh O'Brien, the city's first Irish mayor, died in 1894. Patrick Donahoe, philanthropist and publisher of the Boston *Pilot*, died in 1901. Mayor Patrick Collins died in office at the height of his popularity in 1905. James Jeffrey Roche, *Pilot* editor and biographer of O'Reilly, died in 1908.

These were the immigrants who laid the groundwork for what would become the Boston Irish Century in the twentieth century and made it the world's greatest Irish city. They restored a social cohesion that had been stripped away during the great migration from Ireland, implanting a powerful sense of ethnic identity in the city's Irish community. They laid claim to a hyphenated Irish-American identity that offered the best of both worlds to the Irish community. From that dual identity a special brand of Irish-American patriotism emerged, wrapped around the American flag while waving the Irish tricolor. It was a patriotism celebrated by George M. Cohan, politicized by James Michael Curley, and practiced by the thousands of Irish Americans who enlisted in the American military from South Boston, Charlestown, Dorchester, and other Irish neighborhoods throughout the century.

Boston's Branch of Irish Independence

The city's distinctive Irish persona made Boston a headquarters for Ireland's political exiles, aspirants, agitators, and leaders between the 1880s and the 1920s, a critical time in the history of Ireland. By the late nineteenth century, Ireland's politics were roughly divided between constitutional nationalists, who sought to win Home Rule from Britain through political pressure and negotiation, and militant nationalists, who held that the British would leave Ireland only when driven out by physical force. A third category, the Unionists, insisted on allegiance to Britain, but their leaders rarely ventured to Boston to state their case.

The nationalists did come to Boston—frequently. Charles Stewart Parnell, Fanny Parnell, John Redmond, John Devoy, John Dillon, and Michael Davitt all journeyed to the city with three goals in mind: to muster political support, to raise money, and to create publicity for their various causes.

Maud Gonne had set the standard in 1900, accomplishing all three goals with relative ease in Boston, Fall River, and Lowell. She had raised more than fifty thousand dollars in pledges and had achieved front-page news coverage in the major papers. Others followed, with varying degrees of success, and with their own particular agendas. Home Rule advocate John Dillon came in 1903 on behalf of the United Irish League and raised ten thousand dollars at a meeting at Faneuil Hall. In December 1904, when Douglas Hyde, founder of the Irish language movement, visited Boston to promote cultural nationalism, he was introduced by Fred Norris Robinson, an Irish language enthusiast who initiated the Celtic studies program at Harvard University. In 1914 Home Rule leader John Redmond was introduced at a United Irish League rally by abolitionist William Lloyd Garrison. Francis Sheehy-Skeffington, a militant pacifist who espoused women's rights, vegetarianism, and Irish independence, came to Worcester and Boston in 1915. James Larkin, the trade union leader from Belfast, spoke at the Tremont Temple in February 1915, when he was described as "more of a poet and idealist than a red-handed agitator."

The Ancient Order of Hibernians, the Clan na Gael, and the Irish Progressive League had chapters in Boston, supporting an emerging physical force movement. The United Irish League of America seemed to attract more middle-class, respectable Irish Americans who were worried by the worldwide advance of socialism and other radical movements. In Charlestown the Parnell Literary Club kept the Home Rule leader's memory alive, and the John Boyle O'Reilly Club had branches from Boston to Springfield. Despite the various shadings of political activism, it looked to casual observers as though the Irish were coming together at last. Even the headlines of the *Boston Globe* commented on the development:

> *TORY ALARM At the Uprising of the Irish People*
> *Celtic Race United in a Most Surprising Manner*

Irish Rebels and Irish Yankees

The outbreak of World War I in August 1914 interrupted the momentum that the Home Rule movement had gained in Ireland, setting up a quandary for Irish Americans. Would they root against the British in the war, heeding Maud Gonne's slogan from her Tremont Temple speech: Any Enemy of England Is a Friend of the Irish? But once America entered the war in 1917, most Irish-American feelings of ambiguity toward fighting alongside Britain were put to rest. Senator David I. Walsh, who had been elected the state's first Catholic governor in 1914, then became the state's first Catholic senator in 1919, put it best when he said, "Let every man of Irish blood face his duty as an American citizen in passing judgment on national and international questions. Let us remember to be Americans first."

That's exactly what Boston's Irish community did. Colonel Edward L. Logan of South Boston, after whom Logan International Airport is named, led the city's famous Irish Ninth Regiment, which had been reorganized into the 101st Regiment of the Yankee Division. Logan and his men went to the front lines in France and fought at the Argonne Forest and other battles. One of his men, Mickey Perkins from South Boston, singlehandedly took over a German machine gun nest and captured the twenty-five soldiers inside.

George M. Cohan gave musical expression to American patriotism during World War I. Cohan's father Jeremiah was born to Irish immigrants on Blackstone Street in Boston in 1848; his mother, Nellie Costigan, was from Rhode Island. George, his sister Josephine, and their parents toured the minstrel and vaudeville circuit for two decades before they made it in New York, where George would become the toast of Broadway.

A trilogy of Cohan compositions became America's theme songs during World War I. The first was "Yankee Doodle Dandy," which Cohan wrote in 1904 for his play *Little Johnny Jones*, appropriating an old jingle that British troops had sung to lampoon the ragtag colonial army at Lexington and Concord in 1775. According to Cohan biographer John McCabe, "The audience was electrified. They had never heard a song like this—patriotically stirring, yet funny." The second tune, "You're a Grand Old Flag," was written in 1906, after Cohan met a Civil War veteran at a funeral who reminisced about his love of America and inspired the song. Two days after President Woodrow Wilson declared war on Germany on April 6, 1917, Cohan completed the trilogy with a song that became the American anthem during the war, "Over There."

Hungering for the Truth

When the war came to an end on November 11, 1918, Irish leaders in Boston turned their attention back to Ireland. Riding the coattails of Irish-American valor and patriotism during the war, they created an advertising campaign to promote an Irish Victory Drive for Freedom of Ireland:

> *Let us pay our debt! Remember what you owe to Ireland. As you honor the Irish blood shed for American liberty, help the cause of liberty— NOW!*

The Irish managed to connect the Ireland issue with the postwar negotiations taking place in Europe, especially the right of small nations to be free, thanks to the astute leadership of Éamon de Valera, the New York–born son of a Spanish father and an Irish mother. In various roles as rebel, political leader, and statesman, de Valera visited Boston numerous times over a period of nearly five decades and received the most enthusiastic welcomes ever accorded a foreign leader, Irish or otherwise. In 1919 de Valera escaped from a British jail, smuggled himself aboard a ship, and made his way to America, where he spent the next nineteen months raising funds and lobbying for Ireland's independence. When he arrived in Boston on Saturday, June 28, 1919, twenty thousand people greeted him at South Station. The *Irish World* reported:

> The crowd was so dense and so demonstrative that the automobile in which the Irish leader was conveyed from the station to Copley Plaza Hotel had great difficulty in getting through. The difficulty was solved by the crowd itself, forming into a procession behind the car, every man and every woman carrying the Stars and Stripes and the Irish Republican flag.

At the banquet that evening, de Valera called upon America to "take up the responsibility for the moral leadership of the world" by ensuring the rights of all nations, particularly small ones. Referring to Boston's own colonial history, de Valera told his rapt audience, "Your fathers fought and broke the chains that bound you to George III. We ask you, their sons, to assist us in breaking the chains that bind Ireland to George V."

The next day de Valera spoke at Fenway Park before a crowd estimated at fifty to sixty thousand people. It was the largest gathering for a foreign politician in Boston's history, surpassing even the visit of Lafayette in 1825. Governor Calvin Coolidge sent a letter "expressing strong support with Ireland's Cause." Boston mayor Andrew Peters and Mayor Edward Quinn of Cambridge gave rousing speeches, and Senator David I. Walsh, who would become close friends with de Valera, gave what the *Boston Post* called "the best speech of his life," comparing de Valera with Abraham Lincoln and predicting he would be as successful.

De Valera addressed his comments directly to President Woodrow Wilson: "Let America and America's President take the fortunes that fate clearly indicates for them—emancipate and save the world. . . . Let [America] lead—true democracy will organize itself the world over to press on to salvation and happiness behind her."

De Valera returned to the United States in 1927, visiting Boston three times that year. His first visit, on March 20, 1927, was a triumph. James T. Sullivan of the *Boston Globe* wrote, "It was undoubtedly the greatest reception any Irish leader ever got in Boston for an indoor meeting."

Irish leader Éamon de Valera (in glasses) always drew a large crowd when visiting Boston.

De Valera was speaking at Symphony Hall, the famous concert hall renowned for its acoustic brilliance. By 7:00 p.m. five thousand people had already crowded into the hall, and police shut the doors. Another twenty thousand people surrounded Symphony Hall, in the snow and rain, on "one of those mean and miserable nights when people have to be strongly tempted to leave the comforts of their own homes," wrote the *Irish World*. The organist hired to lead the crowd in patriotic songs had to be escorted to the building by police, forty-five minutes late for her gig. De Valera was not able to speak until nearly 11:00 p.m. and first had to quell the noise outside the hall by addressing the crowd waiting in the snow. When he finally walked onto the stage, the *Irish World* reported,

> *Men and women rose and cheered again and again. There were old men there too, men who have followed the fortunes of Ireland through many a weary length of years. And there were white haired old women who gazed up at the tall, spare figure of the man with tears in their eyes, their lips quivering as they called to him and blessed him and prayed that he*

> *must lead their nation to the so long deferred victory. . . . All through*
> *his speech . . . the people listened to every word with an almost painful*
> *intensity. They were hungry for the truth.*

After touring the United States, de Valera again returned to Boston, where his ship, the *Republic,* was sailing to Ireland. There he received another joyous and frenzied welcome. He addressed a farewell banquet hosted by the chamber of commerce, invoking America's history:

> *Instead of getting its liberty, Ireland has been partitioned and mutilated.*
> *Lincoln fought a great civil war in this country to prevent the partition of*
> *the United States and that is just what we are opposing today in Ireland.*

On April 30, the day of his departure, de Valera spoke at the Parkman Bandstand on Boston Common before thousands of Bostonians, who were "clutching at his coat and struggling with each other to shake him by the hand." The Saint Ambrose Fife and Drum Corps led a procession to Commonwealth Pier, where the *Republic* was docked. At the pier de Valera's car was closed in by thousands of supporters, "many of them with children held high in their arms to give them an opportunity to shake hands with the leader," wrote the *Irish World.* He stood up in the car and spoke to the crowd in Gaelic and English, and they finally let him board the ship, which sailed out of Boston Harbor "to the skirling of the bagpipe music of the Irish Republican Band playing the Soldiers Song."

Ireland's success in the 1920s in forming a nation separate from Great Britain had unexpected consequences for immigration to America. The Irish spent the decade nation-building, and a stabilized political environment helped to improve economic conditions in Ireland, making it unnecessary to leave. Also, many Irish opted to stay home to help strengthen their nation and implement changes they had been advocating for centuries. This was compounded by the US Immigration Act in 1924, which limited the number of immigrants to 2 percent of the total number of people of each nationality from the 1890 US census. Its intent was basically to preserve the Anglo-Saxon character of the United States. The act was revised in 1928, increasing the annual quota for the Irish Free State from 13,862 to 17,427.

But even those quota allotments weren't used by the Irish. Speaking to the Clover Club in Boston in 1930, Michael MacWhite, a minister of the Irish

Free State, said that "emigration dropped from 24,544 in 1928 to 17,672 in 1929, a decrease of 28 percent in a single year. The Free State was one of the few European countries that did not take full advantage of the emigration quota."

The Great Depression of the 1930s had a further effect on Irish immigration, and it wasn't until the 1940s that there was an uptick in Irish immigrants.

CHAPTER ELEVEN

Musical Stages: Symphony Hall and Hibernian Hall (1900–1940)

WHEN IRISH TENOR John McCormack burst onto the music scene in the early 1900s, the Boston Irish rejoiced. Here at last was a worthy purveyor of the ancient melodies of Ireland, and he could also sing opera! After winning the Dublin Feis Ceoil (music festival) in 1903 at age twenty, the Athlone-born singer embarked on a forty-two-year career that placed him in the pantheon of the world's greatest singers. Novelist James Joyce, a fair tenor himself, wrote that McCormack had "a voice from beyond the world." Even Italy's great tenor Enrico Caruso considered McCormack the best tenor alive, which he told the young Irishman to his face when they met by chance in the lobby of the Copley Plaza Hotel.

The Boston Irish agreed wholeheartedly with Joyce and Caruso. The *Republic* newspaper noted McCormack's "superb presence, magnetic personality and rare voice," hailing him as "about as potent an influence for the conservation of what is distinctly Irish . . . as any that has appeared in our time. He makes people glad they are Irish."

McCormack made his first Boston appearance in April 1910, performing at the Boston Theatre in the Manhattan Company's production of *La Traviata*. The following year, on February 5, 1911, he made his debut at Symphony Hall, one of the great concert venues of the world. Between 1911 and 1936 he performed there sixty-seven times, more than any other singer.

Irish tenor John McCormack, who had "a voice from beyond the world"

McCormack's arrival on the music scene was timely, since the Irish influence on America's songbook was beginning to wane. Ireland's ancient melodies had been retrieved during the Celtic Revival of the 1880s, but they were being overshadowed by what author Mark Sullivan has called "melting pot songs," as discussed in his popular American history book *Our Times: 1900–1925*. These songs were usually written by Americans about newcomers—or greenhorns—whether they were Irish, German, or Italian. They fed into the stereotypes of each group with "a sophisticated air of humorous condescension," Sullivan wrote. Songs about the Irish, predictably, often involved drinking, fighting, stubbornness, and ineptitude. In the 1900s the mass production of sheet music and the emergence of the recording industry flooded the marketplace with these songs.

John McCormack temporarily reversed this trend by restoring a high standard for Irish melodies. He also added credibility to Irish-American songsters like Chauncey Olcott and Ernest Ball, who cowrote McCormack's first hit, "Mother Machree," in 1910. Of McCormack's rendition of "Mother Machree," Sullivan observed, "true Irish songs enabled a singer to be sentimental without causing shivers to the discriminating listener."

The Boston Irish loved McCormack's ability to enthrall mainstream audiences, since they themselves were moving into mainstream society at a time when other immigrant groups—Italians, Poles, and Lithuanians—were being considered the greenhorns of America. His vast repertoire combined the old Irish songs he had learned as a boy with the classical arias of Italy, France, and Germany. He favored the melodies of Thomas Moore, Ireland's great nineteenth-century bard and poet, and relied upon the arrangements of fellow Irishman Herbert Hughes. Hughes described Irish songs as having "the rarest beauty and distinction, with more variety of mood than can be found in any other European language" in his two-volume set *Irish Country Songs*, published in 1909. H. Earle Johnson's book *Symphony Hall, Boston* notes that McCormack "often went to the Public Library in Copley Square" hunting for new songs and "came away with the prizes of research."

McCormack also developed a distinct patriotism toward America that was consistent with Irish-American sensibility at that time. Like Patrick S. Gilmore and George M. Cohan, McCormack was unabashed about his admiration for what America offered to him and his family. During World War I he did a musical tour for the American Red Cross and recorded such songs as "God Be With Our Boys Tonight," earning him popularity with the troops in Europe. In 1914 he took out papers to become an American citizen, further endearing him to his American audience.

During his visits to Boston, McCormack got to know many well-known artists of international stature, such as Enrico Caruso and Dr. Karl Muck, the Boston Symphony Orchestra's celebrated conductor. In April 1925 he met John Singer Sargent, the prolific painter whose murals grace the Boston Public Library and the Museum of Fine Arts. The two artists hit it off at once, recalls McCormack's wife Lily in her charming memoir *I Hear You Calling Me*. Sargent told Lily he would paint McCormack's "magnificent head and sensitive mouth" later that fall, but Sargent died in London before that work got under way.

A devout Catholic, whose "inner life was built upon his faith," McCormack was befriended by William Cardinal O'Connell and devoted time to various Catholic causes in Boston, doing benefit concerts for the Knights of Columbus War Fund, Emmanuel College, and Saint Mary's Infant Asylum in Dorchester.

McCormack's final Symphony Hall concert in 1936 was a benefit for the Guild of Saint Elizabeth's on Dudley Street in Roxbury, which did "benevolent work among children," according to the program book. "There was a poignant realization in those brief hours," H. Earle Johnson writes, "that he was standing on hallowed ground, as it were, for the last time. He seemed to linger with the audience, and people applauded when they would rather have wept."

Dancing on Dudley Street

Roxbury was a fitting place for McCormack to direct his charitable donations, since it had become an epicenter of Boston's Irish-American community. Saint Patrick's Church was established there in 1836, followed by Saint Francis de Sales and the Mission Church, which became anchors for the Irish community moving out of inner-city Boston in the nineteenth century. The Sisters of Notre Dame moved to Roxbury in 1853, followed by the Carmelite nuns and the Sisters of Charity.

The Roxbury venue that represented the region's Irish cultural scene for nearly half a century was Hibernian Hall at 184 Dudley Street. It was one of two dozen Hibernian Halls built around the state at the turn of the century by the Ancient Order of Hibernians (AOH), the largest Irish Catholic fraternal group in the country. Plans for the building started in 1906, when the Hibernian Building Association of Boston Highlands was incorporated, representing fourteen divisions of the AOH and four Ladies Auxiliary chapters. The dream was to create a social headquarters for ten thousand Boston AOH members in the area. Shares were sold for ten dollars each, and before long there were over five hundred shareholders. In 1911 the group acquired the land on Dudley Street near Warren Street, right next to the Dudley Street terminal of the elevated train. Cambridge architect Edward T. P. Graham was engaged to design the building, and in January 1913 the group broke ground.

When the organizers made plans to lay the cornerstone for Hibernian Hall on May 30, 1913, they asked themselves, who better to place the stone than the local Irish political maestro himself—Roxbury native son James Michael Curley? Indeed, there was no one better than the up-and-coming politician, who had already been mayor and was currently serving as the US congressman for Boston. Curley was born on Northampton Street in 1874, and he and his wife Mary (née Herlihy) still lived on Mount Pleasant Street. He was a proud and dedicated member of the AOH. Rumor was that Curley had planned his Niagara Falls honeymoon in 1906 so he could swing by the national AOH convention at Saratoga Springs on the way back to Boston.

At the cornerstone ceremony the crowd of five thousand Irish Americans cheered and waved tiny American flags as Congressman Curley laid the stone with a silver trowel. Patrick J. Larkin, head of the Hibernian Building Association, placed a copper box inside the stone with "a copy of the deed, pictures, newspapers, and other things . . . of interest in the future." Local papers reported that Curley launched into impassioned oratory about the Irish community and what it meant to Roxbury, to Boston, and to the nation.

"Congressman Curley said the Irishman today stands for liberty and progress and his daily life is the most highly developed form of American citizenship," reported the *Roxbury Gazette*. "He spoke of the character, purity and honesty of the Irish, who came here at the time of the thirteen colonies and made such a republic possible. He told of the Irish in the Civil War."

It was vintage Curley: preaching to the converted, laying another Irish brick atop the cobblestoned city of Puritans, extolling Irish virtues while wrapping around himself his own patriotism. Curley came of age at the very beginning of the Boston Irish Century, when his ethnicity, religion, politics, and worldview seemed perfectly suited for transforming the city from a stifled seaport town of crusty Puritans into a vibrant Celtic city where robust men roared through life with a vengeance and built a future their recent ancestors had been denied. He was ambitious and tough enough to wield power and to dominate politics for half a century, with a flair that was often charming but also brutal at times. The quid pro quo of promising favors for votes became the formula for Curley and others to maintain their post atop the city on a hill. The notion of using local government to help friends, neighbors, and relatives certainly was not an Irish invention: the Yankees had been doing it for generations. The practice gave the Irish a leg up in the early days, when they needed it. But by the time they were fully in control and an Irish ethos dominated Boston government, the motto All Politics Are Local had become a thinly veiled ruse for patronage, nepotism, and cronyism. In the end, political office became a feeding trough for political appointees, coat holders, and sign hangers, who ultimately detracted from rather than contributed to the more noble Boston Irish persona that O'Brien, O'Reilly, and Collins had envisioned a generation earlier.

Hibernian Hall was officially opened on October 1, 1913, by Lieutenant Governor David I. Walsh, and it quickly became the main venue for large Irish social and charitable events. Because so many Irish were involved in politics and in trade unions, the hall also became a gathering place for rallies, meetings, and events. In December 1913 the Ward 14 Tammany Hall Club held its banquet, and over thirty-five hundred people packed the hall, cheering wildly when Congressman Curley, who was running for mayor, entered the ballroom and tore into Mayor Fitzgerald and Thomas Kenny, eliciting the *Boston Globe* headline "Curley Turns Ball into Rally." In February 1914 the Galway Men's Benevolent Association event had such an overflow of crowds that the police sent over ten officers just to clear the streets of more than three hundred people waiting to get in. In February 1914 over a thousand new members were inducted into the AOH, the largest initiation in recent years.

Politics and popular culture intersected frequently in Boston during the twentieth century, as politicians trolling for votes went looking for voters looking for favors. The often uproarious theater of Boston Irish politicians recalls Curley biographer Jack Beatty's observation of the Irish tendency to "see life in a comic light." So it would have been charming and all in good fun to see James Curley puffing into a set of highland bagpipes or donning elaborate Indian headgear for the photographer, or John "Honey Fitz" Fitzgerald standing on a chair to sing "Sweet Adeline" in his mellifluous voice. Fitzgerald later recalled, "When I was mayor of Boston, I learned that everywhere a mayor went, he had to make a speech, and no one really wanted to hear a speech every time, so I sang." Even nonelected officials such as Richard Cardinal Cushing had a go at the Scottish bagpipes or played a few tunes on the button accordion at Blinstrub's in South Boston while a couple of old-timers danced the Kerry set.

Hibernian Hall would become a Mecca for traditional Irish dance music so popular among the Boston Irish. The music got a terrific boost in the 1890s when brothers Michael and William Hanafin emigrated from County Kerry, bringing a rich repertoire of Irish tunes that had been passed down orally for centuries. Here they met up with Patsy Touhey, the uilleann piper from South Boston whose exceptional playing brought him to such national platforms as the Chicago Exposition in 1894 and the St. Louis World's Fair in 1902. The Hanafins' brand of

Richard Cardinal Cushing plays the accordion at Blinstrub's in South Boston.

dance music—jigs, reels, hornpipes, quadrilles, and polkas—was popular with middle-class Irish Americans seeking authenticity and with newly arrived Irish immigrants from a rural background familiar with the repertoire.

There were plenty of places in Boston to hear good music, thanks to the expansion of Irish organizations in Boston between 1900 and 1920. At the Gaelic League of America convention in 1900, local musicians presented Feis Ceoil Agus Shanachus (Festival of Irish Minstrelsy, Song, and Story), featuring "Gaelic folk songs, gems of Irish opera, Irish harp, and bagpipe music" at the Hollis Street Theatre. County club functions often drew twelve hundred people or more and featured both modern American dance music and traditional Irish music. On January 11, 1910, the newly formed Boston Irish Pipers Club held a concert at Wells Auditorium. Joining Touhey and local pipers were Sean O'Nolan, originally from Wexford and now a recording star with Columbia Records, and Sergeant William Early, a Chicago cop who had formed a piper's club in the Windy City.

The Boston Irish were constantly on guard against the Stage Irishman, who was still winding his way across the American landscape. Local Irish papers proudly reported that the Stage Irishman was hounded out of Butte, Montana, in 1905 for portraying the Irish as baboons.

But just as in Ireland, Boston politicians and clergy were overly vigilant about protecting the people from themselves when it came to music, dancing, and cultural expression that might have immoral consequences. In 1904 Boston mayor Patrick Collins appointed John M. Casey as the city's licensing clerk for theatrical productions coming to town. Casey held the job until 1932 and in effect served as an official censor, helping to popularize the term "Banned in Boston." In 1910 Mayor Fitzgerald told the press that he had directed Casey "to notify all the managers of theatres in Boston that they must have a proper regard for public decency . . . in the dialogues and stage costumes." When Dublin's Abbey Theatre came to Boston in 1911 with their production of J. M. Synge's *Playboy of the Western World,* rumblings came from some Irish that the play was too risqué. A riot had broken out in Dublin when the play was performed, and critics assailed it as a slight upon the Irish character. Ireland's foremost poet William Butler Yeats and playwright Lady Gregory traveled with the troupe to Boston to defend it against potential protests from the Irish community. But the *Boston Globe* reported that the play elicited "some hisses, some cheers," but overall had not caused "the excitement that some people had feared."

"Banned in Boston" became a national joke of sorts with occasionally ludicrous rulings. The Wilkes-Barre *Times Leader* in Pennsylvania ran a story on March 17, 1917, headlined "Declares Bare Legs Shocking Unless as Part of Bag Piper":

> *When the Harvard Hasty Pudding Club applied for permission to have some of its actors at the home talent show next month dance a bare-legged back to nature affair, censor John M. Casey put his foot down on their legs, as it were. "Men's legs or women's legs," said he, "makes no difference. Bare legs are shocking, unless as part of a bag-pipe player. As women's legs, men's legs cannot appear."*

This kind of censorship prompted Boston's Methodist minister Frank Case to smirk in 1925, "The Irish make good Puritans."

In a larger context Irish music appeared to be losing ground to America's changing tastes in music. Jazz and swing swept through the nation in the early part of the century, offering rhythms, tempos, and improvisations that broke free of traditional music idioms. The new sound centered on urban black music that drew from such influences as Creole roots, brass band, minstrelsy, jigs, blues, and ballads. It arrived during a decade in which postwar angst and Prohibition drove people to excess.

The jazz movement put some Irish music lovers on the defensive. The Reverend Francis P. Donnelly, SJ, a Boston College professor and song composer, gave a lecture on Irish music in all its glory. He concluded that "it is degradation for America to pass by this rich Irish inheritance and to adopt the monstrosities of China, Japan, of Hottentot and Hawaiian and American savages. Let us drive out, therefore, these vaudeville reversals to barbarism and bring up your children in the music of civilization and of art, in the folk music of Ireland."

In Ireland itself judges "launched a campaign against jazz dances, making it a condition for dance hall licenses that 25% of each program shall be Irish dances," according to an Associated Press report in October 1933.

Nevertheless, Irish music had become part of Boston's mainstream cultural offerings. In 1932 Boston Symphony Hall presented Irish Night, featuring solos by tenor Arthur O'Shea and soprano Christine Gallagher of Dublin. And in July 1934 an Irish Rhapsody concert presented by Arthur Fiedler and the Boston Pops took place on the Esplanade. The concert drew upward of fifteen thousand people, who listened to "The Harp That Once Through Tara's Halls," a Thomas Moore melody orchestrated by Victor Herbert, and other standards such as "The Londonderry Air" and "Molly on the Shore."

By the late 1930s a new generation of Irish Americans came of age and began frequenting the dance halls in Dudley Square, Roxbury. In January 1938 the Fermanagh, Mayo, Cork Ladies, Saint Brendan's, Roscommon, and Sligo associations all held events at Hibernian Hall, and the Central Council of Irish Clubs held its Saint Patrick's Day dance there in March. As the social scene at Hibernian Hall picked up, other venues along Dudley Street, including Intercolonial Hall, Dudley Street Opera House, Winslow Hall, Palladio Hall, Deacon Hall, and Rose Croix Hall, were also hosting Irish activities.

In the early 1940s the *Irish World*, a national Irish-American paper based in New York, hired three columnists to report from Boston. Dan Horgan, who later ran a Celtic cigar shop in front of Hibernian Hall and coached a women's camogie team, covered the downtown and Dudley Street scene; M. J. Upton reported as the Cambridge Traveler; and accordion player Eva Connors,

COURTESY OF JOSEPH JOYCE

The Irish Social Club gathering at Hibernian Hall, 1949

known as the Irish Rambler, had free rein to report on whatever she wished. A typical edition of the *Irish World* in the early forties devoted five to seven thousand words to Boston coverage.

The columnists were diligent in reporting every single aspect of the Boston Irish community. They covered the county clubs, concerts, lectures, and the Gaelic classes, along with weddings, funerals, births, and baptisms. The *Irish World*'s Boston pages provided a steady stream of gossip, news, schedules, and activities that provided a continuity and definition to the Irish from the 1940s through the early 1960s.

Even as Irish music remained secondary to mainstream American tastes, the caliber of Irish music in Boston was extremely high in the 1940s. Dozens of local musicians emerged, including Joe Derrane, Billy Caples, Tom Senier and his sons, Jack Storer and his sons, Joe Joyce, Jack Concannon, Johnny Powell, Johnny Bresnahan, and Virginia Doherty. After the war they were joined by immigrant musicians like Larry Reynolds, Brendan Tonra, Mike Landers, and Paddy Cronin. These musicians presided over a fabulous era in which it wasn't unusual for thousands of people to converge on Dudley Street on any given weekend, going from one hall to the next, standing out in the street as crowds of dancers streamed down from Dudley Street station.

The scene was further elevated when Justus O'Byrne DeWitt started a small recording label called Copley Records and began publishing local musicians like Joe Derrane and Paddy Cronin. Irish radio programs on WBOS, WHDH, and WTAO featured such stars as singer Terry O'Toole and Myles O'Malley, a talented saxophonist and clarinetist in the 1940s who was popular live and on the radio, especially when he played a few novelty tunes on the tin whistle. O'Malley spent four years in the navy and in 1947 returned to Boston. Decca Records gave him a contract, and soon the Tin Whistle King was playing jazz nightly while setting aside Thursdays as Irish night.

Pianist Dick Senier recalled that many Irish musicians, including his father Tom, were comfortable playing in various musical styles, from traditional Irish and Scottish to swing and jazz. Saxophones, trumpets, and drum sets were regularly used in Irish ensembles, and most Irish-American sidemen were able to play the popular tunes of the day.

Not all Irish Americans, of course, stuck with Irish music. Jimmy McHugh of Jamaica Plain became a noted writer of popular melodies, composing over five hundred songs, including such hits as "I'm in the Mood for Love" and "On the Sunny Side of the Street." Newspaper columnist George Frazier, who grew up in a South Boston three-decker, was a virtuoso wordsmith who crafted a style of jazz writing at the *Boston Herald* and *Boston Globe* that rings true today. In the 1950s Norman J. O'Connor, chaplain at Boston University, was a board member of the first Newport Jazz Festival and became known as "the jazz priest." According to his 2003 obituary in the *New York Times*, O'Connor saw "nothing wrong with using jazz in religious services," though he apparently encountered criticism from "lay Catholics who viewed the music as disreputable."

The Irish were probably among O'Connor's critics, since many of them preferred Irish melodies to anything else. When Connie Foley, a traditional singer from County Kerry living in Worcester, recorded "The Wild Colonial Boy" for Copley Records, "letters evaluating the tenor's performance—both pro and con—rolled in," according to a 1951 profile in *Newsweek* magazine. One of Foley's fans was quoted as saying, "Let those who don't enjoy Connie turn to the old English stations for their jazz and silly songs."

Ironically, the preservation of Irish traditional music in Boston during the 1950s was somewhat compromised by a new musical fad coming out of Ireland called "show bands." These bands played a hybrid of rock 'n' roll, Irish, and

Hibernian Hall Revival

The beloved landmark Hibernian Hall, designed by architect Edward T. P. Graham and located at 184 Dudley Street in Roxbury, fell into disrepair in the middle decades of the twentieth century. It was nearly torn down in the 1990s to make way for new construction. In fact, a group of musicians who had played there in the 1950s returned in 1998 for a final set of tunes before the building was to be demolished. But the Massachusetts Historical Commission designated the building a historic property, and it was spared. The Roxbury Consortium of Arts, Culture and Trade (ACT), along with the Madison Park Development Corporation, turned the building into a multi-arts facility for residents of the Dudley Square area and kept the name Hibernian Hall in tribute to the building's Irish roots. For more information call (617) 541-3900 or visit hibernianhall.org.

country-western tunes that captured the growing Americanization of music worldwide. They began arriving in Boston in the late 1950s with their horn sections and gyrations imitative of Elvis Presley. Before long, the Irish crowds followed the show bands from Dudley Street to the New State Ballroom on Massachusetts Avenue in Back Bay. By then popular music was being changed fundamentally by folk music and ultimately by rock 'n' roll. With the Dudley scene in demise, it would be nearly two decades before Irish traditional music returned to its former glory in Boston.

Irish Culture Rebounds

Michael Cummings got his shot at the American Dream when he was just twenty-two years old. The six-foot-one-inch football star from Ballygar, County Galway, arrived in Boston in June 1947 to play in the season's final game for Boston's Galway football team, a match it handily won. The following season Cummings was elected team captain and led his squad to five successive championships between 1948 and 1952 at Dilboy Field in Somerville.

The end of World War II launched an exciting phase of the Boston Irish experience, as thousands of Irish-American soldiers returned home from their duty and a wave of new immigrants from Ireland settled in Boston. Newcomers such as Mike Cummings waded into the future with optimism and resolve. Mike settled in Dorchester and took a job with Boston Consolidated Gas. In 1956 he married the lovely Noreen McSweeney from Saint Gregory's parish and started a family, eventually moving to nearby Milton to raise their two boys and two girls.

Not since the 1880s had there been such an Irish revival in Boston as the one that took place between 1945 and 1965. Dudley Street, full of music and dancing and socializing, was just part of the revival. Third- and fourth-generation Irish Americans became interested in knowing more about Ireland, and they formed groups such as the Eire Society to reestablish their roots. Harvard University, the Museum of Fine Arts, and the Boston Symphony Orchestra were involved in Irish projects in the 1950s, and even Jordan Marsh, Boston's main department store, ran some highly publicized marketing campaigns to promote Irish goods.

One reason for the enthusiasm was that Ireland had finally become an independent nation. Éamon de Valera, who served as Ireland's prime minister from 1933 through 1948, had remained forceful in calling for the unification of Ireland and for breaking away from the British Commonwealth. De Valera got part of his wish in December 1948, when the Irish Parliament passed the Republic of Ireland Act, in tandem with the British Nationality Act, declaring that "People born in Eire in the future will be Eire subjects and not British subjects." On April 18, 1949, Ireland officially became the Republic of Ireland and severed its ties to the British Commonwealth. Northern Ireland chose the right to remain with Great Britain, cementing the partition of Ireland that remains to the present day.

Sean MacBride and Sean Lemass were two Irish officials who stood out during this time. MacBride, minister of external affairs for Ireland, was the son of Captain John MacBride and Irish rebel Maud Gonne. He understood that gaining worldwide sympathy for the new Ireland was more than a political venture; it was a public relations exercise, too. In a speech to the Eire Society in 1950, MacBride said, "Whether it be in the field of international politics, foreign trade, or tourism, one of the first tasks to be achieved is to make the people of other countries interested in our island and to make them feel kindly to us."

Thus began a government-supported initiative of exporting Irish culture to America, which continues today. In 1950 Ireland's Cultural Relations Committee sent an Irish photo exhibit to Boston as part of Jordan Marsh's hundredth anniversary. The following year an exhibit of paintings by Jack Yeats, brother of the poet W. B. Yeats, opened at the Institute of Contemporary Art on Newbury Street.

Meanwhile Sean Lemass, minister of commerce, worked on the business front to open up investment and travel opportunities. Irish journalist Seamus Malin wrote that it took Lemass ten years to bring to fruition a transatlantic air route connecting Shannon Airport to Boston and New York. It finally happened on October 5, 1958, when the first Aer Lingus flight left Boston's Logan International Airport, filled with such dignitaries as Lieutenant Governor Robert Murphy, Boston mayor John Hynes, and the Reverend Timothy O'Leary, superintendent of Catholic schools. On the return flight Lemass and Robert Briscoe, Dublin's lord mayor, came to Boston to further develop the Boston-Irish connection. Aer Lingus offered two flights each week from Logan Airport, on Thursdays and Sundays, with return flights from Ireland on Mondays and Fridays.

The new wave of immigrants helped to reinvigorate Irish clubs that had been the staple of Boston's Irish community since the turn of the century. After the war Mary Concannon and Nora Hart founded the Irish Social Club to provide cultural activities in a family setting. Every Sunday evening at Hibernian Hall the social club hosted a dance that featured a junior ceili band of budding musical stars such as Joe Derrane. In Cambridge accordionist Tom Senier taught Irish dances to the Harvard Folk Club. Cummings, along with Walter Norris and Walter O'Regan, gave dance instruction to Eire Society members along Commonwealth Avenue.

In the summer of 1950, the Central Council Irish Clubs presented an Irish *feis,* or festival, at Malden Municipal Stadium, modeled on popular gatherings in Ireland. More than five hundred entrants registered to compete in seventy-five competitions, including uilleann pipes, the fiddle, the accordion, dancing, oratory, Gaelic singing, storytelling, and sports. The *feis* attracted thousands of people and flourished throughout the decade.

The vitality of Boston's Irish community attracted national attention. In 1956 the NBC television series *Wide Wide World* arrived to film an Irish field day at Dilboy Field. The crew interviewed the versatile Cummings on the fine points of set dancing and football. It filmed a joint performance by the Kevin Barry Pipe Band and the Saint Joseph's All-Girl Pipe Band and filmed a hurling match and "Irish-American colleens" dancing the Kerry set in full traditional costume.

The Eire Society of Boston, composed of mostly teachers, lawyers, academics, and artists, created a robust program of cultural activities. In 1947 the society commissioned composer Leroy Anderson to write the *Eire Suite,* which was performed and later recorded by Arthur Fiedler and the Boston Pops. In 1953 the society partnered with Harvard University to raise funds to microfilm the National Library of Ireland's collection of rare manuscripts and scholarly material. At a time when the Irish-American newspapers were covering almost exclusively the social scene, the *Eire Society Bulletin* offered insightful snippets about Irish culture, education, theater, and the emerging bond between Irish Americans and the Irish. Contributors such as Dr. Regina Madden, James J. Ford, and George E. Ryan made the bulletin a must-read publication. The society held its events at the Copley Plaza Hotel, creating an environment for the area's sprawling middle-class Irish Americans who had moved away from the dance halls in the old neighborhoods.

A lively literary scene sprouted up during this era. In November 1951 the Dublin Players had a two-week run at John Hancock Hall, where they performed plays by Michael MacLiammoir, Lennox Robinson, and Paul Vincent Carroll. Molly Manning Howe, a Dublin-born novelist and playwright who taught drama at Radcliffe College, founded the Poets' Theatre in Cambridge to encourage young writers. In 1957 Irish actress Siobhan McKenna performed in *The Rope Dancers* and was honored by the Eire Society.

From Last Hurrah to Camelot

During this time writer Edwin O'Connor published his novel *The Last Hurrah*, a fictionalized account of James Michael Curley, the legendary Boston politician whose reign in public office stretched from 1900 to 1950. The best-selling novel became a Book-of-the-Month Club selection and was later made into a movie staring Spencer Tracy. When Curley stepped away from public life, or rather was rejected by Boston voters—he served his fourth and final term as mayor from 1946 to 1949—pundits such as O'Connor

Official portrait of Governor James Michael Curley

suggested that Curley's demise marked the end of an era.

Voting "early and often," as Mayor Curley used to quip, was the rallying cry for those politicians, whose constant goal was to get reelected. But while some voters objected to Curley's particular brand of identity politics and ethnic favoritism, many Bostonians remained devoted to him for years to come. In 1979 *Boston Globe* letter-writer Mary Sullivan wrote that Curley represented "actual salvation to many Irish immigrants. He helped them find jobs, provided them with financial assistance, guided them through daily problems and always fought against the humiliating discrimination the Irish faced." In 1980 Mayor Kevin White unveiled twin statues of Curley in Union Park in front of Boston City Hall, and in 1988 Boston Mayor Raymond L. Flynn tried to turn the Curley mansion on the Jamaicaway into an Immigrant Museum.

Boston Mayors of Irish Ancestry	
Hugh O'Brien	1885–88
Patrick Collins	1902–5
John F. Fitzgerald	1906–7
	1910–13
James M. Curley	1914–17
	1922–25
	1930–33
	1946–49
Frederick W. Mansfield	1934–37
Maurice Tobin	1938–44
John Kerrigan	1945
John B. Hynes	1950–59
John Collins	1960–68
Kevin H. White	1968–83
Raymond L. Flynn	1984–93

In addition to controlling the mayor's office for most of the twentieth century, Irish Americans served five terms as governor between 1914 and 1953: David Walsh, James Curley, Charles Hurley, Maurice Tobin, and Paul Dever. In the 1950s South Boston's John McCormack, the consummate deal maker, and Thomas "Tip" O'Neill, the cigar-chomping storyteller from Cambridge, were in Washington, DC, bringing home the bacon, as it were, to their constituents, and they had become accomplished legislators on the national stage. And the backslapping, camera-mugging Irish politicians who once roamed the streets of Boston looking for handshakes or shakedowns were no longer de rigueur. By the 1950s they were being replaced by a more sophisticated generation of public officials who sensed that the curtain was coming down on the Irish burlesque routine that earlier Irish-American politicians had perfected. Mayors John B. Hynes and John Collins represented the new generation of Irish-American politicians who brought a sense of purpose to local politics in the 1950s and 1960s.

CHAPTER TWELVE

The Camelot Era: JFK Seizes the Day (1945–1965)

THE RISING STAR of the postwar generation in Boston was John Fitzgerald Kennedy, the young war hero who had saved his crew members when his PT-109 was sunk in the Pacific Ocean. He had an impressive Irish-American pedigree: His father Joseph, a successful businessman, had been ambassador to Great Britain and was well connected in Washington, and his paternal grandfather, Patrick Kennedy, was a state representative and senator but was better known as a successful businessman and ward boss of East Boston. JFK's mother, Rose Fitzgerald Kennedy, was the daughter of John "Honey Fitz" Fitzgerald, one of Boston's most colorful politicians, who was mayor of Boston for six years and had served as a United States congressman for six years.

John Kennedy's first foray into politics came in 1946, when he ran for the US Congress. His mother Rose proved to be a valuable asset to the campaign; as a young woman she had campaigned for her father, Honey Fitz, and knew about wards and precincts better than anyone on the campaign. Rose and her daughters hosted tea parties designed to capture the women's vote. When Rose would finish speaking on the campaign trail, Kennedy aide Dave Powers noted, "She got a standing ovation."

Kennedy handily won the election and took the congressional seat of the eleventh district, once held by his grandfather Fitzgerald. He held that seat until 1952, when he ran for the US Senate against Henry Cabot Lodge Jr., a scion of Boston's Brahmin class who traced his ancestors back to the Puritans. Apart from the interesting dynamic between the Anglo-Saxon and Celt tribes of the state, this was a personal grudge match, since Lodge's grandfather had defeated Kennedy's grandfather, John Fitzgerald, for this same Senate seat in 1916. Kennedy unseated the incumbent Lodge by just seventy thousand votes. Though educated in private, non-Catholic schools, Kennedy was aware of the dynamic between the old-line Bostonians and the Irish immigrant stock, and he himself sensed anti-Irish feeling among some of his Harvard classmates.

Kennedy was also aware of the transition being made in Boston within the Irish-American establishment and recognized that he was part of that transition. "John F. Kennedy succeeded James Michael Curley in Congress—a fact often forgotten about both men's careers," wrote Martin Nolan in a *Boston Globe* article called "The Last Hurrahs Are Fading."

Many hailed John Kennedy as a new breed of Irish-American politician, unhindered by ward politics and backroom deals. Given the complex problems emerging in world politics with the spread of communism, voters were seeking leaders of the highest caliber. He was a war hero whose wealth and political pedigree enabled him to travel the world, meet influential leaders, and observe firsthand the problems of other nations. He was well educated and had gained modest acclaim as a reporter and later as an author with his books *Why England Slept* and *Profiles in Courage*. He was young, handsome, witty, and charming, and politics was in his blood.

Kennedy's run for president in 1960 raised the thorny issue of his Catholic religion, a cross that the Boston Irish had had to bear since the city was founded by the Puritans in 1630. The innuendo that a Catholic would somehow subvert the American system of government by paying allegiance to a foreign pope was as ludicrous in 1960 as it was in 1830, when preachers and plebeians fretted about a popish invasion, and in 1700, when priests were banned from the Bay Colony. Kennedy handled the issue with a firm confidence and graciousness that silenced his critics, and no one objected when his friend and confidant Richard Cardinal Cushing officiated at Kennedy's inauguration on January 20, 1961.

His inaugural speech on a cold winter day in the nation's capital was a tour de force in which Kennedy mapped out the ambition and certitude of the postwar generation, while also placing in context the moorings of tradition so important to the American psyche.

> *The world is very different. . . . And yet the same revolutionary beliefs*
> *for which our forebears fought are still at issue around the globe—the*
> *belief that the rights of man come not from the generosity of the state,*
> *but from the hand of God. We dare not forget today that we are the heirs*
> *of that first revolution. Let the word go forth from this time and place, to*
> *friend and foe alike, that the torch has been passed to a new generation*
> *of Americans—born in this century, tempered by war, disciplined by a*
> *hard and bitter peace, proud of our ancient heritage.*

President Kennedy's thousand days in office marked an epoch in the Boston Irish story, of one man stepping forth from a marginalized community that had struggled mightily for so many generations, facing hostility and surviving on the edge of society, driven to success by fear of hunger and anger at prejudice, determined to right the wrongs for the sake of the children and future generations. JFK was the future generation that his parents, grandparents, and great-grandparents had daydreamed about as they were toiling in America, saving their pennies, getting stronger, wiser, and warier. He may have represented the hopes and dreams of the world, and of a nation, but in essence JFK represented the pinnacle of immigrant dreams for millions of Irish around the world.

Kennedy's optimism and resolve was emblematic of the American mind of the twentieth century, but he also brought a new level of sophistication to public life. Louis M. Lyons wrote, "The elevation of the tone of the national life may be John Kennedy's most enduring contribution to his country." Along with his beautiful, stylish wife, Jacqueline Bouvier Kennedy, JFK brought a savoir faire to the White House and created a magical mood that later moved Jacqueline to use the word "Camelot" to refer to her husband's presidency. Both the president and his wife were lovers of the arts, and they surrounded themselves with singers, poets, dramatists, artists, and dancers. In a well-deserved nod to the power of poetry, Kennedy invited New England poet Robert Frost to read at his inauguration. Frost later told Kennedy, "You're something of Irish and something of Harvard. Let me advise you, be more Irish than Harvard."

On October 26, 1963, Kennedy gave a compelling address at Amherst College called "On Poetry and National Power," in which he laid out a vision of American life to which the Irish, the politician, and the poet could relate.

> *When power leads man towards arrogance, poetry reminds him of his*
> *limitations. When power corrupts, poetry cleanses, for art establishes*

*the basic human truths which must serve as a touchstone for our
judgment. . . . I look forward to a great future for America—a future
in which our country will match its military strength with our moral
strength, its wealth with our wisdom, its power with our purpose. I look
forward to an America which will not be afraid of grace and beauty. . . .
And I look forward to an America which commands respect throughout
the world not only for its strength but for its civilization as well.*

Kennedy had shown more than a casual interest in Ireland, according to
Arthur Mitchell, whose book *JFK and His Irish Heritage* traces the president's
youthful interests. Kennedy made the first of his six trips to Ireland in 1939
and in 1945 had had the opportunity to meet Éamon de Valera, forging a
friendship that lasted through Kennedy's life. Kennedy had interviewed de
Valera during that trip and submitted a thoughtful piece titled "De Valera
Aims to Unite Ireland" to the *New York Journal-American* in July 1945. He wrote,
"De Valera is fighting the same relentless battle fought in the field during the
uprising of 1916, in the war of independence and later in the civil war. He
feels everything Ireland has gained has been given grudgingly and at the end
of a long and bitter struggle. Always, it has been too little too late." When de
Valera visited Boston in 1948 to promote Irish unification, Kennedy met him
at Logan Airport, even though his flight arrived after midnight. Kennedy also
cosigned a bill sponsored by Rhode Island congressman John E. Fogarty in
1951 calling for Irish unification, and he supported a similar Senate resolution.

A high point of the president's time in office was his official visit to Ireland in June 1963. It captured the world's imagination and shone a spotlight
on the new Republic of Ireland. The visit was a triumphant, emotionally
charged promenade in which the entire population of Ireland seemed to participate. Kennedy's motorcade passed regally through the streets of Dublin,
Cork, and Galway as thousands of proud Irish cheered him with tears of
joy in their eyes, and the twin flags of Ireland and the United States waved
madly for him. He visited the modest town of New Ross, Wexford, which
twenty-five-year-old Patrick Kennedy had left in 1848 on a ship bound for
Boston. On June 29, 1963, in Limerick, Kennedy told the crowds of cheering
Irish, "This is not the land of my birth, but it is the land for which I hold the
greatest affection, and I will certainly come back in the springtime." It was a
sentiment wrought with love, promise, friendship, and possibility, and it was

almost unbearable to recall when the
president was assassinated in Dallas
on November 22, 1963.

Having followed the president's
visit to Ireland with immense pride,
reveling in how he had turned the
world's attention to their small island
off the coast of Europe, the Boston
Irish community was stunned by
the tragedy. They knew that he had
grown up in a different society, one
of privilege and wealth. But they
considered him one of their own. To
that postwar generation in particular,
John F. Kennedy would always be one
of them.

Shortly after his death the Kennedy family took up the task of creating a presidential library and formed
a committee in 1964 to raise funds for

*Presidential candidate John F. Kennedy is
portrayed as young and confident in this 1960
poster.*

the project. An Irish American Committee for the John F. Kennedy Memorial
Fund was set up in Boston, led by Cornelius O'Connor, Humphrey Mahoney,
and Michael Cummings. Its motto was "Modest Donations by Many Rather
Than Large Endowments of a Wealthy Few." As they had done for generations, the Boston Irish envisioned that the library would be built by the small
cash donations of thousands of ordinary believers, the same way they had built
their churches, parish schools, and colleges. The committee held a fund-raiser
at the New State Ballroom on Massachusetts Avenue on May 17, 1964, and
proudly donated $6,550.20 to the Kennedy Library Fund.

The family had selected Harvard Square in Cambridge as an ideal site
for the John F. Kennedy Presidential Library, but numerous delays occurred in
securing the land because of "bureaucratic red tape and political infighting."
The Library Committee looked at other possible sites, including Hyannis and
the Charlestown Navy Yard. Finally in 1975 the committee formed an alliance with city and state leaders to select a parcel of land at Columbia Point in
Dorchester, home of the University of Massachusetts, on nine acres of land

and three acres of mud flat, overlooking Boston Harbor as well as Boston's skyline. State Senator Joseph B. Walsh of Dorchester introduced legislation for the land transfer, and in August 1976 Governor Michael Dukakis signed a bill permitting construction of the library. *Boston Globe* reporter Robert Campbell described the design by architect I. M. Pei: "The Kennedy Library is lonely as a lighthouse or a boat. . . . It was Pei who chose this lonely site. . . . it's a place you see from afar, a place you sense yourself journeying toward."

President John F. Kennedy

The John F. Kennedy Presidential Library and Museum was formally dedicated on October 20, 1979, before seven thousand people. The event was described as "a sedate ceremony . . . sandwiched by a kind of affectionate hobnobbing and backslapping that characterized the JFK era. With the same emotional mix that accompanies a jazzman's funeral, the sobriety seemed only a loud whistle away from a friendly touch football game on the library's landscaped grounds."

Guest speaker President Jimmy Carter said:

> *President Kennedy understood the past and respected its shaping of the future. [He] entered the White House convinced that racial and religious discrimination was morally indefensible. He never failed to uphold liberty and condemn tyranny. . . . The essence of President Kennedy's message—the appeal for unselfish dedication to the common good—is more urgent than ever.*

The podium that day was crowded with President Kennedy's loved ones: former first lady Jacqueline Kennedy and her children John Jr. and Caroline,

JFK Library and Museum

The **John F. Kennedy Presidential Library and Museum** at Columbia Point in Boston is the official library of the nation's thirty-fifth president. The president's thousand days in office are recreated in the exhibits revealing the legacy of Kennedy's short but historically significant administration. The JFK Library continues to offer insight about the nation's first Irish Catholic president and also his Irish-American background. A significant companion of the library is the Kennedy Library Foundation, led by Caroline Kennedy and headed by Thomas McNaught, which keeps the spirit of President Kennedy alive with engaging lectures and forums; a Profiles in Courage Award, given to public servants who demonstrate courage in their work and lives; and a New Frontier Award, given to a person under forty whose public service exemplifies the spirit of John F. Kennedy.

The library/museum is open from 9:00 a.m. to 5:00 p.m. daily. For more information call (617) 514-1600 or visit the website www.jfklibrary.org.

his brothers and sisters, nephews and nieces, cousins and in-laws. Any of them could have glanced out at Boston Harbor and settled their gaze on Deer Island, the last island separating the United States from Ireland. This is where their ancestors—the Kennedys, Fitzgeralds, Murphys, and Coxes—would have been stopped at the quarantine station before they were allowed to enter Boston, where history could then take its course.

CHAPTER THIRTEEN

The Irish on the Move (1965–1985)

THE 1960s were a transition decade for the Boston Irish. The Dudley Street dance hall scene had fizzled out, as people moved away from the neighborhood. In 1960 the Union Savings Bank of Boston foreclosed on Hibernian Hall, which had been owned by the Hibernian Building Association of Boston Highlands, and sold it for seventeen thousand dollars. Intercolonial Hall stayed open for several more years, staging ceili dances and televising the occasional All-Ireland football finals from Croke Park. But many Irish had already shifted away from Dudley Street and over to the Donnelly Memorial Theater at 209 Massachusetts Avenue, which had been purchased by Richard Cardinal Cushing and the Boston Archdiocese in 1959. The 3,450-seat theater booked everyone from Bob Dylan to Stevie Wonder, as well as Irish groups such as the Clancy Brothers and Tommy Makem, and held fundraisers, especially for Catholic groups such as the Sisters of Notre Dame. Right next door was the State Ballroom, which had presented jazz bands such as Artie Shaw and Glenn Miller going back to the late 1920s. By the 1960s it was bringing in Irish show bands through Irish promoter Bill Fuller, the husband of singer Carmel Quinn. But when the State Ballroom closed in 1968, the Irish music scene scattered into neighborhood and suburban venues such as Metropolitan Hall in Roslindale and the Norwood Irish Music Hall.

The most significant factor affecting the Boston Irish in this decade was the Immigration Act passed by the US Congress in 1965. Immigration reform had been championed by President Kennedy, and after his assassination this legislation had been shepherded through Congress by Massachusetts senator Edward M. "Ted" Kennedy and his brother, New York senator Robert Kennedy.

The 1965 act eliminated the "national origins" criteria that had favored Europeans for so long, substituting a "family reunification" preference that favored immigrants from Latin America, Asia, and Africa. The bill was opposed by many conservative congressmen because it threatened to open the doors to immigrants other than white Europeans.

Along with other European nations, Ireland's annual allotment of visas to the United States was cut drastically. Between 1955 and 1965, 70,000 visas were issued to Ireland, an average of 7,000 per year. After 1965 the number dropped to 1,000 a year, and by 1985 the annual Irish allotment of visas was 515. The Kennedys were roundly criticized by Irish leaders in New York and Boston for shutting down the Irish quotas, and in 1968, when Robert Kennedy was running for president, Ted Kennedy had this to say:

> The present laws unintentionally discriminate against the Irish because
> of the historic pattern of Irish immigration. I share the distress felt by
> many in this matter and I am working to remedy the situation.

It would take Kennedy and others another quarter century to remedy the situation for the Irish, but in the meantime the Irish discovered a loophole in the law. Though permanent visas were scarce, the United States was issuing up to fifty thousand holiday visas each year. Once the Irish made their way into the country on a 90-day visitor's visa, they could disappear into the vast network of Irish enclaves from Boston to San Francisco and stay in America indefinitely. But there was a price to pay: the illegal Irish lived in constant fear of getting caught, and if they went home for a holiday, wedding, or funeral, they risked not being allowed back into the States for three to ten years.

In 1985, when the media broke the story that fifteen thousand to thirty thousand illegal Irish immigrants were living clandestinely in Boston, the public was shocked. This was America's most Irish city, where the Irish had been coming since the 1700s. This was the home of Kennedy and O'Neill and the headquarters of the newly formed American Ireland Fund, which was collecting millions of dollars to send back to Ireland. How could Boston have overlooked a generation of young Irish living a frightful existence, afraid to open a bank account, get a driver's license, or start a business for fear of being deported?

In truth Irish-American leaders, especially the successful ones who worked downtown and lived in the suburbs, had become disconnected from Irish immigrants living in Dorchester, Quincy, and Brighton. The Irish government, accused of using migration as a safety valve against high unemployment, was also mute on the issue. And the illegals themselves were silent, not wishing to draw attention to themselves at a time when Boston's construction industry was booming, with such large-scale projects as the Boston Harbor cleanup and the Big Dig—a revamping of Boston's roadways—in full swing.

Grassroots leaders learned quickly to address the problem. Bill McGowan, a former Irish priest and Gaelic Athletic Association (GAA) official whose small insurance company on Dorchester Avenue served Irish immigrants, was hearing that Irish coming into Logan Airport were increasingly hassled, detained, or deported by immigration officers. Every day rumors swirled that the Immigration and Naturalization Service might raid a job site, a pub, or an apartment and arrest illegal Irish. McGowan's office was getting constant calls for help. People were looking for advice.

McGowan contacted his congressman, Brian Donnelly, who had also been receiving similar reports about Irish being detained at Logan. Donnelly's four grandparents came from Roscommon and Galway, and his Eleventh Congressional District included Dorchester and Quincy, making it one of the most Irish districts in the country. As he told one reporter, "Of the twelve houses in my street, six have families who have emigrated directly from Ireland."

In May 1985 Donnelly submitted HR Bill 2606, "to make additional immigrant visas available" for Irish and other groups who had been shut out by the 1965 Immigration Act. Two months later, encouraged by Donnelly's proposal, McGowan convened a meeting at the Irish Social Club in West Roxbury, attended by sixty representatives of Irish groups in Boston, and announced a national effort to reform immigration laws.

The group, called the Massachusetts Immigration Committee, set about amending the 1965 Immigration Act. Joining McGowan in the campaign were Mike Joyce, a Connemara native working at the statehouse, GAA official Joe Lydon, attorney Paul Kilgarriff, and Mike Cummings, who had helped jumpstart the Irish revival of the 1950s. Throughout 1986 the committee contacted hundreds of elected officials across America by tapping into the national networks of the Gaelic Athletic Association and the Ancient Order of Hibernians.

Michael Cummings and Thomas Flatley traveled to Washington, D.C., to lobby for immigration reform.

They established relations with Italian, Greek, Canadian, and German groups. They took out ads in the paper and set up hotlines for illegal aliens.

Cummings approached his close friend Thomas Flatley, a successful real estate developer, about getting involved in the campaign. Flatley agreed to match all funds raised by the Massachusetts Immigration Committee and began working with Donnelly's office. On July 26, 1986, Flatley and Cummings traveled to the nation's capital to testify in favor of the Donnelly bill that was before the House subcommittee. Flatley reflected on his own successful career as a Boston businessman:

> *In no other country in the world but America could I have realized my*
> *dream of pursuing the entrepreneurial spirit. It saddens me . . . [that]*
> *had I been born 25 years later, I too might not have been able to realize*
> *my dream.*

Finally, with great fanfare and relief, the Donnelly bill passed in fall 1986 as part of the US Immigration and Control Act. The Donnelly visa program allocated 40,000 permanent visas to Europeans, of which 18,363 were given to Irish immigrants, including many who had been living illegally in the United States. It provided temporary relief to the problem of illegal immigration.

But the allotment barely dented the number of illegal Irish who were already here, and besides, upward of 25,000 Irish were still coming into the country annually, using holiday visas to get here, then going underground when those temporary visas expired. In response to the ongoing crisis, a group of Irish immigrants in New York City formed the Irish Immigration Reform Movement, and in the summer of 1987 a Boston chapter opened. Like the Massachusetts Immigration Committee, the IIRM became part of a broad alliance of Irish and Irish Americans trying to help the Irish stay in America. That autumn, Boston Mayor Ray Flynn opened an Immigrant Office at City Hall to provide free, confidential legal advice to illegal immigrants. He also vowed to provide free health care at Boston City Hospital for immigrants who had no insurance.

On the national scene, the effort was led by Connecticut congressman Bruce Morrison, a Yale-educated attorney with Ulster Protestant roots. He had taken a genuine interest in Ireland during a 1987 fact-finding mission to Northern Ireland, according to *Irish Echo* editor Ray O'Hanlon, whose book *The New Irish Americans* provides a fascinating account of the Irish visa bill as it worked its way through Congress. As chair of the immigration subcommittee, Morrison steered the visa bill past countless obstacles, negotiating support with Asian and Hispanic lobby groups while keeping IIRM and other Irish groups in the loop.

In 1991 it appeared that the Morrison bill, HR 4300, would languish in Congress, but Boston's congressman Joe Moakley came to the rescue. A few years earlier Morrison had supported Moakley's congressional investigation into the murder of American nuns in El Salvador, O'Hanlon reported, and now Moakley would return the favor. As chairman of the Rules Committee, Moakley was able to maneuver Morrison's bill for a final House and Senate vote, and it passed into law.

The Morrison visa bill was more ambitious than the Donnelly bill, providing the Irish with 51,715 Morrison visas in a three-year period, effectively solving the problem of Irish illegals in the 1990s. Morrison was feted in Boston by grateful Irish immigrants now able to get on with their lives and was considered a genuine hero in the Irish community. So too were the hundreds of grassroots leaders who had dedicated years of their lives to securing a future in Boston for new Irish immigrants.

The Boston Irish now turned their attention to the considerable amount of paperwork and legal advice that Morrison visa recipients needed to become legal in America, and two groups came to the fore. The Irish Pastoral Centre, formed in 1987 by Father Dan Finn and Sister Veronica Dobson, was part of the Boston Archdiocese. It offered the new Irish spiritual advice, marriage counseling, and information on health, housing, and jobs. Its offices were based in the Irish parishes around Boston—Saint Mark's in Dorchester and Saint Columbkille's in Brighton—and provided a familiar setting for anyone seeking a connection with the Catholic Church, long a steadfast anchor of Irish life. Today the Pastoral Centre is run out of St. Brendan's Parish, headed by Father John McCarthy and immigration specialist Kieran O'Sullivan. The Centre continues to help new Irish families get acclimated to life in Boston.

The second group was initiated in 1989 by young immigrants operating out of a basement in Dorchester. The Irish Immigration Center offered a hotline for illegals worried about their status. Under the energetic leadership of Sister Lena Deevy, Patrick Riordan, and others, the Center set up workshops on citizenship and health care and offered counseling and other services the new Irish needed. As the Morrison visa holders became acclimated to American society, the Center expanded its mission to help other immigrants. Deevy, who had worked in poor neighborhoods in Dublin, Belfast, and Glasgow, recognized the need to find a common ground among immigrants from other parts of the world as a way of resolving inner-city tensions. She initiated an annual event called Black and Green, which connected the Irish with Haitian, Cape Verdean, and other immigrants living in Dorchester. She knew, as Irish leaders in the past knew, that for this generation of Irish to settle into Boston in a fruitful way, they needed to learn to live in harmony with other Bostonians.

Chapter Fourteen

The Gaelic Roots Revival (1985–2000)

WHEN BOSTON COLLEGE hired Irish fiddle champion Seamus Connolly in 1991, musicians from around the world began showing up on campus, instruments in hand. They came from Boston, New York, Philadelphia, and Chicago, and from Sweden, Holland, and Japan. The ten-time All-Ireland fiddle champion from County Clare was hired to develop a new Irish music program for one of the nation's most Irish, Catholic institutions. With characteristic zeal, charm, and dedication, Connolly built a Gaelic roots music program that was extraordinary for its breadth, scope, and quality.

The college needed some good, authentic Irish music to stay grounded in its roots. Founded in 1863 by businessman Andrew Carney and Jesuit priest Rev. John McElroy, SJ, Boston College was originally located next to the Immaculate Conception Church on Harrison Avenue in the South End. The college was modest at first, supported by the pennies of Irish immigrants who put their dreams into their children's futures. In 1909 Boston College purchased land in Chestnut Hill and built a full-size campus drawing on the area's substantial Irish-American and Catholic community for faculty, staff, and students.

By the 1980s the pennies of immigrants were replaced by endowments from wealthy Irish businessmen, and this enabled the college to create an Irish studies program. Cochaired by history professor Kevin O'Neill and English professor Adele Dalsimer, the program swiftly became one of the finest in the

Seamus Connolly has spent the last
decade compiling *Music: My Life*, a
collection of over three hundred Irish
tunes that he has assembled over the
past fifty years, from field recordings,
old 78s found in basements, and
reel-to-reel tapes of sessions recorded
from Clare to Cape Breton and
from Boston to the Appalachian
states. In 2013 the Burns Library at
Boston College presented an exhibit
entitled *The Musical Roots of Seamus
Connolly, Sullivan Artist in Residence,*
which portrayed the influences and
milestones in Connolly's music career.
In May 2013, Connolly received
the Ellis Island Medal of Honor for
"his significant contributions to the
United States." And Connolly has also
been awarded the 2013 National
Heritage Fellowship from the National
Endowment for the Arts for his accomplishments on the fiddle.

*Clare fiddler Seamus Connolly, founder of Gaelic
Roots program at Boston College*

United States. It established a junior-year-abroad program at Cork University
and developed ties with Dublin's prestigious Abbey Theatre. The John J. Burns
Library became a leading repository for important collections belonging to
poet William Butler Yeats, novelist Samuel Beckett, singer John McCormack,
athlete James Brendan Connolly, and many other Irish notables. In 1987
BC hosted the annual meeting of the American Conference for Irish Studies
(ACIS), bringing a national spotlight to its program.

By hiring Irish musician Connolly, considered one of the premier Irish
fiddlers of his generation, Boston College elevated its Irish studies program on
an academic and community level. Connolly had collected decades of music
recordings he had made in the field, of local musicians from the west of Ireland to the Canadian Maritimes. Because of his status in the Irish music scene,
he also attracted people from the Irish community who had never stepped foot
on BC's campus before.

Along with archivist Beth Sweeney, he created the Irish Music Archives at the John J. Burns Library, soliciting old recordings from his friends across the country. He and musicologist Micheal O'Suilleabhain from University College Cork staged a concert with sixteen of the world's best Irish fiddlers, recording a compact disc called *My Love Is in America*. The concert was a tour de force, and Connolly quickly followed it with an impressive gathering of harpists and a convention of uilleann pipers.

In 1993 Connolly launched Gaelic Roots: A Music, Song, and Dance Summer School and Festival. Noted music writer Earle Hitchner hailed it as an unprecedented and historic event. Indeed it was, growing stronger annually for the next decade. For a full week each June, the world's finest Celtic musicians, dancers, singers, and scholars came to Boston College, where they taught classes and gave concerts. Hundreds of students registered for the program, living in the dormitories and eating in the school cafeteria. Most importantly, they played together in both classes and casual music sessions in the quiet repose of the beautiful campus. The master musicians gave two evening concerts through the week, open to the general public. Students came from as far away as Australia, and the classes typically filled six months in advance.

Along with the organizational and operational skills of his wife Chrysandra Walter, Connolly developed Gaelic Roots into the best program of its kind in the Celtic world. It combined hands-on instruction and performances with lectures and research, while showcasing the school's vast collection of Irish materials and Irish studies experts. It brought old music masters from remote areas of Ireland who specialized in regional styles, while integrating Scottish, Cape Breton, and Appalachian musicians and dancers to underscore the roots of the music. In the finest Irish tradition, it encouraged adult students who had always wanted to learn an instrument while inspiring a whole generation of young people to take up Irish music and dancing.

To the surprise and dismay of the Irish community at large, Boston College announced in June 2003 that it was eliminating Gaelic Roots, just as the program was celebrating its tenth anniversary. Budgetary constraints combined with the new difficulty of securing temporary visas for foreign artists caused school officials to terminate the weeklong summer school in favor of ongoing workshops, lectures, and concerts during the academic year.

A Boston Irish Renaissance

Gaelic Roots was part of a larger Irish cultural revival taking place in Boston, noted by *Boston Globe* music reporter Scott Alarik in his 1990 article "Keeping Ancient Irish Culture Alive." Alarik described "an Irish renaissance in Boston, a resurgence not just of music, but of dance, language and lore." He pointed to the popularity of Irish set and ceili dancing hosted by Comhaltas Ceoltoiri Eireann (Irish Musicians Association) at the Canadian American Club. He cited the popularity of genealogy and the Irish Ancestral Research Association. He mentioned the proliferation of Irish language courses in local colleges and the success of local storyteller Sharon Kennedy.

Authenticity became the cornerstone of the new revival. Irish immigrants and Americans alike were frustrated by how beer and greeting card companies had hijacked the Irish identity in America, especially around Saint Patrick's Day. Green plastic derbies, shamrock-shaped beer coasters, and tacky T-shirts were hawked by shameless hucksters cashing in on sentimental icons of Irish culture. Boston's Irish community wanted something more, and partly as a response to the stale and commercialized stereotyping of the Irish in America, they embraced Irish culture, especially music and dance, theater and literature.

Irish troupe Sugan Theatre injected a new vitality into Boston's community theater, staging Irish and Scottish plays that fought the image of a romanticized Ireland by displaying an often disturbing reality of Irish society. The Sugan flourished from 1992 through 2006. Nora Hussey at Wellesley College directed a number of Irish plays, while the Huntington Theatre produced nationally acclaimed productions by leading Irish playwrights. The Poets' Theatre in Cambridge, founded in the 1950s by Irish actress Mary Manning Howe, hosted poet Seamus Heaney and novelist John McGahern. And the City of Boston teamed up with the Waterstone Bookstore, led by Scotsman Bert Wright, to create an Irish Writers Series featuring novelists Peter Quinn and James Carroll, scholar Angela Bourke, and poets Nuala Ni Dhomhnaill and John Montague.

At Stonehill College, president Bartley MacPhaidin and Richard Finnegan formed an Irish studies program that included a year-abroad program at University College Dublin while building a collection of Irish government documents valuable to historians and students. Harvard's Celtic Department celebrated its centenary of Celtic studies in 1996, and chairman Patrick Ford and alumnus Philip Haughey formed a Friends group to aid graduate students in their scholarly pursuits. Elizabeth Shannon convened conferences on women from Northern Ireland at Boston University. At University of Massachusetts Boston, Padraig O'Malley, along with Catherine Shannon of Westfield State College, brought in the Northern Irish to discuss their troubles, while Thomas O'Grady and Sean O'Connell brought Irish poets to discuss their verse.

A literary ambience even showed up in the city's new wave of Irish pubs. A generation of Irish bartenders, many of whom apprenticed at the Black Rose Pub at Faneuil Hall, opened their own pubs, offering traditional music, healthy food, a hip jukebox, and a friendly, intimate ambience. It was fashionable to christen these pubs with a literary or cultural name—the Brendan Behan, Flann O'Brien's, Mr. Dooley's, and the Midnight Court as well as the Kells, Claddagh, and Druid. By the 1990s, these pubs, along with the Burren, O'Leary's, and the Green Briar, ushered in a robust era where the pubs became the cornerstone of Irish nightlife in the city.

The pub scene was the place where Irish music next took hold in Boston after the demise of the Dudley Street dance halls left a gap in the social scene. It started around 1976, when Phil Sweeney and Richard McHugh opened the Black Rose on State Street and George Crowley opened the Plough & Stars on Massachusetts Avenue. Both became hot spots for Irish music sessions, with Dublin musicians Shay Walker, Declan Hunt, Alan Loughnane, and Johnny Beggan leading the tunes. The Plough attracted a crowd of rugby players but quickly became a hangout for Irish poets Desmond O'Grady, Seamus Heaney, and raconteur Peter O'Malley, who started *Ploughshares* magazine. The Black Rose attracted an eclectic, energetic mix of City Hall types, tourists, and businessmen. The murals of Donegal painter David O'Docherty adorned the walls.

In Brookline Village, Henry Varian opened the Village Coach House, where Connolly and Galway fiddler Larry Reynolds held court at the Monday night sessions. The weekly session attracted a new generation of musicians such as Helen Kisiel, Kevin McElroy, Willie Mahon, Andy Hanley, Skip McKinley, Claudine Langille, and Maureen Kelly. It became a showcase for Comhaltas Ceoltoiri Eireann, which trained a whole generation of outstanding traditional players. In 1991 Connolly's prize student Brendan Bulger of South Boston won the All-Ireland fiddle championship. A few years later accordionist Colm Gannon of Dorchester, whose Connemara-born father and brother are excellent box players, won the All-Ireland title. Championship dancers frequented the

Galway fiddler Larry Reynolds, founder of Boston's Comhaltas Ceoltoiri Eireann

scene, including Deirdre Goulding and Liam Harney. Sean Curran, son of radio personality John Curran and his wife Kitty, became a lead dancer in the Bill T. Jones dance troupe in New York City and later started his own troupe.

Comhaltas helped restore the atmosphere that many immigrants missed about Ireland. The group met the first Sunday of every month at the Canadian American Club in Watertown. The club had a bar but also offered coffee, tea, and soda bread, turning the music session into a family affair that sometimes included participants from four generations. One could hear white-haired flutist Gene Preston, who emigrated from Sligo in the 1920s, playing alongside fiddler Roger Burris, who came from County Clare in the 1980s. They played with accordionists Mike Reynolds from Waltham and Chris Bulger from South Boston. The session also attracted Canadian players Sally Kelly and Mary Irwin and Scottish fiddler Johnny Cunningham, which led to the beginnings of a pan-Celtic scene that included Irish, Scottish, and Cape Breton musicians.

The explosion of music coming out of Ireland and Scotland buoyed Boston's music scene, and soon dozens of Irish radio programs flourished in the

Comhaltas Ceoltoiri Eireann

Comhaltas Ceoltoiri Eireann (Irish Musicians Association) is an international group formed in 1951 that promotes traditional Irish music and dance in more than twenty countries. The Boston chapter was formed in 1975 by fiddler Larry Reynolds, John Curran, Pat and Mary Barry, and Billy Caples, and has since become one of the largest chapters in the world. Comhaltas holds regular Irish ceilis (dances) and offers set dance instructions at the Canadian American Hall at 202 Arlington Street in Watertown. Comhaltas also has a fine year-round teaching program on fiddle, flute, tin whistle, accordion, harp, and other traditional instruments. For more information visit cceboston.org.

Boston area. Longtime radio hosts John Curran, Bernie McCarthy, John Latchford, and Tommy Cummings were joined by a new generation of radio hosts like Brian O'Donovan, Bud Sargent, Gail Gilmore, and Seamus Mulligan. Tom Clifford's popular cable TV show *Ireland on the Move* was joined in 1995 by Celtic Vision, a full-time but short-lived Irish television station.

In publishing, Quinlin Campbell Publishers issued its third edition of *Guide to the New England Irish* in 1994, listing twelve hundred Irish organizations and activities in the region, more than tripling the size of the first edition published in 1985. In 1991, when Don Mooney's *Boston Irish News* went defunct, Ed and Mary Forry launched the *Boston Irish Reporter,* a bright monthly newspaper that catalogued the activities and personalities of the Irish community. The *Reporter* added editor Peter Stevens, a noted author with a unique appreciation of Boston Irish history. Connell and Siobhan Gallagher of Donegal launched the *Irish Emigrant* green pages in South Boston, providing a weekly update on the bustling pub scene in Greater Boston. For a time the two New York City papers, the *Irish Echo* and the *Irish Voice,* ran news bureaus in Boston that flourished but then faded after several years. Paul Feeney of Dorchester launched the *Boston City Paper,* which covered topics like immigration, politics, and music on Dudley Street.

A number of books about the Boston Irish emerged during this time. Political and social histories of the Boston Irish by Thomas H. O'Connor, RuthAnn Harris, and Dennis P. Ryan charted the nineteenth-century Boston Irish experience. Historian James M. O'Toole weighed in on the Catholic Church, while Sean O'Connell and Charles Fanning wrote about Irish-American literature. Jack Beatty's biography of James Michael Curley and William Bulger's political memoirs added considerable insight into Boston Irish politics.

Preserving the Culture

Despite the flourishing of Irish activity in Greater Boston, the Irish community yearned for a central gathering spot that drew everyone together, the way Dudley Street had.

The 1965 immigration laws had cut off the flow of new Irish coming into Boston, stripping away the vibrancy that newcomers brought to stock Irish neighborhoods like South Boston, Dorchester, Charlestown, and Brighton. In the mid-1970s several Irish neighborhoods in Boston got ensnared in a

A Cultural Hub for the Irish

The Irish Cultural Centre in Canton was established in 1989 as a headquarters for the promotion and preservation of Irish culture for the New England region. The forty-six-acre campus includes a new state-of-the-art building with function rooms, a library and genealogical research room, a pub, classrooms, and a banquet room for large events. Irish sports are played here, including football, soccer, rugby, hurling, and camogie. The center has more than four thousand members, who enjoy a year-round schedule of classes, performances, competition, and gatherings in the areas of music, dance, theater, and athletics. Educational programs and social activities are also common throughout the year. The Centre is celebrating its twenty-fifth anniversary in 2014. For details about the Irish Cultural Centre, call (781) 821-8291 or visit irishculture.org.

school busing controversy that pitted working-class blacks and whites against each other. The ensuing white flight from Boston to the suburbs contributed to the ebbing of the city's Irish population that had been taking place throughout the century.

The dispersion caused a tangible sadness about losing the community cohesiveness that had come to define the Boston Irish persona since the 1840s. Irish leaders began discussing the notion of building a cultural center as a way of recreating that sense of community being lost. Other cities—Chicago, Pittsburgh, and San Francisco—had created Irish centers with much smaller populations. Why couldn't Boston?

The idea for an Irish Museum and Hall of History was floated as early as 1959, when advertising executives in Boston proposed building a Celtorama: Irish Museum and Hall of History to attract tourists to the city. "Picture a shamrock-shaped building—containing Irish art, handicraft, industrial exhibits and even a replica of the Blarney Castle, including a chip from the Blarney stone itself," John B. Fisher told a group of hotel managers.

The *Boston Globe* endorsed the idea:

> Behind the proposal there is a fundamental issue that is a matter of concern. The cultural beginnings of many of our immigrant families are being lost completely to their children and their children's children. Relics and records of those first arrivals, mementoes of the countries of their origins, the bridge of letters that spanned the Atlantic, photographs, costumes—these should not be lost.

An Irish hurling exhibition at the Boston Irish Festival on the grounds of the Irish Cultural Centre in Canton

The idea languished for two decades until Bill McGowan, immigration leader and Gaelic Athletic Association official, outlined his ideas to "establish a Gaelic Center in Boston" during an interview with Vincent O'Sullivan of the *Boston Irish Press* in 1981. A few years later Comhaltas Ceoltoiri Eireann proposed a Traditional Irish Music Center "as a means of cultural identity and as an influence on the development of America's own music."

In 1989 a committee of Irish leaders announced plans to build an Irish Cultural Centre, led by Noel Connolly, Mike O'Connor, Tom Gallagher, Eddie Barron, and others. Their goal was to create a place "where present and future generations can participate in activities that promote Irish cultural, education, sporting and social events." The group launched an annual Irish Festival at Stonehill College and a golf tournament to raise funds and within five years had pulled together enough funds for a down payment on some land.

Where to locate such a center was a point of discussion. The organizers believed that a location south of Boston would be most convenient to the greatest number of Irish Americans. Those who had stayed in Boston were pushing for a site within the city, with Mayor Ray Flynn offering to locate city property that could suffice. Even the *Boston Globe* weighed in on the debate with an editorial in 1993 stating:

> *The Irish center belongs in Boston, where émigrés like trade unionist*
> *Daniel Tobin and folk hero John Boyle O'Reilly served the cause*
> *of social justice, a city that was home to the beloved Irish-American*
> *president John F. Kennedy. It is time to collect and preserve local Irish*
> *artifacts, books and museum-quality pieces now in private hands.*

But after examining dozens of sites, including the Water & Sewer facility at Columbia Point and an old rope building at Charlestown Navy Yard, the group purchased a plot of land in Canton, about twenty miles southwest of downtown Boston in 1995. Organizers of the cultural center joined forces with the Gaelic Athletic Association, which had outgrown Dilboy Field in Somerville, to create the forty-six-acre campus that both organizations could use. Between 1995 and 1998 thousands of volunteers—laborers, carpenters, electricians, painters, and tradespeople—cleared the land, cut the road, created the playing fields, and built a seventeen-thousand-square-foot two-story facility. The Irish Cultural Centre officially opened in 1997 and today is a bustling, year-round gathering place as originally envisioned.

Remembering the Famine

Despite demographic shifts to the suburbs, downtown Boston still mattered to the Irish, if not for the future then at least for the past. As the 150th anniversary of the Irish Famine approached in the late 1990s, a number of Famine commemorations took place around Boston. In June 1997 a religious service was held on Deer Island in Boston Harbor to remember the five thousand immigrants who had been quarantined there in the mid-nineteenth century. The City of Cambridge commissioned Maurice Harmon of Derry, Northern Ireland, to create its memorial on Cambridge Common. It was unveiled in July 1997 before five thousand people, including Ireland's president Mary Robinson and Massachusetts governor William Weld.

When mayor Ray Flynn left Boston to become US ambassador to the Vatican, Irish-born real estate developer Thomas Flatley stepped forward to organize the city's memorial. On May 1, 1997, he convened a meeting of leaders from the Irish community and business world to undertake the $1 million project. Flatley and Mike Cummings walked the city of Boston and settled upon the perfect spot for the memorial at the corner of Washington and School

Streets. It was across from the Old South Meeting House and a few yards away from the International Institute of Boston, which helps new immigrants and refugees settle in Boston. It was steps from the place where the first Catholic Mass in Boston was publicly celebrated in 1788. The committee chose noted sculptor Robert Shure to create the twin statues, depicting a family in Ireland and one stepping onto American soil. The memorial was unveiled on June 28, 1998, before seven thousand people. The eight narrative plaques encircling the statues were read aloud by four Irish and Irish Americans along with a Vietnamese girl, a Rwandan boy, a Medal of Honor winner, and a survivor of the Jewish Holocaust.

In a poignant way the worldwide commemorations of the Great Hunger helped to knit together, even if only for a brief time, Ireland's sprawling diaspora. It focused attention on the famines still taking place in many African countries, and in the broadest sense it reminded the world of the pain, loss, promise, and redemption inherent in the human condition.

CHAPTER FIFTEEN

Who's Irish?

FICTION WRITER Gish Jen posed the poignant question "Who's Irish?" in her 1999 short story about interethnic marriages. Jen's modern-day tale about a Chinese grandmother's snobbery toward her Irish-American in-laws strikes a chord with anyone who has married outside his or her own racial, religious, or ethnic group and discovers the tension that underlies assimilation.

In a humorous exchange the Chinese daughter defends her Irish husband's clan, saying, "You know, the British call the Irish heathen, just like they call the Chinese. . . . You think the Opium War was bad, how would you like to live right next door to the British?"

As it turns out, the Chinese and Irish lived next door to each other in Boston and began intermarrying around 1875, when there was an abundance of single Irish women and single Chinese men. Sarah Deutsch's book *Women and the City* recounts a *Boston Globe* story in 1895 in which a group of conventioneers wondered why a "rather good-looking" Irish girl was riding her bike around Chinatown, when suddenly a Chinese man opened a nearby door and called out, "Lil, come quickly." The reporter explained that "the girl was probably the Chinaman's wife and that there were several more of her kind in the colony."

In 1908 a Boston Catholic almanac reported that the Irish were converting local Chinese, who crossed over the bridge from Chinatown to become Catholics in South Boston. The Reverend Walter J. Browne of Saints Peter and

Paul Church had "twenty-six baptized converts and fourteen neophytes," who "looked very well in European dress." The religious instructors were Muldoon, Coholan, Whalen, Conboy, Breen, and Cunningham.

After the Civil War, John Boyle O'Reilly and others cultivated Irish solidarity with blacks, Chinese, Jews, and American Indians. A shared sense of oppression and proximity among these groups led to interracial alliances. Deutsch writes, "In the 1870s and 1880s, black Bostonians married whites— largely Irish women—at a higher rate than Irish Catholics married Yankee Protestants."

What it means to be Irish in Boston has evolved over the past three centuries. President Theodore Roosevelt predicted that Irish immigrants would eventually become more American than Irish. In an 1897 letter to James J. Roche praising the newly formed American Irish Historical Society, Roosevelt wrote:

> We [Americans] are a new people, derived from many race strains, and different from any one of them, and it is a good thing to have brought before us our diversity in race origin. . . . In time the different strains of blood will all be blended together, English and Irish, German and French. When that time comes, and before it, the chief thing for all of us to keep in mind is that we must be good Americans, purely as such, no matter what be our creed or our ancestry in Europe.

Others objected to the notion of race unions. Charles William Eliot, the president of Harvard University, said there should be "no admixture of racial stocks," while lecturing in Alabama in 1909. "I believe, for example, that the Irish should not intermarry with the Americans of English descent; that the Germans should not marry the Italians; that the Jews should not marry the French. Each race should maintain its own individuality. In the case of the negroes and the whites the races should be kept apart in every respect."

But the "admixture of racial stocks" was taking place well before Eliot's objections, and not just among Europeans. In the eighteenth century Irish and Scottish servants escaping into the wilderness with Indians and Africans began a process of racial intermingling that became the stock for America's melting pot. Race and religion emerged as the twin methods of establishing some definition of American society. The Irish, as "papists and foreigners," were perceived as twin threats to a fledgling Anglo-American nation and were

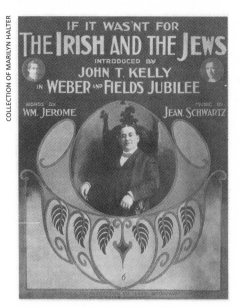

Ethnic sheet music in the early twentieth century attests to the American melting pot concept.

stigmatized on both counts. Other groups—notably blacks, Chinese, and Italians—faced similar rejection by nativists, who were hoping that America might remain a homogenous white Anglo-Saxon Protestant nation. Those hopes were not realized.

Boston's demographics have dramatically changed since the time of Mr. Eliot's address. Today 28 percent of Boston is foreign born, representing a hundred different nations. You can chart Boston's changing urban landscape by monitoring its mix of grocery stores, retail shops, funeral homes, pubs and restaurants, and churches. Sociologists call it ethnic succession. The rule of thumb is that funeral homes represent the declining ethnic group, while shops and grocery stores represent the up-and-coming groups. There was a time when Irish gift shops were ubiquitous in Boston, for example, but those too have vanished with the changing demographics and the shift to online purchasing.

These types of neighborhood shifts have occurred throughout Boston's history. The Irish who first settled in the North End, West End, and East Boston made their way to the South End, South Boston, Dorchester, and Roxbury before moving farther out to Jamaica Plain, West Roxbury, Milton, and Dedham and ultimately taking over much of the South Shore. Other immigrant groups—Italians, Jews, Vietnamese, Haitians, and Central Americans—took their place, and they too have moved onward and outward to suburbs and small towns beyond the city.

A *Boston Globe* story in 1924 titled "One Irish Family Left in North End" profiled the McNabbe family as the lone survivor of a once-Irish and now Italian neighborhood. A *Globe* story in 1925 noted that "Anyone familiar with South Boston has known that the region ceased long ago to be the stronghold it once was for families of Irish descent. . . . As the families of Irish immigrants grew up . . . they persuaded the old folks to move to Dorchester or Brighton . . . or waited until the old folks passed away, and then moved."

South Boston was further affected in the 1970s, when Judge W. Arthur Garrity Jr. imposed a federally mandated school busing order that shuttled working-class black and white students across town in hopes of creating an equitable school system That decision caused a steady exodus of white residents out of South Boston and other neighborhoods to nearby cities and towns. That exodus of long-time Southie residents continued in the 1990s as rising real estate costs prohibited many young residents of the neighborhood from buying homes there. Jack Hart, who represented South Boston as its state senator for many years, told the *Boston Globe*, "Families would love to stay, but they can't afford to, paying the taxes and tuition for private school."

In Dorchester, you still find pockets of Irish activity in places like Adams Village. The Eire Pub, run by the Stenson family, has been an anchor to the community for half a century, a place where workingmen can have a drink and talk about politics and sports. In 1983 President Ronald Reagan had a pint there, and in 1992 presidential candidate Bill Clinton stopped by there too. Across the street, Greenhill's Irish Bakery, Gerard's, and the Butcher Shop Market form a nucleus for Irish people shopping for imported and homemade products or meeting up with friends. Nearby, the Irish Pastoral Centre at St. Brendan's Parish ministers to Irish Catholics living in the area. And the Boston Irish Festival that takes place in Adams Village each fall attracts people from across the region, who return for the music, dancing, and socializing.

The decline of Charlestown's Irish community has been similar to South Boston's. The mid-nineteenth-century Irish Famine migration transformed Charlestown into an Irish enclave, with a strong contingent of Donegal and Mayo descendants settling there. Such a noted leader as Irish poet John Boyle O'Reilly lived on Winthrop Street with his wife Mary Murphy and their four daughters. In the early twentieth century Charlestown had a thriving Irish cultural scene centered around Hibernian Hall and a number of fine musicians, including accordionist Veronica Doherty.

By the 1960s the Irish gangs of Charlestown had appropriated the town's Irish persona, and the town's cultural scene took a backseat. School desegregation in the 1970s followed by gentrification in the 1980s eroded the solid Irish ambience even further. In response, three Charlestown residents—Ed Callahan, Arthur Hurley, and Jimmy Walsh—came together in 2006 to make a

Massachusetts Mostly Irish

Between 1900 and 2000 Boston's Irish population dropped from 40 percent to under 20 percent. Where did everyone go? Mostly, Bostonians of Irish descent moved beyond the Hub to surrounding cities and towns. The US Census Bureau reports that Massachusetts is the most Irish state in the USA, with 23.7 percent of all residents claiming Irish ancestry. That's over 1.5 million people in a state with 6.5 million residents. Here are the twenty-one most Irish cities and towns in Massachusetts.

47.5 % Scituate	43.4 % Weymouth
46.5 % Braintree	43.3 % Hingham
45.8 % Hull	43.0 % Walpole
45.6 % Marshfield	42.2 % Holbrook
44.9 % Avon	41.4 % Duxbury
44.9 % Pembroke	41.2 % Norwell
44.6 % Milton	40.8 % Hanson
44.5 % Abington	38.7 % Halifax
44.3 % Whitman	38.7 % West Newbury
44.2 % Hanover	38.4 % Westwood

documentary of the Charlestown Irish before the memories of that heritage slipped away entirely. They engaged filmmaker Maureen McNamara and writer Dan Casey to make a one-hour video called *The Green Square Mile*, which charts the illustrious Irish community from the 1820s to 2006, when the film was released.

In recent years, young Charlestown residents Sean Boyle and Caitlin Sullivan have reinvigorated local Irish traditions by forming the Townie Association and bringing back the Charlestown to Charlestown program, which ran from 1982 to 1998 before fading away. Twinned with Charlestown in County Mayo, the program elects an honorary mayor from the neighborhood, who then travels to Ireland to participate in various activities, including the Rose of Tralee pageantry. Boyle is also involved in the Bunker Hill Day parade as a way of keeping Charlestown rooted in its history.

Recasting the Boston Irish

As the narrative shifts away from politics and religion, there has been a recasting of the Boston Irish persona, led by writers, musicians, and filmmakers. In general fiction, Irish-born Áine Greaney's novel *Dance Lessons* examines dynamics between Irish immigrants and Americans in Boston over the last quarter century. J. Courtney Sullivan's novel *Maine* traces three generations of the Kelleher women, a Boston Irish family trying to find its way. J. G. Hayes depicts Irish-American gays living in South Boston in his short story collection *This Thing Called Courage*. James Redfearn's novel *The Rising at Roxbury Crossing* revisits the 1919 Boston Police strike as seen through the eyes of Irish cops.

In nonfiction, Michael Patrick MacDonald's now classic book, *All Souls: A Family Story from Southie*, lovingly depicts his accordion-playing single mother and her eleven children growing up in the Old Colony housing project in South Boston. It is a brilliant treatise of how working-class ethnic families are marginalized and exploited by law enforcement, media, and local thugs. In a similar vein, Irish Micky Ward's memoir, *A Warrior's Heart*, tells the gritty story of the journeyman boxer's life in Lowell, Massachusetts, where drugs, family squabbles, and low expectations threatened to derail Ward's dream of being a world-class athlete.

But it is crime literature—fiction and nonfiction—that largely depicts the Boston Irish today. Following in the footsteps of the late crime novelist George V. Higgins, writers like Dennis Lehane, Chuck Hogan, Casey Sherman, and Brian Wallace have explored the gritty underside of Boston Irish neighborhoods, revealing a sordid tale of gangsters, drug trafficking, child abuse, and family dysfunction. A cottage industry of books about South Boston crime lord James "Whitey" Bulger continues to thrive, and there has been renewed interest in Irish-American gang wars from the 1960s, along with bank robberies, gun running, gambling, and more.

As an outgrowth of this literature, Hollywood has discovered the Boston Irish, dramatizing the dark side of the community, not unlike how Italians were depicted through several decades of Mafia movies. Hollywood had toyed around with the Boston Irish genre in earlier decades, producing such classics as *The Great John L.*, which portrayed Boston boxer John L. Sullivan, produced by Bing Crosby in 1945; John Ford's film of Edwin O'Connor's *The Last Hurrah* in 1958, a profile of James Michael Curley starring Spencer Tracy; Higgins's *The Friends of Eddie Coyle* in 1973, starring Robert Mitchum; and *The Verdict* in 1982, starring Paul Newman.

The new generation of films has used South Boston, Charlestown, Dorchester, and ethnic enclaves such as Lowell to examine working-class angst and dreams of redemption, cops and robbers, lovable rogues, and inner city antics. *Blown Away, Good Will Hunting, Monument Avenue, The Boondock Saints, The Departed, Gone Baby Gone, The Town, Mystic River,* and *The Fighter* are all recent films that have shaped, for better and worse, a distinctive Irish persona that is both exaggerated and occasionally recognizable.

Beyond Hollywood, academic research by Professor Rob Savage at Boston College and Peter Flynn, founder of the Boston Irish Film Festival, presents a more nuanced investigation of how Irish and Irish-American themes and personas have evolved in film both in Ireland and in Boston. In theater, local playwrights at the Huntington Theatre Company present a dramatic counter-point to Hollywood. Irish-born Ronan Noone explores the outsider, immigrant perspective of living in America; David Lindsey-Abaire looks at the tensions of class, success, and neighborhood loyalty in his native town of South Boston, while Kirsten Greenidge captures the complex dynamics between Irish and black families learning to live side by side in twentieth-century Boston.

There was a time when Irish music was a mainstay of vaudeville, Broad-way, and film soundtracks, in the first half of the twentieth century, and artists with Boston roots—from song and dance man George M. Cohan to composer Jimmy McHugh—played a role. But eventually other musical forms, espe-cially African-American and Latin music, surpassed Irish music in America's popular imagination, and it became secondary. Occasionally a Boston Irish band still hits the big time, like the Dropkick Murphys, a punk rock band with an Irish flair formed in Quincy in 1995. Led by singer/bassist Ken Casey, the Dropkicks exude the scrappy, sentimental, hard-driving Boston Irish that came out of neighborhoods, straddling both traditional and progressive sentiments. The band scored a hit with its song "I'm Shipping Up to Boston," which was featured in Martin Scorsese's film *The Departed*. The song has become Boston's unofficial anthem at Red Sox, Bruins, and Celtics games.

Traditional Irish music, though still a minor genre of popular culture, gets a contemporary recasting in Boston, thanks to Irish-born radio personality Brian O'Donovan, host of the popular weekly show *A Celtic Sojourn* on WGBH-FM. O'Donovan has broadened the region's appreciation of Irish music by placing it in a larger context that includes roots music, country-western, folk, and world music. His holiday show, "A Christmas Celtic Sojourn," captures the timeless quality that music brings to memory, pageantry, and tradition, and his live music series at the Burren Pub in Davis Square brings audiences up close with some of the most accomplished musicians now performing.

Jazz pianist Paul Sullivan puts an exciting new twist on Irish traditional music with his album *Irish Soul*. Sullivan, who grew up in Saint Gregory's Parish in Dorchester and won a Grammy for his work with the Paul Winter Consort, blends the Irish melodies he heard growing up as a child with the depth and technical skill he's accrued as a career musician playing in concert halls around the world. He elevates songs such as "Danny Boy," which has been unduly exploited from vaudeville circuits to karaoke bars, while reintroducing underappreciated Gaelic tunes such as "Spirit Seeking Light and Beauty." It is this process of recasting traditional Irish melodies in a contemporary light that broadens the appeal of the music over time.

From the minstrel and vaudeville eras to the present day, Boston continues to be a mecca for Irish dance. Teachers like Rita O'Shea of Galway, who has been teaching Irish step dancing in greater Boston since the 1960s, have created a solid network of Irish dance academies throughout the area that teach students the fine art of dance. At least twenty-five of O'Shea's students have gone on to open studios of their own, a testament to her teaching skills and her ability to instill passion for dance.

O'Shea, Michael Smith, Liam Harney, and others were the reason why Boston was selected to host the World Irish Dancing Championships in March 2013, attracting seven thousand champion dancers from around the world. New England has its share of world champions, such as Harney, who won the coveted trophy in 1984 and again in 1987. Harney, who now runs his own dance academy in Walpole, passed the baton to one of his young students, Melissa McCarthy, who won the All Ireland Championship title in 2012.

In academics, Irish studies programs at Boston College, Stonehill

PHOTO BY HARRINGTON

Irish step dancer Melissa McCarthy won the World Irish Dancing Championships in 2012.

College, UMass/Boston, Harvard University, and other schools continue to explore Irish history, politics, and literature. And recently Boston University has launched a new Institute for the Study of Irish Culture that advances scholarship in history, politics, religion, literature, music, and the arts. The Institute offers courses on the Kennedys and the Boston Irish, as well as on Irish poetry, film, and theater. Among the faculty is Professor Carrie Preston, who has done important research on the connection between William Butler Yeats and Japanese Noh theater.

Trading with Ireland

Trade relations between Massachusetts and Ireland have been important since the 1950s, when Sean Lemass, Ireland's minister of commerce, began seeking investment opportunities. The Aer Lingus route between Boston and Dublin, which launched in October 1958, opened up business relations between the two cities, and President Kennedy's 1963 trip to Ireland ushered in a new era of trade and commerce. In the 1980s, Boston mayor Ray Flynn launched the Boston Ireland Ventures, which twinned Boston with the city of Derry/Londonderry in Northern Ireland. Economic opportunity in Northern Ireland became a dividend of the peace treaty.

In recent years, Senate president Therese Murray has been at the forefront of creating partnerships between Massachusetts and Ireland and Northern Ireland, involving government, academia, and business leaders. In 2011 she helped create the Northern Ireland Massachusetts Connection, initiating research partnerships between universities, encouraging Irish companies to relocate to Massachusetts, and strengthening trade between the countries.

Massachusetts governor Deval Patrick, the state's first African-American governor, has also indicated that he has Irish roots going back to his great-grandmother in Kentucky. In May 2013 Patrick joined Senate president Murray on a trade mission to Ireland, attending a Life Sciences Trade Summit and meeting with Ireland's prime minister, Enda Kenny.

In 2008 the *Irish Echo* newspaper initiated an annual Golden Bridges event in Boston that connects the city's business community with leaders from Derry and Donegal in Northern Ireland. Local leaders of this effort include state representatives Martin Walsh and Eugene O'Flaherty and Boston business leader David Greaney. The Boston Irish Business Association, led by president A. J.

Gerritson, has developed strong partnerships with some of the leading Irish companies seeking to do business in Massachusetts.

In 2012, Ireland was Massachusetts's fourteenth largest export partner, shipping more than $509 million in goods and services to Ireland. Massachusetts is Ireland's sixth largest import partner, importing over $1.2 billion worth of goods and services from Ireland last year.

Ireland's Nativists and the Diaspora

The issue of who is Irish and who is not has become more complex in Ireland since the 1990s, when immigrants from countries like Nigeria, Poland, Romania, and China began settling there. Though generally well received by a majority of Irish, many new immigrants endure hostility, violence, and racist comments on a daily basis. There have been a few efforts to promote a White Only Ireland amid charges that immigrants bring disease, crime, and lawlessness from abroad. Curiously, these are the same charges the Irish faced in nineteenth-century Boston.

Irish begrudgery and intolerance raise the uneasy question of whether Ireland is too parochial for its own good. It's a discussion that's taking place in Ireland itself and throughout the Diaspora, as concerned citizens try to grapple with a sensitive topic: Has an inherent narrow-mindedness made Ireland a backward nation of begrudgers? Many Irish expatriates who emigrated because of economic conditions have been asking for the right to vote in Ireland's elections, in hopes that Ireland's political malaise and corruption can be corrected by a broader Irish voting population.

The Internet age has revealed a subset of vigilantes in Ireland who zealously monitor a relatively minor issue: who deserves to be called Irish and who doesn't. They believe that only people born in Ireland can be referred to as Irish, and there must be no hyphenated-Irish usage of any form. These staunch guardians are like nineteenth-century Boston nativists who insisted that you couldn't be an American unless you were born here or had Puritan roots. Their begrudging invective is aimed at the Irish Diaspora in England, Australia, Canada, and the United States. Their favorite insult is Plastic Paddy, a term that originated in Britain in the 1980s to describe the thousands of first- and second-generation English who returned to Ireland looking for their family connections. Such a harsh indictment of people connecting in a sincere way to

President Barack Obama greeted over one million people at College Green, Dublin, on his brief visit to Ireland in 2011.

their Irish ancestry seems a hypocritical stance to take, since a prevailing Irish trait throughout history is an insistence on planting the Irish flag wherever they go, proclaiming their Irishness, holding on to their customs, and encouraging their children and grandchildren to do the same. Now they are criticizing Diasporans for embracing this trait?

There is a largesse about people of all nationalities who retain affection for the land of their ancestors, and it is a common feature of the American perspective, applicable not just to Irish but to hundreds of ethnic groups in America. There is something small-minded about Irish people who prefer to mock this impulse rather than celebrate it.

In a broad sense, who is Irish today has more to do with sensibility than birthplace or geography. As Ireland's former president Mary Robinson noted, "Irishness is not simply territorial."

That became apparent in 2011 when President Barack Obama visited Ireland on his way to the G-8 summit in France. During the 2008 presidential campaign, genealogists had discovered Obama had distant Irish connections on the side of his mother, Ann Dunham. It turns out President Obama's great-great-great-grandfather, Falmouth Kearney, emigrated from Moneygall, County Offaly, and settled in Ohio. Obama was rightfully tongue-in-cheek about the scant Irish connection, but the people of Ireland came out by the hundreds of thousands when he arrived for a twenty-four-hour stopover, as part of a European visit that included stops in England, France, and Poland.

In a speech in Dublin before one million people, President Obama said,

> *Falmouth Kearney . . . left during the Great Hunger, as so many Irish did, to seek a new life in the New World. He traveled by ship to New York, where he entered himself into the records as a laborer. He married an American girl from Ohio. They settled in the Midwest. They started a family. It's a familiar story because it's one lived and cherished by Americans of all backgrounds. It's integral to our national identity. It's who we are, a nation of immigrants from all around the world.*

President Obama returned to Northern Ireland in June 2013 to attend the G-8 summit in Belfast, strengthening his commitment to the peace process and the trade partnerships between American and Northern Ireland companies.

CHAPTER SIXTEEN

The Late Great Irish Generation

I N NOVEMBER 2010 state senate president Therese Murray presided at the opening of a photography exhibit called *To Love Two Countries: Ireland's Greatest Generation in America* at the Massachusetts State House. Sponsored by the Irish Arts Center in New York City, the exhibit profiled some thirty-six Irish emigrants who had settled in Massachusetts, Rhode Island, and Connecticut between the 1920s and 1950s, from all counties in Ireland, and from all walks of life. In the exhibit's program book, award-winning photographer John Minihan writes of being moved as he got to know this brave generation of immigrants who had left home not knowing if they would ever return:

> *They posed for me in their homes with artifacts of identity behind them: snapshots of loved ones, grandchildren in Irish dance costumes, sons and daughters in US Military uniforms taking pride next to a picture of the Blessed Mother holding the baby Jesus. In every home there are reminders of who they are and where they come from.*

The Irish depicted in the exhibit are part of a grand tradition—a legacy really—that stretches back to the early days of the Irish in Boston. Like their forefathers of ten generations past, these Irish immigrants loved two countries, never forsaking one for the other. They remained devout Catholics, standing by the Church even when it faltered. They proved their patriotism to the United States by joining the military, fighting in wars not of their making. They raised large families and kept traditions alive that were lovingly brought over from the old country. They sent money home to Ireland and brought their siblings to join them. They taught their children and grandchildren to love Ireland and America with an equal heart.

Many of those characteristics of Irish immigrants have shifted in the twenty-first century: The traditional values that were once so important to the Irish are in flux. The Catholic Church no longer holds the authority it once did. Patriotism is viewed cynically in some quarters and not seen as necessary to prove one's merits as a newcomer. Irish families are smaller and more mobile than before. Irish social and fraternal clubs have aging memberships and lack marketing expertise to reach younger generations. The children and grandchildren of this generation have moved to the leafy suburbs, rightly assimilating into American life.

The immigrants profiled in *To Love Two Countries* flew the Irish flag with pride in Boston for half a century or more, but their generation's work is near completion. Many of Boston's tireless Irish community leaders have passed away in recent years: Irish-born Michael Cummings of Milton, John Curran of Belmont, and Larry Reynolds of Waltham, along with American-born Dave Burke of Lawrence, Joe Joyce of Jamaica Plain, Rita O'Connell of Duxbury, and Kathleen Lawlor of Milton. Losing them has affected the vigor and vibrancy of Boston's Irish community, making it more faded, less green.

In politics the Last Hurrah of the Boston Irish had already begun a decade earlier, with the death of Congressman Thomas "Tip" O'Neill of Cambridge in 1994, followed by Congressman Joe Moakley of South Boston in 2001 and Boston mayor Kevin White in 2012. Congressman Joe Kennedy II quit politics to run a successful nonprofit that provides heating oil to low-income families. Boston mayor and Vatican ambassador Ray Flynn retired from politics and became involved in Catholic issues; Congressman Brian Donnelly left politics and moved out of the limelight; state senate president Bill Bulger served as president of the University of Massachusetts, and then settled into retirement. State senator Jack Hart of South Boston left politics to earn a better living for his young family. The emergence of a new generation of Irish Americans has slowed, with only Joseph Kennedy III, recently elected as US congressman for the Fourth District, stepping onto the national stage from Massachusetts.

The Vanished Immigrant

"They're all gone," Irish publican Peter Nash told *Boston Globe* reporter Kevin Cullen in 2008, for Cullen's article "The Fading of the Green." "They've all gone home." Nash, from County Kerry, was talking about the Irish immigrants who swelled his once popular Irish pub on Dorchester Avenue—the construction workers, nurses, office and retail workers who packed the joint for televised Irish football games and on weekends always with ready cash in hand to buy a round.

But his clientele left, drifted away, or moved back to Ireland, and Nash sold the property to a Vietnamese-American couple who opened an Asian fusion restaurant called Van Shabu & Bar that is doing well. The changeover reflected the evolution of a neighborhood, the decline of one ethnic group and the rise of another, the ebb and flow of life in an urban city, in America itself.

The steady demise of Boston's Irish immigrant community came as a mild surprise to many, since Irish immigrants had been a ubiquitous presence from the earliest days of the Bay Colony. Even as fluctuations in US immigration laws and Ireland's shifting economy and political situation affected immigration in the twentieth century, the Irish continued to settle in Boston regularly, even if they had to do so illegally.

The twenty-first century has been a different story. After September 11, 2001, it became tougher for the Irish to just show up at Logan International Airport on a ninety-day visitor visa—as they had done since the 1970s—then disappear into an Irish enclave in Dorchester, Quincy, or Brighton when the visa expired. Heightened Homeland Security and law enforcement made it nearly impossible for the illegal Irish to return home for a holiday, a wedding, or a funeral, and they risked deportation with any minor traffic accident or infraction. Once caught overstaying their visas, the Irish were denied entry back to the States for up to a decade. An end to Boston's mega construction projects—the Central Artery Project and the Boston Harbor cleanup—also discouraged Irish workers from counting on Boston for steady work, and they began heading to Canada or Australia or staying home in Ireland.

The Celtic Tiger

There was a brief period when a generation of new Irish entering the workforce could actually stay in Ireland to work, thanks to the Celtic Tiger, an economic boom that lasted from about 1997 to 2007. In fact, Irish who had emigrated in earlier generations were being enticed by the strong economy and job growth to return home, including many Irish expatriates living in Boston. In 2005 there were more Americans—forty-three hundred—emigrating to Ireland than the seventeen hundred Irish who emigrated to the United States, according to FAS, Ireland's training and employment agency.

But the Celtic Tiger was not the king of the financial jungle, and it became yet another Celtic myth in Ireland's history. Irish banking and financial titans, self-described masters of the universe, were living large on other people's money, promising a pot of gold, then trying to slip out the door when the debt was due. They were flimflam artists, full of blarney and bluster. In Boston, Anglo Irish Bank executives had a "reputation for lavishly entertaining clients," dining at Radius and other fancy restaurants, "flying Boston clients by private jet to some of Ireland's better-known courses," a *Boston Globe* story notes.

A 2010 National Public Radio report depicted the country's mood: "The Irish are spitting with rage after discovering that the final costs of bailing out their errant banks is potentially $69 billion."

Today, Ireland struggles with double-digit unemployment, a massive debt to the European Union and international finance agencies, and an outraged and discouraged population. The age-old pattern of Irish immigration continues into the twenty-first century, and leaving Ireland remains a primary option of young people just coming into the workforce. But strict immigration laws prevent them from settling in the United States; instead they're looking to England, Canada, and Australia as places to settle, start a new life, as previous generations did before them.

In the United States, Ciaran Staunton, Bart Murphy, Bruce Morrison, and other members of the Irish Lobby for Immigration Reform have put in place a grassroots campaign to ensure that the Irish get a fair share of visas in the next round of immigration reform.

Lion of the Senate

Someone they'll miss in the immigration battles in Washington is Senator Edward M. Kennedy, a champion of Irish causes for all of his career, and a formidable ally to have had on your side in the nation's capital. Kennedy's death of brain cancer in August 2009 closed one more chapter in the Boston

Irish annals, marking a changing of the guard, the official end of the Camelot era, the last of the Last Hurrahs.

As Massachusetts's senator for forty-seven years, Kennedy had an extraordinary career, and at times a troubled and troubling life. He nearly squandered himself to misery and mishaps, but in the end he returned to the core values that helped his family endure their many tragedies, values that defined the Boston Irish community for over two centuries.

"I grew up in a large Irish Catholic family as the youngest of nine children," he once wrote. "By their words, their actions, and their love, our parents instilled in all of us the importance of the ties that bind us together—our faith, our family, and our love of this great country."

Born in 1932, Ted Kennedy as the youngest of the nine children was overshadowed early by his exceptional and ambitious brothers, Joe, John, and Bobby, and by his talented and beautiful sisters, Rose, Kathleen, Eunice, Patricia, and Jean. Only two generations removed from struggling immigrant families trying to make their way in East Boston and the North End, he grew up a privileged, pampered child, and he took it for granted, attending the best schools and vacationing around the world at an early age, living in Boston, New York, Cape Cod, Palm Beach, and London. His older siblings were blazing the path that he could readily step onto whenever the time was right, so he was cavalier about his life. After graduating from Harvard, he won his first political seat as a US senator from Massachusetts, not on the basis of his experience or character but because of his name.

"If your name was simply Edward Moore instead of Edward Moore Kennedy," his opponent Edward McCormack told him during a televised debate, "your candidacy would be a joke."

But throughout his life and illustrious career as a US senator, Ted Kennedy proved to his adversaries, and to himself, that he was no joke. He took a long and winding road, peppered with poor judgment and an excessive lifestyle. He endured the indelible sadness of having four siblings—Joe, John, Kathleen, and Bobby—die in the most tragic fashion before he turned forty. When it became clear to him that he would never be president of the United States, Kennedy pulled himself together and devoted the final three decades of his career to being the best US senator he could possibly be. He vigorously pursued the social causes that were dear to him: health care reform; civil rights for minorities, women, gays, and the disabled; protecting jobs and economic opportunity for working people; human rights around the world; and immigration reform here in America.

History will show that Ted Kennedy was instrumental in helping to end the Troubles in Northern Ireland, even though his initial efforts were checkered. He entered the fray in 1970, when peaceful protests in Northern Ireland were met with police violence from authorities. In October 1971 he called for withdrawal of British troops from Northern Ireland and the reunification of the thirty-two counties, saying that "Ulster is becoming Britain's

Senator Edward M. Kennedy

Vietnam." After he was roundly criticized by the British and Irish governments, Kennedy stepped back and took a more constrained, nuanced approach. Some Irish-American activists accused him of falling in line with British Government propaganda that violence was the cause of the Troubles, instead of failed British policies and poor governance. But Kennedy stayed the course and remained outspoken through the hunger strikes of the 1980s and into the 1990s, when the election of President Bill Clinton gave new hope to solving the Troubles.

Kennedy was approached by Sinn Fein emissaries about a possible end to the violence. Along with his sister Jean Kennedy Smith, then the US ambassador to Ireland, he believed the entreaties were legitimate. Senator Kennedy enlisted his foreign policy advisor, Trina Vargo, and her former colleague Nancy Soderberg, chief of staff of Clinton's national security team, to help secure a visa for Sinn Fein leader Gerry Adams to visit the United States. That visit opened the doors to a wider dialogue and negotiation about a cease-fire and enabled President Clinton and special envoy George Mitchell to jump-start, then solidify, the peace process.

Just as he reached across the aisle in Congress, Senator Kennedy reached across the community divide in Northern Ireland to bring everyone into the conversation for peace. He picked up the phone frequently to ensure that

party leaders in Northern Ireland
stayed the course in their search
for a lasting resolution. In January
1998 Kennedy traveled to Northern Ireland to speak directly to the
nationalists and unionists. Vargo
traveled with Kennedy and his wife
Vicki on that trip, and she recalled
that he "went out of his way to meet
with all and visit both communities
. . . both in the Nationalist Bogside
where he was a hero and even in
the Unionist Fountain and Ebring-
ton where he was welcomed for his

> The Edward M. Kennedy Institute for
> the United States Senate, slated to open
> right next to the John F. Kennedy Library
> in Dorchester, is dedicated to educating
> the public about the American system
> of government and inspiring the next
> generation of citizens and leaders to
> participate in public service. The Institute
> will portray Senator Kennedy's life and
> his work on behalf of immigrants and
> the peace process in Northern Ireland, as
> well as broader issues such as health care
> reform and human rights. emkinstitute.org

gesture of coming to them and making clear his goal was a Northern Ireland
where both communities flourished." In April 1998 the Northern Ireland Peace
Agreement was signed, ending decades of fighting and putting in place a political structure for the opposing sides to govern together. Vargo later went on to
create the nonpartisan US-Ireland Alliance and George J. Mitchell program to
send future American leaders to study in Ireland and Northern Ireland.

Kennedy also led the charge on immigration reform during his career.
In 1965, along with his brother, Senator Robert Kennedy, he helped craft the
Immigration Act, which ended the system of national quotas that favored
European countries and opened up immigration to people from around the
world. Many Irish disapproved of the shift in American policy because it meant
Europe would have to share coveted visas with a larger pool of nations from
South America and Asia. Kennedy continued to fight for immigration reform
through his life and came close in 2007 to pushing through a bill with Republican senator John McCain. He wasn't able to complete the task, and his death
left it up to a different generation of leaders to solve the aching problem of illegal and stunted immigration to the United States.

The Last Hurrah?

There have been many "Last Hurrahs" in the story of the Boston Irish, perhaps
a sign of the community's durability, or the wishful thinking of adversaries. The

Irish were deemed a scattered and inconsequential community through much of the eighteenth century, marginalized by the dominant Puritan ethos, relegated to servitude with occasional outbursts of rebellion and war-time heroics.

In the nineteenth century, new generations of Irish arrived traumatized, impoverished, and seemingly ill-equipped to make a contribution to a bustling Boston. They were regarded as more of a threat than a promise for a city seeking a certain caliber of citizenry. Their shortcomings were exaggerated and their downfall was predicted by nativists, preachers, and politicians alike. Even after the Irish fought in the Civil War, returning veterans still picked up local newspapers and read "No Irish Need Apply" advertisements into the 1870s. Successive generations of Bostonians devised laws to exclude the Irish, or at least to slow them down.

By sheer tenacity—and overwhelming numbers—the Irish hit their stride in the twentieth century, finally gaining parity, some would say the upper hand, in terms of political, social, economic, and educational opportunities. It is sometimes referred to as the Boston Irish Century, since an Irish ethos pervaded so many aspects of the city's life. Indeed, that designation almost seemed preordained; in 1906 journalist Herb Classon wrote that "Boston, not Dublin or Belfast, is now the greatest Irish city in the world."

Classon was exaggerating, of course, but Boston came to be known as the capital of Irish America, a place that wore its Irishness on its sleeves, that relished its rascals and rogues, that obeyed its priests and politicians, that produced great athletes, singers and dancers, writers, educators, and war heroes. In this era, the Irish helped to accentuate the city's attributes that had never fully developed under the Puritan regimes of earlier times: empathy and loyalty, community service and volunteerism, plus humor and optimism.

Boston's Irish community has certainly produced a pantheon of political leaders who commanded their troops with an iron fist and occasionally a velvet glove. Many of them verged on caricature, full of blarney and song mixed with flashes of temper and vows of revenge, tribal in nature, vengeful when crossed. The pride of the pack—the Kennedys, Tip O'Neill, John McCormack, and Joe Moakley—rose above their surroundings and moved onto the national stage, where they helped shaped the nation itself. Ray Flynn, Brian Donnelly, and Joe Kennedy II played an important national role in rallying the American Irish Diaspora behind Irish causes like immigration reform and peace and justice in Northern Ireland. And there were and are hundreds of others who made their mark in more modest but still meaningful ways, and their names are scattered around the city as milestones to their influence—Logan Airport, Morrissey Boulevard, Tobin Bridge, and Callaghan Tunnel.

Not everyone has been enthralled with the Boston Irish. There have been recurring charges of corruption, patronage, and nepotism against reigning politicians in various decades. Others objected to the Irish clannishness that often inspired intolerance for others, especially blacks, Italians, Jews, and other groups who lived in proximity to Irish enclaves. The fatal affliction of Irish Alzheimer's—forgetting everything but the grudges—has been endemic among certain locals. More recently, Catholic Church officials, many of them with Irish surnames, have been castigated for behaving so sanctimoniously while their most innocent parishioners were abused behind closed doors.

The Boston Irish story in the twenty-first century is a work in progress. It is unlikely that new waves of Irish immigrants will ever have enough cachet to influence an entire city as their predecessors did in earlier generations. It is doubtful that the Boston Irish will ever again wield the pervasive political power they enjoyed throughout the twentieth century. And it is unlikely that the Irish will find another institution—like the Catholic Church—that it could dominate for so many decades.

But in other arenas, the Boston Irish spirit flourishes, such as in the ranks of soldiers, policemen, firemen, and first responders who are unwavering and courageous in the line of duty. Irish-American soldiers have won more Medals of Honor than any other ethnic group in the military, with neighborhoods like South Boston having a disproportionate number of war heroes. Local leaders like Tommy Nee, a US Marine, have worked tirelessly to commemorate the Vietnam Veterans from South Boston and Dorchester who made the ultimate sacrifice for their country.

On the municipal front, there has always been a robust tradition of serving in the city's police and fire departments that runs through generations of Boston Irish families, many of whom were at the scene of the Boston Marathon bombings in April 2013. Not all of them were Irish, of course, but all of them were tough, brave, and compassionate as they put their lives on the line to save the victims and track down the killers.

In the days after the bombing, Kevin Cullen of the *Boston Globe* published a column entitled "The Names I'll Remember," in which he wrote, "I want them [the bombers] to vanish from my memory bank, which is too busy trying to remember the names that matter. I want to remember the names of O'Brien and other firefighters from Engine 7 . . . and Lieutenant Joe Roache from Ladder 15 . . . Jimmy Hooley and his EMTs and paramedics . . . Watertown cops Joe Reynolds and Sergeant John MacLellan . . . MBTA police officer Dick Donohue . . . Boston police officer Ricky Moriarty . . . FBI agent John Foley . . . I want to remember all those names. And I want to see Janey Richard dance again."

Jane Richard was a seven-year-old Irish step dancer from Dorchester, who lost her left leg in the bombing. Her eight-year-old brother Martin William Richard was killed at the finish line. Boston's Irish dancing community immediately held a fund-raiser in support of the Richard family, and the effort was taken up by Irish dance groups across the country. Twenty-nine-year-old Krystle Campbell died at the finish line waiting for her boyfriend to finish. Krystle was a regular at the Burren Pub in Davis Square, and the owner, musician Tommy McCarthy, has dedicated one of his songs, "Listen I Know," to raise money for the family. Richard Donohue, a transit policeman, was wounded at the scene of the shoot-out in Watertown the night the bombers were tracked down. His femoral artery was shattered and he went into cardiac arrest from loss of blood. He has been praised for his bravery and dedication in the line of duty.

Bravery and dedication—these traits are universal but also consistent with the Boston Irish persona dating back to colonial times and continuing through the centuries. The Boston Irish could always be relied upon to step forward and be counted, to never walk away from a fight, to earn their rightful place in a city that wasn't entirely happy to see them arrive.

In retrospect, the Boston Irish experience harkens back to an age-old narrative, of strangers perpetually arriving from somewhere else, seeking shelter from the storm, looking for a place to call home. That is the Puritan narrative too, and the story of all immigrant, indigenous, and enslaved peoples who have made Boston their home.

Perhaps because of his own family's odyssey from Ireland to Boston, President Kennedy understood these truths to be self-evident: the journey is as important as the arrival, what you become matters more than where you come from, and each generation must build upon the work of previous generations.

History will judge whether future generations of Boston Irish heed the sentiments President Kennedy voiced in his inaugural speech in January 1961, when he said to his fellow Americans, to this nation of immigrants, "So let us begin anew. . . . With a good conscience our only sure reward, with history the final judge of our deeds, let us go forth to lead the land we love."

Bibliography/Notes

Chapter One

Adams, James Truslow. *Provincial Society, 1690–1763*. Vol. 3 of *A History of American Life*. Edited by Arthur M. Schlesinger and Dixon Ryan Fox. New York: Macmillan, 1927.

Barker, Charles A. *American Convictions: Cycles of Public Thought, 1600–1850*. Philadelphia: J. B. Lippincott, 1970.

Boston Registry Department. Selectmen's Minutes. City documents no. 77 (August 9 and September 15, 1736) and no. 87 (December 3, 1739, and February 11, 1740). In *Records Relating to the Early History of Boston*, vol. 15. Boston: Rockwell and Churchill, 1886.

Boston Gazette, July 13, 1742.

Boston News-Letter, May 8, 1704; September 6, 1714; August 2, 1750.

Burke, Charles T. *A History of the Charitable Irish Society*. Boston: Charitable Irish Society, 1973.

Cullen, James Bernard. *The Story of the Irish in Boston*. Boston: J. B. Cullen, 1889.

Doherty, J. E., and D. J. Hickey. *A Chronology of Irish History Since 1500*. Savage, MD: Barnes and Noble, 1990.

Donovan, George Francis. *The Pre-Revolutionary Irish in Massachusetts, 1620–1775*. Menasha, WI: George Banta, 1932.

Dunn, Richard S. *Sugar and Slaves: The Rise of the Planter Class in the English West Indies, 1624–1713*. New York: W. W. Norton, 1972.

Erikson, Kai T. *Wayward Puritans: A Study in the Sociology of Deviance*. New York: Wiley, 1966.

Fender, Stephen. *American Literature in Context: 1620–1830*. New York: Methuen, 1983.

Ford, Henry Jones. *The Scotch-Irish in America*. Princeton, NJ: Princeton University Press, 1915.

Howe, M. A. DeWolfe. *Boston Common: Scenes from Four Centuries*. Boston: Riverside Press, 1910.

Jennings, Francis. *The Invasion of America: Indians, Colonialism, and the Cant of Conquest*. New York: W. W. Norton, 1975.

Johnson, Harriett E. *The Early History of the Arlington Street Church*. Boston: Arlington Street Church, 1937.

Kenny, Kevin. *The American Irish: A History*. Boston: Longman, 2000.

Lepore, Jill. *The Name of War: King Philip's War and the Origins of American Identity*. New York: Alfred A. Knopf, 1998.

Leyburn, James G. *The Scotch-Irish: A Social History*. Chapel Hill: University of North Carolina Press, 1962.

Linebaugh, Peter. *The London Hanged: Crime and Civil Society in the Eighteenth Century*. New York: Cambridge University Press, 1992.

Lucey, Charles. *Harp and Sword, 1776: The Irish in the American Revolution*. Washington, DC: Charles Lucey, 1976.

McDonnell, Frances. *Emigrants from Ireland to America, 1735–1743*. Baltimore: Genealogical Publishing, 1992.

Meltsner, Heli. *The Poorhouses of Massachusetts: A Cultural and Architectural History*. Jefferson, NC: McFarland, 2012.

Miller, Perry. *Errand into the Wilderness*. Cambridge, MA: Belknap Press of Harvard University Press, 1956.

Moorhead, Rev. John. "Marriages Performed at Church of Irish Presbyterian Strangers." 1730–70. Harvard University Divinity School.

Morgan, Edmund S. *The Puritan Family: Religion and Domestic Relations in Seventeenth-Century New England*. Rev. ed. New York: Harper & Row, 1966.

Murdock, Kenneth B. *Literature and Theology in Colonial New England*. Cambridge, MA: Harvard University Press, 1949.

Nellis, Eric, and Anne Decker Cecere, eds. *The Eighteenth-Century Records of the Boston Overseers of the Poor*. Boston: Colonial Society of Massachusetts, 2007.

New England Courant, August 21, 1721; January 25, 1725.

New England Weekly Journal, November 6, 1727; March 31, 1729; September 4, 1732; November 22, 1737; January 23, February 28, March 17, May 23, June 20, September 26, and November 28, 1738.

O'Connor, Thomas H. *The Irish in New England*. Boston: New England Historic Genealogical Society, 1985.

Quinlin, Michael P. *Finding Your Irish Roots in Massachusetts*. Boston: Boston Irish Tourism Association, 2004.

Records of the Suffolk County Court, 1671–1680. 2 vols. Boston: Colonial Society of America, 1933.

Riley, Arthur J. *Catholicism in New England to 1788*. Washington, DC: Catholic University of America, 1936.

Sellin, J. Thorsten. *Slavery and the Penal System*. New York: Elsevier, 1976.

Simmons, R. C. *The American Colonies: From Settlement to Independence*. New York: David McKay, 1976.

Smith, Abbot Emerson. *Colonists in Bondage: White Servitude and Convict Labor in America, 1607–1776*. Chapel Hill: University of North Carolina Press, 1947.

Sweetser, M. F. *King's Handbook of Boston Harbor*. 1882. Boston: Applewood Books, 1989.

Thomas, Evan. "To Write History for the Masses." Interview by Fred L. Schultz. *Naval History Magazine* 17, no. 3 (June 2003)..

Whitmore, William H. *Notes Concerning Peter Pelham: The Earliest Artist Resident in New England*. Cambridge, MA: John Wilson and Son, 1867.

Winthrop, John. *Winthrop's Conclusions for the Plantation in New England*. Boston: Old South Meeting House, 1894.

Chapter Two

Adams, John. *Diary and Autobiography, 1775–1804*. 4 vols. Cambridge, MA: Harvard University Press, 1961.

Adams, Thomas Boylston. *A New Nation*. Chester, CT: Globe Pequot Press, 1981.

Boston Globe, March 5, 2001.

Boston Registry Department. Selectmen's Minutes. City document no. 42 (October 5, 1769, and January 5, 1775). In *Records Relating to the Early History of Boston*, vol. 23. Boston: Rockwell and Churchill, 1893.

Bruun, Erik, and Jay Crosby, eds. *Living History America: The History of the United States in Documents, Essays, Letters, Songs and Poems*. New York: Tess Press, 1999.

Bucke, Gerald L. "The Irish Contribution to the American Nation." *Eire Society Bulletin*, December 1976.

Cahill, Robert Ellis. *The Irish of Old New England*. Peabody, MA: Chandler-Smith, 1985.

Colonial Society of Massachusetts. *Boston Prints and Printmakers, 1670–1777*. Boston: The Society, 1973.

Copley, John Singleton. Letter to Henry Pelham, August 1775. In *Letters & Papers of John Singleton Copley and Henry Pelham, 1739–1776*. Boston: Massachusetts Historical Society, 1914.

Chastellux, François Jean, Marquis de. *Travels in North America in the Years 1780, 1781 and 1782*. Edited by Howard C. Rice. 2 vols. Chapel Hill: University of North Carolina Press, for the Institute of Early American History and Culture, 1963.

Danforth, Mildred E. "The Indomitable Sullivans." *Eire Society Bulletin*, January 1977.

Doyle, David Noel. *Ireland, Irishmen and Revolutionary America, 1760–1820*. Dublin: Mercier Press, 1981.

Draper's Gazette, September 21, 1775.

Fleming, Thomas. *Now We Are Enemies: The Story of Bunker Hill*. 1960. Franklin, TN: American History Press, 2010.

Ford, Henry Jones. *The Scotch-Irish in America*. Princeton, NJ: Princeton University Press, 1915.

Irish Association for Documentation and Information Services. *Ireland and Irishmen in the American War of Independence*. Dublin: Academy Press, 1976.

Jones, E. Alfred. *The Loyalists of Massachusetts: Their Memorials, Petitions and Claims*. London: Saint Catherine Press, 1930.

Maas, David Edward. *The Return of Massachusetts Loyalists*. New York: Garland, 1989.

McCullough, David. *1776*. New York: Simon & Schuster, 2005.

O'Brien, Michael J. "America's Debt to Ireland." *Gaelic American*, June 21, 1919.

————. *A Hidden Phase of American History: Ireland's Part in America's Struggle for Liberty.* 1919. Baltimore: Genealogical Publishing, 1973.

————. *The Irish at Bunker Hill.* New York: Devin-Adair, 1968.

————. "The Kellys, Burkes and Sheas of the Massachusetts Line." *Journal of the American Irish Historical Society* 21 (1922): 107–10.

Pelham, Henry. Letters John Singleton Copley, May 1775. In *Letters & Papers of John Singleton Copley and Henry Pelham, 1739–1776.* Boston: Massachusetts Historical Society , 1914.

Prown, Jules David. *John Singleton Copley.* Cambridge, MA: Harvard University Press, 1966.

Ryan, George E. "The Eire Society Bulletin." *Eire Society Bulletin,* March 1978.

————. "Patrick Carr." *Eire Society Bulletin,* November 1, 1970.

Stark, James H. *The Loyalists of Massachusetts and the Other Side of the American Revolution.* Boston: James H. Stark, 1910.

Thomas, Evan. *John Paul Jones: Sailor, Hero, Father of the American Navy.* New York: Simon & Schuster, 2003.

Washington, George. "Letter to Reverend Francis Adrian Vanderkemp." *Teaching American History,* May 22, 1788.

Whitmore, William H. "The Early Painters and Engravers of New England." *Proceedings of the Massachusetts Historical Society* 9 (1867): 197–216.

Zobel, Hiller B. *The Boston Massacre.* New York: W. W. Norton, 1970.

Chapter Three

Bartlett, John. *Familiar Quotations.* 15th and 125th anniv. ed. Boston: Little, Brown, 1980.

Boston Catholic Directory. Boston: Archdiocese of Boston, 1995.

Callaghan, Ed, and Casey, Dan. *The Green Square Mile: Story of the Charlestown Irish.* Boston: Charlestown Historical Society, 2006.

Catholic Intelligencer, March 23, 1832.

Coyle, Henry, Theodore Mayhew, and Frank S. Hickey. *Our Church, Her Children and Institutions.* 3 vols. Boston: Archdiocese of Boston, 1908.

Crimmins, John D. *St. Patrick's Day: Its Celebration in New York and Other American Places, 1737–1845.* New York: privately printed, 1845.

Cullen, James Bernard. *The Story of the Irish in Boston.* Boston: J. B. Cullen, 1889.

Daly, Marie. Interview by Michael P. Quinlin. Boston, June 26 and December 8, 2003.

Dauwer, Leo P. *I Remember Southie.* Boston: Christopher Publishing House, 1975.

Ellis, John Tracy, and Robert Trisco. *A Guide to American Catholic History.* 2nd ed. Santa Barbara, CA: ABC-Clio, 1982.

Fenwick, Benedict. Letter to Massachusetts General Court, March 1832. Archdiocese of Boston Archives.

Gurney, William J. *A Short History of St. Augustine's Cemetery*. South Boston, 1953.

Jesuit, March 16 and 23 and November 23, 1833.

Mooney, Thomas. *A History of Ireland from Its First Settlement to the Present Time*. Vol. I. Boston: Patrick Donahoe, 1853.

Murray, Thomas. *See* Thomas Murray Family Papers.

O'Connor, Thomas H. *Boston Catholics: A History of the Church and Its People*. Boston: Northeastern University Press, 1998.

———. *South Boston, My Home Town*. Boston: Quinlan Press, 1988.

O'Toole, James M. "Sources for Irish-American History in the Archives of the Archdiocese of Boston." *Eire Society Bulletin*, November 1982.

Pilot, February 19, 1853.

Quincy, John, Jr. *Quincy's Market: A Boston Landmark*. Boston: Northeastern University Press, 2003.

Thomas Murray Family Papers, 1817–1857. John J. Burns Archives, Boston College.

Zinn, Howard. *A People's History of the United States, 1492–Present*. Rev. ed. New York: Harper Perennial, 1995.

Chapter Four

Adams, John Quincy. *Dermot MacMorrogh; or, The Conquest of Ireland*. Columbus, OH: Isaac N. Whiting, 1834.

Bunker Hill Aurora, November 30 and December 12, 21, and 28, 1833; January 18, 1834. Court transcripts.

Catholic Intelligencer, March 23, 1832; November 23, 1833; January 18, 1834.

Ellis, John Tracy. *The Pilot: 1829–1979*. Boston: Archdiocese of Boston, 1979.

Grimes, Robert R. *How Shall We Sing in a Foreign Land?* South Bend, IN: University of Notre Dame Press, 1996.

Grund, Francis J. *The Americans in Their Moral, Social, and Political Relations*. 2 vols. London: Longmans, 1837.

Handlin, Oscar. *Boston's Immigrants, 1790–1880: A Study in Acculturation*. Cambridge, MA: Harvard University Press, 1941.

Johnson, Tyler V. *Devotion to the Adopted Country: U.S. Immigrant Volunteers in the Mexican War*. Columbia: University of Missouri Press, 2012.

Jones, Howard Mumford, and Bessie Zatan Jones, eds. *The Many Voices of Boston: A Historical Anthology, 1630–1975*. Boston: Little, Brown, 1975.

Lord, Robert H., John E. Sexton, and Edward T. Harrington. *History of the Archdiocese of Boston*. Vol. 2. New York: Sheed & Ward, 1944.

Schultz, Nancy Lusignan. *Fire and Roses: The Burning of Charlestown Convent, 1834*. Boston: Northeastern University Press, 2000.

Stevens, Peter F. *Hidden History of the Boston Irish: Little-Known Stories from Ireland's "Next Parish Over."* Charleston, SC: History Press, 2008

Tager, Jack. *Boston Riots: Three Centuries of Social Violence.* Boston: Northeastern University Press, 2000.

Walsh, Francis. "The Boston Pilot: A Newspaper for the Irish Immigrant, 1829–1908." Thesis, Boston University, 1968.

Whittier, John Greenleaf. "The Emerald Isle." *Newburyport Free Press,* 1826.

Wolkovich-Valkavicius, William. *Immigrants and Yankees in Nashoba Valley, Massachusetts.* W. Groton, MA: St. James Church, 1981.

Chapter Five

Abbott, Edith. *Historical Aspects of the Immigration Problem: Selected Documents.* Chicago: University of Chicago Press, 1926.

American Signal, May 20 and July 24, 1847.

Boston Daily Bee, January 1, February 18, and May 10, 1847.

Boston Daily Whig, May 25, 1847.

Boston Herald, April 24 and 28, 1851; May 5, 1853.

Boston Medical and Surgical Journal, March 3, 1847.

Boston Society for the Prevention of Pauperism. Annual Report, 1865.

Clark, Henry Grafton, MD. *Typhus Fever: Its History, Nature and Treatment.* Boston: Ticknor, Reed, and Fields, 1850.

Drake, Dan, MD. "The Irish Immigrants' Fever." *Boston Medical and Surgical Journal,* August 27, 1847.

Forbes, H. A. Crosby, and Henry Lee. *Massachusetts Help to Ireland During the Great Famine.* Milton, MA: Captain Robert Bennet Forbes House, 1967.

Forbes, R. B. *An Interesting Memoir of the* Jamestown *Voyage to Ireland.* Boston: J. B. Cullen, 1890.

Loughran, William J. "Calamity off Cohasset." *Eire Society Bulletin,* November 1987.

Lover, Samuel. "War Ship of Peace, an Irish Melody." New York: Firth and Hall, 1847.

Maguire, John Francis, MP. *The Irish in America.* London: Longmans, Green, 1868.

McColgan, John. "Boston 1847: What Really Happened?" *Boston Irish Reporter,* August 1997.

Oldman, Ellen M. "Irish Support of the Abolitionist Movement." *Boston Public Library Quarterly,* 1958.

Pilot, March 16, 1850; February 12, 1859; March 15, 1862; August 29, 1863.

Quinlin, Michael P. "The Boston Medical Society's Response to Typhus Fever During the Irish Famine." Paper delivered at American Committee for Irish Studies conference, Suffolk University, October 1997.

Sullivan, Louis H. *The Autobiography of an Idea.* New York: Press of the American Institute of Architects, 1924.

Upham, J. B., MD. *Records of Maculated Typhus, or Ship Fever.* New York: John F. Trow, Printer, 1852.

Woodham-Smith, Cecil. *The Great Hunger*. New York: Harper & Row, 1963.

———. "Ireland's Hunger, England's Fault?" *Atlantic Monthly*, January 1963.

Chapter Six

Boston Evening Transcript, August 3, 1868.

Boston Herald, April 185l; May 1853.

Clark, Dennis. *Hibernia America: The Irish and Regional Cultures*. Westport, CT: Greenwood Press, 1986.

Coffey, Michael, and Terry Golway. *The Irish in America*. New York: Hyperion, 1997.

Coyle, Henry, Theodore Mayhew, and Frank S. Hickey. *Our Church, Her Children and Institutions*. 3 vols. Boston: Archdiocese of Boston, 1908.

Curran, Michael. *Life of Patrick Collins*. Norwood, MA: Norwood Press, 1906.

Daily Evening Traveller, August 19, 1853.

Garrison, Webb. *Brady's Civil War: A Collection of Memorable Civil War Images*. Rev. ed. New York: The Lyons Press, 2008.

Hale, Edward Everett. *Letters on Irish Emigration*. Boston: Phillips, Sampson, 1852.

Harris, Ruth-Ann M., and Donald M. Jacobs, eds. *The Search for Missing Friends: Irish Immigrant Advertisements Placed in the Boston* Pilot. 7 vols. Boston: New England Historic Genealogical Society, 1989–99.

Jensen, Richard. "No Irish Need Apply: A Myth of Victimization." *Journal of Social History* 36 (November 2, 2002).

Knobel, Dale T. *Paddy and the Republic: Ethnicity and Nationality in Antebellum America*. Middletown, CT: Wesleyan University Press, 1986.

Lane, Roger. *Policing the City: Boston, 1822–1885*. New York: Athenaeum, 1971.

Lears, Jackson. *Rebirth of a Nation: The Making of Modern America, 1877–1920*. New York: HarperCollins, 2009.

New Englander Magazine. "Brothel Groggeries in Boston." July 27, 1850.

New York Times, July 11, 1853.

Norton, Charles Eliot. *Letters*. Edited by Sara Norton and M. A. DeWolfe Howe. Vol. 1. Boston: Houghton Mifflin, 1913.

Page, N. Clifford. *Irish Songs: A Collection of Airs Old and New*. Boston: Oliver Ditson, 1907.

Pilot, March 12, 1859.

Quill, Edward. *Deer Island Death/Burial Registry 1847–1850*. Boston: City of Boston Archives, 1990.

Ryan, Thomas. *Recollections of an Old Musician*. New York: E. P. Dutton, 1899.

Von Frank, Albert J. *The Trials of Anthony Burns: Freedom and Slavery in Emerson's Boston*. Cambridge, MA: Harvard University Press, 1998.

Wilson, Susan. *Boston Sites and Insights*. Boston: Beacon Press, 1994.

"A Word for Boston and Anglo-Saxonism." *Common School Journal*, October 1, 1851.

Chapter Seven

Boston Herald, April 14, 1871.

Coyle, Henry, Theodore Mayhew, and Frank S, Hickey. *Our Church, Her Children and Institutions.* 3 vols. Boston: Archdiocese of Boston, 1908.

Douglass, Frederick. *Narrative of the Life of Frederick Douglass, an American Slave.* 1845. New York: Barnes & Noble, 2003.

Gilmore, P[atrick]. S. *History of the National Peace Jubilee and Great Musical Festival.* Boston: P. S. Gilmore, 1871.

———. "When Johnny Comes Marching Home Again." Boston: Lee and Shephard, 1863.

Handlin, Oscar. "Two Distinct Cultures and Both Stubborn." *Boston Globe,* June 11, 1959.

Irish-American Weekly, July 5, 1868.

Kammen, Michael. *Meadows of Memory: Images of Time and Tradition in American Art and Culture.* Austin: University of Texas Press, 1992.

Kenneally, Ian. "The Fenian Invasion of Canada, 1866." theirishstory. com/2011/09/16.

MacNamara, Daniel George. *The History of the Ninth Regiment, Massachusetts Volunteer Infantry.* 1899. New York: Fordham University Press, 2000.

National Peace Jubilee Festival official program, June 15, 1869.

O'Connor, Thomas H. *The Call to Arms.* Vol. 1 of *Massachusetts in the Civil War.* Boston: Massachusetts Civil War Centennial Commission, 1960.

———. *Civil War Boston: Home Front and Battlefield.* Boston: Northeastern University Press, 1997.

Pilot. "Death of Martin Milmore." July 30, 1883.

Roche, James Jeffrey. *John Boyle O'Reilly: Life, Poems and Speeches.* New York: Cassell, 1891.

Rohdenburh, Ernest, III. *A Bid for Immortality: The Sculpture and Life of Martin Milmore.* Chatham, MA: Chatham Historical Society, n.d.

Saint-Gaudens, Homer, ed. *The Reminiscences of Augustus Saint-Gaudens.* New York: Century, 1913.

Samito, Christian G., ed. *Commanding Boston's Irish Ninth: The Letters of Colonel Patrick R. Guiney.* New York: Fordham University Press, 1997.

Shannon, Mary. *Passport to Public Art in Boston.* Boston: City of Boston Printers, 1980.

Chapter Eight

American Irish Historical Society. *Proceedings.* Bowie, MD: Heritage Books, 1991.

Casey, John S. *Journal of a Voyage from Portland to Fremantle on Board the Convict Ship "Hougoumont."* Bryn Mawr, PA: Dorrance, 1988.

Cobbe, F. P. "No Irish Need Apply." *Every Saturday,* July 25, 1868.

Cullen, James Bernard. *The Story of the Irish in Boston.* Boston: J. B. Cullen, 1889.

Cummings, Michael. "100 Years Later, Copley Square Still Echoes Gilmore's Giant Jubilee." *Pilot*, April 19, 1969.

Donahoe's Magazine 12, nos. 1–6 (July–December 1884); 23, nos. 1–6 (January–June 1890); 27, nos. 1–6 (January–December 1892).

Exercises at the Dedication and Presentation of the O'Reilly Monument, June 20, 1897. Boston: Boston City Council, 1897.

Galvin, John T. "Patrick J. Maguire: Boston's Last Democratic Boss." *New England Quarterly* 4, no. 3 (September 1985).

Golway, Terry. *For the Cause of Liberty: A Thousand Years of Ireland's Heroes*. New York: Simon & Schuster, 2000.

Irish-American Weekly, June 15, 1878.

Irish Echo, January 1886; September 1890.

Irish World, August 5, 1881.

Joyce, William Leonard. *Editors and Ethnicity: A History of the Irish-American Press, 1848–1883*. New York: Arno Press, 1976.

Logan, Edward L. *The Clover Club of Boston: Golden Jubilee Year Book*. Boston: Clover Club, 1933.

O'Connell, Shaun. *Imagining Boston: A Literary Landscape*. Boston: Beacon Press, 1990.

Patriot Ledger, September 19–20, 1992.

Pilot, May 6 and September 30, 1871; August 5, 1882 ("Fanny Parnell").

Quinn, Peter. "How the Irish Stayed Irish." *America*, March 16, 1996.

Republic, March 25, 1882; March 18, 1896.

Solomon, Barbara Miller. *Ancestors and Immigrants: A Changing New England Tradition*. Cambridge, MA: Harvard University Press, 1956.

Stein, Charles W., ed. *American Vaudeville As Seen by Its Contemporaries*. New York: Alfred A. Knopf, 1984.

Stevens, Peter. *The Voyage of the* Catalpa: *A Perilous Journey and Six Irish Rebels' Escape to Freedom*. New York: Carroll & Graf, 2002.

Sullivan, Robert E., and James M. O'Toole, eds. *Catholic Boston: Studies in Religion and Community, 1870-1970*. Boston: Roman Catholic Archdiocese, 1985

Chapter Nine

Anderson, Jack. "John L. Sullivan: The First Irish American Boxing Champion." www.irishidentity.com/geese/stories/sullivan.htm.

Boston Globe, March 20, 1891; April 8, 1896.

Boston Sunday Post. "Thomas E. Burke." Obituary. February 15, 1929.

Concannon, Joe. "The Elder's 50th Jaunt." *Boston Globe*, April 18, 1981.

Connolly, James B. *Limelight Magazine*, 1933–34.

Cooper, Pamela. *Twenty-Six Miles in America*. Syracuse, NY: Syracuse University Press, 1998.

Cullen, James Bernard. *The Story of the Irish in Boston*. Boston: J. B. Cullen, 1889.

Daley, Arthur. "Sports of the Times: A Vote from Afar." *New York Times*, January 19, 1949.

Derderian, Tom. *The Boston Marathon: 100 Years of Blood, Sweat and Cheers*. Chicago: Triumph Books, 1996.

Donovan, Charles M. *Irish America*, April–May 2003.

Gershman, Michael, ed. *125 Years of Professional Baseball*. Chicago: Triumph Books, 1994.

Kaplan, Ron. "The Sporting Life: From King Kelly to Mark Maguire." *Irish America*, February–March 2003.

Kissal, Gary. "New Life for an Old Salt? The Renaissance of James Brendan Connolly." *Eire Society Bulletin*, November 1991.

Murnane, Timothy Hayes. "Old Time Baseball." *Boston Globe*, February 23, 1900.

New York Times. "Patsy Donovan." Obituary. December 26, 1953.

Olmsted, Frederick Law. *Civilizing American Cities: Writings on City Landscapes*. Edited by S. B. Sutton. New York: Da Capo Press, 1997.

Power, Jerome W. *The Boston Strong Boy, 1937–38*. In *American Life Histories: Manuscripts from the Federal Writers Project 1936–1940*. Library of Congress. www.loc.gov/collection/federal-writers-project/?q=boston+strong+boy.

Republic, March 25, 1882; May 1882.

Riess, Steven A. *City Games: The Evolution of Urban Society and the Rise of Sports*. Urbana: University of Illinois Press, 1989.

Roche, James Jeffrey. *John Boyle O'Reilly: Life, Poems and Speeches*. New York: Cassell, 1891.

Ryan, Dennis. *Beyond the Ballot Box: A Social History of the Boston Irish, 1845–1917*. Amherst: University of Massachusetts Press, 1983.

Schaefer, John. *The Irish American Athletic Club: Redefining Americanism at the 1908 Olympic Games*. New York: Archives of Irish America, 2001.

Stout, Glenn. *Fenway 1912: The Birth of a Ballpark*. Boston: Houghton Mifflin Harcourt, 2011.

Wilcox, Ralph C. "'The English as Poor Losers' and Other Thoughts on the Modernization of Sport: The Works of James Brendan Connolly, First Modern Olympic Victor and Literator." *Sports Historian* 17, no. 1 (May 1997): 63–92.

Chapter Ten

Ayers, Brenda A. "'Honey Fitz' In Search of a 'Bigger, Better and Busier Boston.'" *Eire Society Bulletin*, March 1981.

Boston Globe, February 16, 18, and 21, 1900; December 20, 1901; December 4, 1905; March 16, 1914; April 25–29, 1916; October 22, 1933; July 30, 1934.

Boston Herald, March 18, 1896.

Boston Sunday Post, September 22, 1912.

Classon, Herbert N. "The Irish in America." *Munsey's Magazine*, April 1906.

Coyle, Henry, Theodore Mayhew, and Frank S. Hickey. *Our Church, Her Children and Institutions*. 3 vols. Boston: Archdiocese of Boston, 1908.

Cummings, Michael. "The Life and Times of Brigadier-General Lawrence James Logan." Unpublished article, 1981.

———. "The Logans of Logan Airport." *Eire Society Bulletin*, November 1983.

Fitzgerald, Thomas A., Jr. *Grandpa Stories*. Aurora, CO: Rundel Park Press, 2006.

Gaelic Alliance of Boston program book. Dublin: National Library, 1912.

Gaelic American, December 30, 1905.

Harty, Patricia. "Irish Americans of the Century." *Irish America*, November 1999.

Irish World, June 22 and July 5, 1919; March 26, May 7, and December 31, 1927; July 2, 1932.

MacManus, M. J. *Eamon de Valera: A Biography*. Dublin: Talbot Press, 1944.

McCabe, John. *George M. Cohan: The Man Who Owned Broadway*. Garden City, NY: Doubleday, 1973.

Norton, Elliot. *Broadway Down East: An Informal Account of the Plays, Players, and Playhouses of Boston from Puritan Times to the Present*. Boston: Boston Public Library, 1978.

O'Connell, Lenahan, and James W. Ryan. *Able, Active and Aggressive: The O'Connell Family of Massachusetts. . .* Boston: Elizabeth-James Press, 1994.

Republic, June 2, 1900; May 5, 12, and 19, 1905; March 22, 1919.

Wayman, Dorothy. *David I. Walsh: Citizen-Patriot*. Milwaukee: Bruce Publishing, 1952.

Wilkes-Barre *Times Leader,* March 17, 1917.

Chapter Eleven

Allen, John. "John McCormack: Master Singer." *Ireland Today,* June 1984.

Beatty, Jack. *The Rascal King: The Life and Times of James Michael Curley (1874–1958)*. Reading, MA: Addison-Wesley, 1992.

Boston City Paper, April 5–18, 1997.

Boston Globe, December 4, 1913

Boston Sunday Globe, October 5, 1958.

Carroll, James Robert. *One of Ourselves: John Fitzgerald Kennedy in Ireland*. Bennington, VT: Images from the Past, 2003.

Cummings, Michael. "Gaelic Athletic Association History." Unpublished, 1983.

Fountain, Peter. *One Man's Poison: The Life and Writings of Columnist George Frazier*. Chester, CT: Globe Pequot Press, 1984.

Garvey, Thomas. "Dancing on Dudley Street." In *Guide to the New England Irish*, edited by Michael P. Quinlin, 2nd ed. Boston: Quinlin Campbell Publishers, 1987.

Gedutis, Susan. *See You at the Hall: Boston's Golden Era of Irish Music and Dance*. Boston: Northeastern University Press, 2004

Hughes, Herbert. *Irish Country Songs*. 4 vols. London: Boosey, 1909–36.

Irish World, September 26, 1931; May 27, 1933; March 29, 1941; June 2, 1947; February 28, 1948.

Johnson, H. Earle. *Symphony Hall, Boston.* Boston: Little, Brown, 1950.

Maier, Thomas. *The Kennedys: America's Emerald Kings.* New York: Basic Books, 2003.

McCormack, John. Papers. Boston Symphony Hall Archives.

———. Papers. John J. Burns Library Archives, Boston College.

McCormack, Lily. *I Hear You Calling Me.* Milwaukee: Bruce Publishing, 1949.

Newsweek, January 8, 1951.

New York Times. "Jazz Priest N. O'Connor Dead at 81." July 7, 2003.

O'Connor, Edwin. *The Last Hurrah.* Boston: Atlantic Monthly Press, 1956.

O'Connor, Thomas H. *The Boston Irish: A Political History.* Boston: Northeastern University Press, 1995.

O'Neill, Francis. *Irish Minstrels and Musicians.* Cork, Ireland: Mercier Press, 1913.

Republic, January 15, 1910; March 26, 1910.

Roxbury Gazette, May 30, 1913; June 7, 1913.

Ryan, George E. "Irish Notes on American Music." *Eire Society Bulletin,* March 1988.

Sullivan, Mark. *Pre-War America.* Vol. 3 of *Our Times: 1900–1925.* New York: Charles Scribner's Sons, 1930.

Swan, John C., ed. *Music in Boston: Readings from the First Three Centuries.* Boston: Boston Public Library, 1977.

Victor Records. Catalog, 1919.

White, Robert. "John McCormack's Recordings." *Cara,* May/June 1984.

Williams, William H. A. *'Twas Only an Irishman's Dream: The Image of Ireland and the Irish in Popular Song Lyrics: 1800–1920.* Urbana: University of Illinois Press, 1996.

Chapter Twelve

Boston Business Journal, October 17–23, 2003.

Boston Evening American, November 27, 1959.

Boston Evening Traveller, October 9, 1956.

Boston Globe, February 28, 1924; October 1, 1958; January 27, 1968.

Carter, Jimmy. Speech. Harvard–National Library of Ireland Irish Manuscripts Microfilm Project. *Eire Society Bulletin,* October 20, 1979.

Central Council of Irish County Clubs. Forty-sixth annual directory, March 17, 1951.

Central Counties Committee, Boston. Feis program book, 1950.

County Donegal Association. Fifty-fifth annual reunion program, November 21, 1963.

Daly, Mary E. "Nationalism, Sentiment, and Economics: Relations Between Ireland and Irish America in the Postwar Years," *Eire-Ireland,* Spring/Summer 2002.

Fahey, Joseph J. *Boston's Forty-Five Mayors.* Boston: City of Boston Printers, 1975.

Feis Mor Greater Boston. Feis program, July 30, 1950.

"First Boston Visit of the Pete Brown Band coming to the New State Ballroom Direct from Ireland." Circular, May 24–26, 1962.

Ford, James J. "Some Records of the Irish Language in the Greater Boston Area." *Eire Society Bulletin*, November 4, 1973.

Gaelic Athletic Association. Annual reunion and ball program., December 3, 1953.

Hennessey, Maurice N. *I'll Come Back in the Springtime: John F. Kennedy and the Irish*. New York: Ives Washburn, 1966.

Ireland Department of Foreign Affairs. "Visit of President John F. Kennedy to Ireland, 26–29 June 1963." Dublin, 2003.

Irish American Committee for the John F. Kennedy Memorial Library Fund in Boston. Correspondence, April 15, 1964.

Irish Echo, April 3, 1982; October 31, November 27, and December 5, 1987; February 13, 1988.

Irish Talent Club. Eleventh annual "Night in Ireland" program book, November 1, 1959.

Irish World, June 22, 1946; August 29, 1950.

Jacqueline Kennedy: Historic Conversations on Life with John F. Kennedy. Foreword by Caroline Kennedy. New York: Hyperion, 2011.

Kennedy, John F. *A Nation of Immigrants*. Rev. ed. New York: Harper and Row, 1964.

———. "On Poetry and National Power." *Massachusetts Review*, Winter 1964.

Kennedy, Rose Fitzgerald. *Times to Remember*. Garden City, NY: Doubleday, 1974.

Lyons, Louis M. "The Legend of John F. Kennedy." *Massachusetts Review*, Winter 1964.

MacBride, Sean. "Greetings to Boston Feis." *Eire Society Bulletin*, 1951.

Mitchell, Arthur. *JFK and His Irish Heritage*. Dublin: Moytura Press, 1994.

Roscommon Herald, July 25, 1969.

Roxbury Citizen, March 8, 1951.

Smith, Amanda, ed. *Hostage to Fortune: The Letters of Joseph P. Kennedy*. New York: Viking, 2001.

Tubridy, Ryan. *JFK in Ireland: Four Days That Changed a Presidency*. Guilford: Lyons Press, 2011.

Chapter Thirteen

Ancient Order of Hibernians. *Guide for the New Irish*. March 1988.

Boston Globe, September 25, 1980; May 5, 2001.

Boston Registry Department. Selectmen's Minutes. City document no. 77 (December 28, 1737). In *Records Relating to the Early History of Boston*, vol. 15. Boston: Rockwell and Churchill, 1886.

Flatley, Thomas J. Testimony before US House of Representatives Subcommittee on Immigration, Refugees and International Law, September 7, 1988.

Irish Echo, April 22, 1989.

Irish Times, February 19, 1985; March 25, May 6, and June 17, 1989.

McGowan, William. "The Irish in Boston Are on the Move." *Boston Irish Press* 1 (January 1981).

———. "Massachusetts Immigration Committee Objectives." 1985.

O'Hanlon, Ray. *The New Irish Americans.* Niwot, CO: Roberts Rinehart, 1998.

Patriot Ledger, March 15–16, 2003.

US Congress. A bill to amend the Immigration and Nationality Act to effect changes in the numerical limitation and preference system. 99th Cong., 2nd sess., S. 2768 by Mr. Kennedy. Congressional Record, vol. 132, no. 114 (August 15, 1986).

———. A bill to amend the Immigration and Nationality Act to provide for additional immigrant visa numbers . . . , 99th Cong., 2nd sess., S. 2219 by Mr. Kerry. Congressional Record, vol. 132, no. 36 (March 21, 1986).

———. Resolution to make additional immigrant visas available for immigrants from certain foreign countries. 99th Cong., 1st sess., H.R. 2606. May 23, 1985.

Chapter Fourteen

Boston Globe, January 15, 1959; March 15, 1990; March 17, 1994; March 11, 1995; March 19, 2001; March 24, 2002.

Bulger, William M. *While the Music Lasts: My Life in Politics.* Boston: Houghton Mifflin, 1996.

Carroll, James. *The City Below.* Boston: Houghton Mifflin, 1994.

Davis, William A. "On the Trail of the Irish." *Boston Globe*, March 17, 2001.

Ford, James J. "From the North End to the Fenway: An Irish Walk Through Central Boston." *Eire Society Bulletin*, December 1991.

Irish Echo, December 30, 1989; September 16–22, 1992; March 8–15, 1995; April 12–18, 1995; March 13–19, 1996; November 27–December 3, 1996; March 5–11, 1997; June 17–23, 1998; November 22–30, 1998; May 28–June 3, 2003.

Quinlin, Michael P. "Irish Music As an Emigrant Language." Paper delivered at ACIS conference, Boston University, October 2001, and at Gaelic Roots, June 2003.

Quinlin, Michael P., and Colette Minogue Quinlin. *Guide to the New England Irish.* 3rd ed. Boston: Quinlin Campbell, 1994.

South Boston Tribune, April 11, 1991.

Symposium on Northern Ireland program. University of Massachusetts, Boston, March 18–19, 1983.

Chapter Fifteen

Boston College Chronicle, March 4, 1993.

Boston Globe, March 9, 1909; March 17 and 19, 1996; July 10, 1999.

Boston Herald, January 8, 2001.

Bowen, Kevin. *In Search of Grace O'Malley*. Dorchester, MA: West Cedar Street Press, 1997.

Christian Science Monitor, December 19, 1994.

Deutsch, Sarah. *Women and the City: Gender, Space, and Power in Boston, 1870–1940*. Oxford: Oxford University Press, 2000.

Dezell, Maureen. *Irish America: Coming into Clover*. New York: Doubleday, 2000.

Fahey, Joseph J., ed. *Boston's 45 Mayors, From John Phillips to Kevin H. White*. Boston: City of Boston Printing Department, 1979.

Greaney, Áine. *Dance Lessons*. Syracuse, NY: Syracuse University Press, 2011.

Halter, Marilyn. *Shopping for Identity: The Marketing of Ethnicity*. New York: Schocken, 2000.

Hayes, J. G. *This Thing Called Courage: South Boston Stories*. New York: Harrington Park Press, 2002.

Home & Away, April 28, 2003.

International Irish Dancing Magazine, July 2002.

Jen, Gish. *Who's Irish?* New York: Alfred A. Knopf, 1999.

Kenny, Kevin. *The American Irish: A History*. Boston: Longman, 2000.

Lincoln, Abraham. *Collected Works*. Edited by Roy P. Basler. Vol. 2. New Brunswick, NJ: Rutgers University Press, 1953.

MacDonald, Michael Patrick. *All Souls: A Family Story from Southie*. Boston: Beacon Books, 1999.

Pilot, March 22, 1834; August 29, 1863.

Redfearn, James. *The Rising at Roxbury Crossing*. Wrentham, MA: Olde Stoney Brook Publishing, 2011.

Republic, February 24, 1900.

Robinson, Mary. Address to the Irish Parliament, February 2, 1995.

Roosevelt, Theodore. Letter, January 13, 1897. *Journal of the American-Irish Historical Society* 1 (1898):27–28.

Sullivan, J. Courtney. *Maine*. New York: Alfred A. Knopf, 2011.

US Congress. Irish Peace Process Cultural and Training Program Act of 1998. 105th Cong., 2nd sess., H.R. 4293 (1998).

———. To amend and extend the Irish Peace Process Cultural and Training Program Act of 1999. 108th Cong., 1st sess., H.R. 2655 (2003).

Wilson, Susan. *The Omni Parker House: A Brief History of America's Longest Continuously Operating Hotel*. Boston: Omni Parker House, 2001.

Chapter Sixteen

Cullen, Kevin. "The Fading of the Green." *Boston Globe*, March 17, 2008.

———. "The Names I'll Remember." *Boston Globe*, April 31, 2013.

Higgins, George V. *The Friends of Eddie Coyle*. New York: Penguin Books, 1987.

Kennedy, Edward M. "Statement of Senator Edward M. Kennedy Opposing the Use of Plastic Bullets in Northern Ireland and Calling for a Ban on the Ulster Defence Association." Press Release, June 15, 1982.

McManus, Sean. *My American Struggle for Justice in Northern Ireland.* Wilton, Cork: Collins, 2011.

Minehan, John. *To Love Two Countries: Ireland's Greatest Generation in America.* New York: Irish Arts Center, 2010.

Reeves, Phillip. "In Ireland, the Death of the Celtic Tiger Leads to Anger, Uproar." National Public Radio, October 2, 2010.

Robinson, Mary. *Everybody Matters: My Life Giving Voice.* New York: Walker & Company, 2012.

Siegal, Nina. "Four Corners: When Shifting Groups of Immigrants Compete for the Same Turf." *New York Times,* July 30, 2000.

Sonne, Paul, and Enrich, David. "A Bedraggled 'Celtic Tiger' Struggles to Retrain Workers." *Wall Street Journal,* April 20, 2012.

Index

About the Author

Michael Quinlin has written several books about the Irish in New England and is editor of *Classic Irish Stories* (Lyons Press). His articles have appeared in the *Boston Globe,* the *Boston Herald,* the *Christian Science Monitor,* the *Irish Echo,* and *Irish America* magazine. A founder of the Boston Irish Tourism Association and creator of Boston's Irish Heritage Trail, he lives in Milton, Massachusetts, with his wife, Colette, and son Devin.